FIFTH EDITION

THE EFFECTIVE USE OF ADVERTISING MEDIA

a practical handbook

About the Authors

Martyn P. Davis BSc (Econ) FCIM FCAM FIPR Dip F Ed

Now an independent Marketing Communications Consultant, Martyn P. Davis has working experience with advertisers, agencies and media-owners, as well as academic institutions in this country and abroad. He attended the Harvard Business School and, on his return, was a founder and Executive Director of the Cambridge International Marketing Programme.

In addition to *The Effective Use of Advertising Media*, Martyn is the author of *Business-to-Business Marketing & Promotion*, the *Handbook for Media Representatives* and *A Career in Advertising* as well as numerous articles, and has contributed to various anthologies.

A former member of the National Council of the Advertising Association, he was also a Senior Examiner for the Chartered Institute of Marketing and Moderator for the CAM Foundation examinations. Martyn is a Course Director for the Chartered Institute of Marketing, and has worldwide international experience.

David Zerdin M. CAM Cert Ed

Following initial experience in market research, David Zerdin worked on various accounts (including Unilever, Milk, Anadin and Norwich Union) at various advertising agencies including Bates Dorland and McCann Erickson.

Subsequently he became a client, managing advertising at Access, where he developed the flexible friend campaign, before becoming responsible for marketing and Public Relations at TSB and marketing and customer relations at Midland Bank. He represented Midland on the Board of The Office of The Banking Ombudsman.

A Diploma holder of the CAM (Communications, Advertising and Marketing) Education Foundation, he is currently a Senior Lecturer at the London College of Printing and Distributive Trades where he specialises in marketing, marketing communications, advertising and media.

FIFTH EDITION

THE EFFECTIVE USE OF ADVERTISING MEDIA

a practical handbook

by Martyn P. Davis
BSc (Econ), FCAM, FIPR, FCIM, Dip F Ed

Marketing Communications Consultant

and David Zerdin
M CAM Cert Ed

Senior Lecturer, London College of Printing and Distributive Trades

C
CENTURY
BUSINESS

This fifth edition was first published in the United Kingdom by Century Ltd Random House, 20 Vauxhall Bridge Road, London SW1V 2SA

Random House Australia (Pty) Limited
20 Alfred Street, Milsons Point, Sydney
New South Wales 2061, Australia

Random House New Zealand Limited
18 Poland Road, Glenfield
Auckland 10, New Zealand

Random House South Africa (Pty) Limited
Box 2263, Rosebank 2121, South Africa

Random House UK Limited Reg. No. 954009

Papers used by Random House UK Limited are natural, recyclable products made from wood grown in sustainable forest. The manufacturing processes conform to the environmental regulations of the country of origin.

ISBN 0 7126 7771 2

Typeset by SX Composing DTP, Rayleigh, Essex
Printed and bound in Great Britain by
Mackays of Chatham plc, Chatham, Kent

Companies, institutions and other organisations wishing to make bulk purchases of any business books published by Random House should contact their local bookstore or Random House direct:

Special Sales Director
Random House
20 Vauxhall Bridge Road
London SW1V 2SA

Tel 0171 973 9000
Fax. 0171 828 6681

Contents

Studiare libro + appunti + schemi
X Recador → + volume
Compiti esam 20 ≤ 1
      6 7 } + compito
      13 14
15 16 adato

v

Preface to the Fifth Edition

The media world and advertising practice have both become increasingly sophisticated in recent years, but people in all branches of advertising – advertisers, agencies and media-owners – often seem hindered rather than helped by the wealth of media data and techniques at their disposal. Immense energy is devoted to gathering information and great skill applied to devising new techniques, but unfortunately all this effort is often undermined by failure to build on a sound base. There appear to be more than a few 'blind spots': some matters are so fundamental they are taken for granted, and therefore receive insufficient attention. The chart overleaf shows the six fundamentals – the media themselves, the criteria by which they can be compared, the principles of media planning, and the three groups of organisations involved: advertisers, agencies and media-owners. Not only must all six operate efficiently in their own right, they must also interact effectively before optimum use can be made of advertising media.

My view is that any book on the use of media must necessarily at the same time be a book on advertising administration. This will no doubt present problems to librarians and booksellers – having ordered it, where should it go on the shelves? Should it go under *Media, Media Planning* or under *Advertising Administration*? Under *Advertisers, Agency Practice* or *Media-owners*? I leave this decision to the booksellers and librarians. If they opt for the safest course and buy more copies than they would otherwise have done, I would prefer, in the interests of modesty and good taste, that the suggestion should not have come from me!

The book is really three books in one:

The first part, 'The World of Media', outlines the range of media

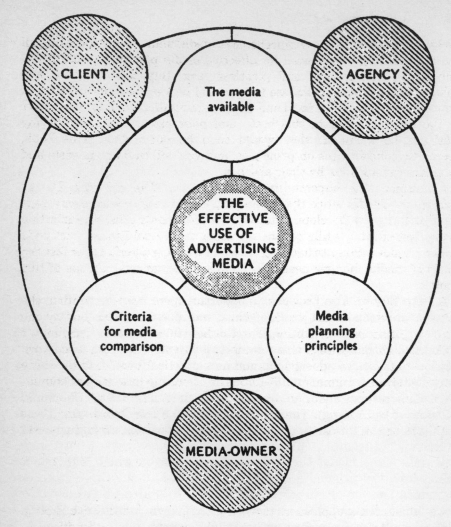

CLIENT

The media available

AGENCY

THE EFFECTIVE USE OF ADVERTISING MEDIA

Criteria for media comparison

Media planning principles

MEDIA-OWNER

THE SIX FUNDAMENTALS

available to communicate your advertising message, reviews the data known about them, and discusses the criteria by which you can compare one with another.

The second part on 'The Organisation of Media' covers the firms and the individuals concerned with these media: the media-owners, the advertisers, their agencies and the media independents.

The third part, optimistically titled 'The *Effective* use of Advertising Media' devotes itself to how the individuals and organisations discussed in the second part can best ensure that the media described in the first part are used to maximum effect.

To attempt to produce a comprehensive media manual incorporating all the facts and figures needed for effective media planning would be an impossible, unnecessary and pointless task. Impossible in that any volume incorporating all these facts would be vast beyond proportion; unnecessary in that the facts and figures are readily available elsewhere in the sources listed in this book, and pointless in that, should any statistics be included, they would soon be out-of-date. This book, therefore, concentrates on principles, and you will find media costs and statistics conspicuous by their absence.

I welcome this opportunity to update the *The Effective Use of Advertising Media* since this makes it possible to give proper coverage of important new developments: some received only a passing mention in the last edition, while others are major structural changes not even under consideration at that time. Anyone wanting proof of how fast the world of media changes need only compare the various editions of this book.

A Fifth Edition also provides an opportunity for me to reconfirm the market for which we are writing, which was alas misunderstood by one reviewer of an earlier Edition. For the benefit of new readers, may I make clear the purpose of this volume. It is intended as a reference work for new entrants to advertising, and as a practical handbook for those working for professional qualifications or attending practitioner courses (hence its recommendation by the CAM foundation and Chartered Institute of Marketing). The book will also serve established executives wishing to make a fresh and detached review of the fast-changing world of media.

MARTYN P. DAVIS

It was an honour and pleasure to work with Martyn on this Fifth Edition of the book he has steered so well through four previous incarnations.

Evidence of the book's importance can be seen in the way that the book has evolved, in line with the coming of age of media, reflecting the more realistic balance between the media and creative aspects of advertising.

There are some constants in media, but far more areas in which change is the only common factor. These are the areas in which the Fifth Edition now reflects the current and future needs of the media practitioner:

International: many media have become 'Pan-European' and are beginning to become global. This edition includes new international research surveys, outlines the differences in international media and describes the different types of client and agency structure available to handle media internationally.

New Media: the established media are still here. They are, without exception, more complex and all continue to evolve. Additionally, new media are identified, not just Ambient media (usually described as miscellaneous outdoor media), but new electronic media particularly the Internet.

Agencies: media departments have, in many cases, evolved into a media dependants and, together with media independents, have spread their wings, beyond the traditional media planning, buying and evaluation functions, into the total communication area.

Research: the book features a number of new research vehicles, reflecting increasing sophistication through techniques such as fusion as well as the growing interest in Europe and new media.

Technology: this book outlines the digital technology which will revolutionise television and radio. It also describes the ways in which advertisers, media and agencies can utilise sophisticated electronic tools, relieving them of the need to undertake calculations mechanically, thus freeing them for the tasks of deciding and implementing strategy.

DAVID ZERDIN

Acknowledgements

Special thanks to Kevin O'Sullivan of DWS Advertising for his dedication in providing constructive comments, criticisms and suggestions, to his secretary Julie, and to the many people in the following organisations for providing valuable information:

The Advertising Association, Advertising Standards Authority, Association of Household Distributors, Association of Media and Communications Specialists, Audit Bureau of Circulations, British Rate and Data, Broadcast Advertising Clearance Centre, Broadcasters' Audience Research Board, BPA International, British Telecommunications plc, BSkyB, CACI, CCN Group Limited, CDMS Marketing Services, Channel One, Cinema Advertising Association, Cinema and Video Industry Audience Research, Cinema Media, Channel 4, Channel 5 Broadcasting Ltd, Commercial Radio Companies Association, Department of National Heritage, Direct Mail Information Service, Direct Marketing International, Donovan Data Systems Ltd, The Economist Newspaper Limited, Exhibition Industry Federation, Exhibition Surveys Ltd, Express Newspapers plc, Financial Times, GMTV, Incorporated Society of British Advertisers, Independent Television Commission, Institute of Practitioners in Advertising, Joint Industry Committee for Regional Press Research, Katz Radio Sales, Laser, Live TV, Leo Burnett Ltd, McGraw-Hill, Maiden Outdoor, Massons, Media Audits, Media Monitoring Services Ltd, Media Sales and Marketing, MediaTel, MTV Europe, National Readership Surveys, National Transcommunications Ltd, NDL International, Newspaper Publishers Association, Newspaper Society, Nielsen Register-MEAL, OPMA, Outdoor Advertising Association, Pearl and Dean, Periodical Publishers Association, Telmar Communications Ltd, The Radio Advertising Bureau, Radio Advertising Clearance Centre, Radio Authority, Radio Joint Audience Research, Radio Times, The Readers' Digest Association, Reed Business Publishing, Royal Mail, Scottish and Irish Radio Sales, Star TV Network, Stepcheck Limited, Target Group Index, TDI Advertising Ltd, J Walter Thompson, TSMS, Verified Free Distribution, Zierler Media.

The authors readily acknowledge their debt to those whose brains they have picked, with or without their knowledge.

Terminology

Throughout this book general terms such as 'advertiser', 'product' and 'purchaser' are used for reasons of simplicity: 'advertiser' may mean a manufacturer, retailer, service organisation or a non-profit government department; 'product' covers services as well as goods; and 'purchaser' must be taken to mean not only the man or woman in the street – in many cases, the buyer may be a large industrial group or some official department.

Other general terms are used when referring to media, again for simplicity. Any mention of advertisement 'size' should be taken to include all variations of the concept and thus covers the length of a television or radio or cinema commercial just as much as press or poster media. Similarly, 'insertions' should be taken to include transmission of commercials, or any other form of appearance of an advertisement. References to advertising copy cover the spoken just as much as the printed word, and design includes moving as well as conventional illustrations. The phrase 'above the line' applies to the five media (press, television, radio, cinema and outdoor) which pay a commission that provides agencies with revenue. 'Below the line' media such as exhibitions, direct mail and display material do not pay this commission so, as explained in Chapter 10, the agency adds a commission-equivalent sum to generate the revenue they need to pay for servicing this type of work. Unless specifically stated, media terms should be interpreted as broadly as possible.

Generally, the reader is addressed as 'You' to avoid reference to any specific job title in any particular type of organisation. Whether your concern is selling advertising space or time, or buying it on behalf of a manufacturer's advertising department or advertising agency, the underlying fundamentals remain the same: you simply approach them from a different standpoint. Where specific posts are mentioned, jobs are sometimes described in terms of their being held by men: this is, again, for simplicity and to avoid cumbersome 'spokesperson-speak' rather than any male chauvinism or discrimination.

Foreword

by *JOHN W. HOBSON, CBE, FIPA, FRSA*
Former President of the Institute of Practitioners in Advertising
Chairman of the Advertising Association
President of the European Association of Advertising Agencies
Author of 'The Selection of Advertising Media'

It is a puzzling fact that, while so much attention and so many books are devoted to the creative and marketing sides of advertising, the media side is so thinly documented. The explanation lies, no doubt, in the glamour element in creative work, and in the commercial interest in effective marketing. Yet the choice of media, the correct analysis of each medium's value, the use of each for its proper purpose, the combination of various media into a powerful orchestration, are not only the governing factors in the wise spending of millions of pounds, but are in themselves a fascinating study and science.

It is, therefore, with particular pleasure that I welcome a new, up-to-date and comprehensive book on this important subject; and I would think that no one is better qualified to write it than Mr Martyn Davis.

I believe I am right in saying that the first analytical study of the subject was my own book *The Selection of Advertising Media* and to many students of advertising it was their first introduction to this side of the business. But the changes in media are so fast-moving that it was out-of-date in detail (though not in its principles) almost from the time of publication. In particular, it was written when television was only a gleam in someone's eye. It was consecutively updated by myself and others, but this could be no more than a process of tinkering.

Martyn Davis' earlier book* was written particularly from the viewpoint of educating the advertisement departments in the techniques of selling media, and it is now high time to have a new coverage of the subject as a whole – seeing it from the advertiser, the agency and the media angles.

* Handbook for Media Representatives.

It is a sobering thought, but one that needs to be constantly impressed, that with a budget of say £1 million, unsound media selection can waste £100,000 or £200,000 – sums that an advertiser would never think of wasting in some other context. The causes are many, and complex. They start with the failure to study the up-to-date figures of readership or viewing, and their value relationship to the target audience for the product. They go on with disregard of the basic 'Concentration – Domination – Repetition' pattern of good media selection. They derive from a slap-happy repetition of some traditional schedule or even from some concession to what the client Chairman's wife likes to see his advertising in. The truth is that scientific media selection can now be based on such a wealth of information about readership, attention values, size and frequency values and so on (not to mention the subjective elements of atmosphere and the company you keep) that it is a very challenging and complex operation to get the answer right.

Equally, in selling space in media, it is not easy to get away from the wishful thinking that expects one's own medium to be acceptable in all cases, and to limit one's own selling operation to those contexts where the statistics show it is an appropriate choice.

For the selfish financial values alone, the knowledge of media selection that this book promotes is essential. But also for the general reputation of advertising, and to avoid the impression of reckless spending in inappropriate contexts, the subject is of importance.

I hope that the book will be well received and well studied, and I wish it all success.

JOHN W. HOBSON

Part 1
THE WORLD
OF MEDIA

Chapter 1

Advertising, and the Media Available

The Advertising Standards Authority once defined advertising as *'The use of paid-for media space or time as a means of persuading people to take a particular course of action, or to reach a point of view.'*

The ASA's *British Code of Advertising and Sales Promotion* is now broader in its coverage, but this is still the best *functional* definition. The key words, as far as this book is concerned, are 'paid-for media', as an essential element in the effective use of advertising media is a contractual agreement with a media-owner, who undertakes to transmit your advertising message in return for a given sum of money. The media-owner has a legal obligation to transmit your message, and you have a legal obligation to pay him for so doing. What that message should be is discussed later. Which media to use (and how best to use them) are the subject of this book.

ADVERTISING AS A MEANS OF COMMUNICATION

This book is aimed primarily at advertising people – whether with advertisers, agencies or media-owners – and there is thus no need to 'defend' advertising against some of the more foolish criticisms. Nevertheless, it is worth reminding ourselves of the benefits it offers in comparison with other means of communication.

Any businessman might justifiably comment that his best advertisements were satisfied customers and ask why he should spend good money on advertising when word-of-mouth recommendation is spreading news of his products to potential purchasers. Most certainly any manufacturer will benefit from new purchasers learning from old about the benefits of his product and should do all he can to encourage this: much public relations activity has this very aim. Nevertheless, the

THE EFFECTIVE USE OF ADVERTISING MEDIA

use of advertising to communicate messages brings certain specific benefits which make more than worthwhile the expenditure involved:

Definite Delivery There is a lack of certainty about the delivery of messages sent via Public Relations that simply does not apply to paid-for advertising. News Releases as part of a co-ordinated promotional campaign can help secure valuable editorial coverage. 'Third party endorsement' can play a major role in securing customer acceptance and keeping possible purchasers up-to-date with news about your product. However, the delivery of such editorial references is necessarily uncertain, being beyond your control. For instance, should events of greater importance occur, your News Release, however well written and targeted, will be consigned to the bin. With paid-for advertising you are certain your message will be delivered.

Completeness On many occasions you will find that, although the media have carried your story, an editor has 'subbed' the News Release rather than printed it in full. Word-of-mouth recommendation is similarly unreliable: those who made a purchase may, in spreading word to their friends, perhaps forget some key points about your product. The same can be said of your sales staff: at the end of a long day on the road, it is perhaps too much to expect tired representatives to deliver *every* sales point. With advertising, you know your chosen message will be delivered in full, simply because you have paid the media-owner to undertake this very task.

Accuracy Word-of-mouth recommendation and News Releases share a common weakness, in that your message could be distorted. With press advertising, you decide precisely which words you wish to use and control how they are to be conveyed. Furthermore, you receive proofs which you correct for accuracy. With other media you have equal control of advertisement content, and there is no possibility of your message being distorted.

Frequency Editorial references in the media may appear only when a company has news to release – how is the market to be stimulated in the meantime? Many manufacturers, particularly those whose goods are purchased on a repeat basis, cannot rely on News Releases or word-of-mouth to stimulate their market. Their products are bought on a weekly or monthly basis and they need to stimulate the market at appropriate intervals: advertising can do just this, simply by booking appropriate appearances as part of your campaign plan.

Speed Advertising communicates rapidly: many manufacturers launching new products need a return on their investment as swiftly as possible or to react swiftly to increased competition. They rely on advertising to help them achieve this, rather than the gradual build-up in sales which word-of-mouth may bring.

Timing Personal recommendations, valuable though they are, may be spread over time in a haphazard way. Equally, it is uncertain when (and indeed if) the media will carry your News Releases in the editorial columns. Advertising, on the other hand, can be used as a precision instrument, stimulating your market when necessary. This may be a matter of seasons, promoting winter goods in the winter and summer goods in the summer, or alternatively may be a matter of days, giving customers a timely boost on a given day of the week.

Selectivity Personal recommendations spread indiscriminately, and you cannot rely on them to achieve full coverage of your particular target market: word often spreads to people with no interest in your product. Advertising, however, can be selective, and aimed at just the people most likely to buy your product. This may be a matter of media selection, choosing those media with good coverage of your target market, and here a fine degree of selectivity such as by age and class is possible, bearing in mind the wide range of media available to you. Alternatively, audience selection may be achieved by advertisement positioning just as much as media choice: an advertisement on the gardening page of a newspaper will select gardeners out of the total readership, and the same is true of other positions which prove equally effective in selecting suitable readers for other manufacturers. Naturally, many advertisers use both methods of audience selection, booking specific positions in selected media.

Economy Advertising media costs spread over a very wide range but, whatever the figure, cost per contact is low in comparison with personal selling. Your company's salesforce plays a vital role and it could be argued that the best way to spread news about your products would be to employ more sales staff. Clearly, however, this would be most uneconomic: salesmen's time can be measured in tens of pounds per call, whereas advertising contacts are usually measured in pennies per thousand. Not only is advertising a more economic way of spreading messages than using your sales force, it can also be most effective in making your sales executives more productive – paving the way before they make their calls, or even providing them with direct leads to follow up.

Table 1
TOTAL ADVERTISING EXPENDITURE BY MEDIA

£ million	1990	1991	1992	1993	1994
National Newspapers	1,187	1,121	1,155	1,220	1,336
Regional Newspapers	1,715	1,628	1,640	1,715	1,871
Consumer Magazines	541	506	466	448	499
Business & Professional	790	708	746	714	828
Directories	492	504	523	551	589
Press production costs	412	417	427	438	478
TOTAL PRESS	5,137	4,884	4,957	5,085	5,600
Television	2,325	2,295	2,472	2,605	2,873
Direct Mail	979	895	945	907	1,050
Outdoor & Transport	282	267	284	300	350
Radio	163	149	157	194	243
Cinema	39	42	45	49	53
TOTAL	8,925	8,532	8,859	9,140	10,169

COMMUNICATIONS MEDIA

Compared with other communications media, such as editorial coverage, word-of-mouth recommendation and even your own sales staff, paid-for advertising has the advantages of definite delivery, completeness, accuracy, frequency, speed, timing, selectivity and economy and – to some extent – *all* media offer these advantages.

To use these media effectively and efficiently, it is essential that you know precisely what you are using. The first four chapters in 'The World of Media' review the range of media available to transmit your message, the next two examine what we know about them, while the seventh chapter discusses the criteria by which you can compare one advertising medium with another.

There are many ways in which your advertising messages can be communicated to potential purchasers. Individual statistics would soon be out-of-date, so this review of media is necessarily limited to broad generalisations about the different categories. These media categories are by no means watertight compartments: some media can be considered under more than one heading, or even shift from one category to another. Some publications, for example, are really magazines in newspaper format, while others originated as newspapers and became magazines, and colour supplements can be considered under the twin headings of newspapers and magazines. The national press often provide regional advertising facilities, while regional newspapers have co-operative facilities for national advertisers. The media market place is a very dynamic one, with existing media continuously adapting and new ones appearing.

The media available to you will be considered in the order listed in the

Table 2
TOTAL ADVERTISING EXPENDITURE: PERCENTAGE OF TOTAL

	1990	1991	1992	1993	1994
National Newspapers	13.3	13.1	13.0	13.3	13.1
Regional Newspapers	19.2	19.1	18.5	18.8	18.4
Consumer Magazines	6.1	5.9	5.3	4.9	4.9
Business & Professional	8.9	8.3	8.4	7.8	8.1
Directories	5.5	5.9	5.9	6.0	5.8
Press production costs	4.6	4.9	4.8	4.8	4.7
TOTAL PRESS	57.6	57.2	55.9	55.6	55.1
Television	26.0	26.9	27.9	28.5	28.3
Direct Mail	11.0	10.5	10.7	9.9	10.3
Outdoor & Transport	3.2	3.1	3.2	3.3	3.4
Radio	1.8	1.7	1.8	2.1	2.4
Cinema	0.4	0.5	0.5	0.5	0.5
TOTAL	100.0	100.0	100.0	100.0	100.0

table above, which shows their importance in terms of overall advertising expenditure. A review of other media will then be made.

PRESS

This overall category covers several distinct types of printed advertising media.

Newspapers

As a group, newspapers permit you to deliver a detailed message on a given day, and at short notice, to a media audience whose size and composition are usually known, as circulation and readership figures are generally available. Space is usually sold by the single-column centimetre (S.C.C.), and in multiples thereof. A wide variety of special positions is usually available, as is classified or semi-display advertising.

Different newspapers appeal to different types of readership, but they fall into three broad categories: qualities, mid markets and populars. The former category, qualities, are usually 'broadsheet' in size, whereas the other two categories are smaller 'tabloid' in format.

Qualities are usually read more by the ABC1 socio-economic grades discussed later, defined as 'managerial, administrative and professional' at higher, intermediate and junior or supervisory levels.

At the other end of the socio-economic scale is the popular press, whose readers are mainly in the C2, D and E socio-economic grades, comprising skilled, semi or unskilled manual workers, and pensioners and casual or lowest grade workers.

Between these two categories of newspapers are the 'mid-markets', which tend to have readership from both ends of the socio-economic scale identified above but are strongest in A, B, C1 and C2 groups.

Another way of classifying newspapers is as national or regional. The dividing line between these two categories is however becoming increasingly blurred. For instance, although they are classified as 'national newspapers', it is often possible to advertise on a regional basis and the regional press featured below can be purchased on a national basis.

National Newspapers In addition to the advantages just mentioned, the benefits of national newspapers can be summarised by considering the two parts of the name – 'national' and 'news' papers. There is a sense of urgency and immediacy about the advertising message which is distributed on a national basis (allowing of course for area variations in penetration). There are different papers to cover different types of readership and British Rate and Data (BRAD: see Chapter 5) lists three 'popular', two 'mid-market' and five 'quality' national mornings. For Sundays, BRAD lists four popular and two mid market newspapers and four qualities. Also listed are two 'sport' national mornings.

The national press has been subject to ups and downs in the circulation/readership patterns of individual publications, but has recently been shaken up by circulation wars, particularly with cover price cuts by one group of papers, followed by cuts by other groups. The subsequent increase in the cost of newsprint (the technical term for the paper used in printing newspapers) has led to a change in the type of competition, away from price towards other promotional activities, but competition is still strong.

Colour advertising is available in all national newspapers either as 'on-the-run' colour, within separate 'reviews' or colour supplements.

An in-depth knowledge of each newspaper is essential as many divide into separate 'themed' sections.

Sunday Newspapers An in-depth knowledge of each paper and its format is again essential but, overall, Sunday newspapers have the additional advantage of being read in a more leisurely atmosphere, and present the advertiser with an opportunity to appeal to partners or the whole family together. The fact that Sunday shopping habits are changing, now that supermarkets and other shops are open for much of Sunday, has not changed the role of Sunday papers to a marked degree. Consumer durables are seldom purchased on impulse and Sunday still has a leisure environment ideal for discussing advertisements and responding to them. In addition, some Sunday newspapers have a longer life, being kept and re-read during the week, being retained for reference (for instance to TV listings) which is rarely the case with most daily newspapers. The exceptions here are the Saturday editions of the quality press, which are developing 'sections' designed to capture readers one day earlier and make it unnecessary for them to buy competitive Sunday newspapers. The various colour supplements often have a 'lifestyle' emphasis, and so can be considered under the twin headings of newspapers and magazines, as discussed below.

As with national newspapers, Sundays have been subject to ups and downs in the circulation/readership patterns of individual publications. Competition focuses on the provision of 'sections', reviews and supplements designed to attract advertisers appealing to particular target segments.

Technological changes In recent years, the press medium has changed in line with developments in printing technology. This has been particularly evident in the field of national newspapers. Fleet Street journalists formerly wrote editorial which was typeset and proof-read by others; copies printed in bulk in London were then physically transported by rail (or other special arrangements). The move from Fleet Street to London's Docklands revolutionised all these practices. 'Direct inputting', by which journalists typeset and check their own material direct resulted in considerable savings. Further cost reductions were achieved by vacating high-cost old-technology premises in Fleet Street and siting new technology facilities in low cost areas such as Docklands. Further economies resulted from sending heavy bulk supplies of newspapers by road rather than rail – or even achieving a double saving in both print and transport costs by printing at provincial centres where there was spare capacity, having sent the 'London set' material there electronically.

London In a category of its own, not truly national but too large to be considered local, is London's evening paper. In that readership figures are included in the National Readership Surveys, it is best considered under that heading – or at least as semi-national. Like other evening newspapers in the regions, the *Evening Standard*, being without direct competitors, is thought to be in a monopoly situation. However, this has been challenged twice in recent years. One challenge was from the new concept of a 24-hour newspaper which cut across the old *morning vs evening* concept. If successful, it could have gone on to challenge the *national vs regional* concept by building a network of 'metropolitan' newspapers to provide national coverage on a regional basis. Another challenge to the *Evening Standard* has come from a 'free distribution' publication. These challenges illustrate yet again that media categories are not watertight compartments. The *Evening Standard* now features a weekly colour supplement.

Regional and local newspapers These sub-divide into two main categories: paid-for and free. They are frequently the mainstay of local retailers' advertising, and are also used by national advertisers for test marketing or boosting particular sales areas, to support local stockists, and to compensate for any weakness in the area coverage of other media such as national newspapers and television. Regional and local newspapers tend to be most effective for advertising close to point of sale, directing customers to local outlets, and providing maps showing the location of such outlets.

As with national newspapers, your advertising message can be quickly spread on a selected day and detailed product and price information included. In common with other press media, most regional and local newspapers have much-improved printing techniques as well as colour facilities.

Verified circulation figures for paid-for newspapers and distribution figures for free newspapers are available for most titles. Readership information is provided by the JICREG database and the Target Group Index shows that nine out of ten people read a regional newspaper. Area fluctuation is small, ranging from 84 per cent in London to 92 per cent in the South West. Chapter 5 gives details of these data sources.

At the time of writing, the breakdown of regional titles was:

Morning and evening dailies	90
Regional Sundays (paid and free)	12
Paid-for weeklies	527
Free weeklies	804
Total	1433

Source: The Newspaper Society

These figures relate to separate buying points for advertising, rather than separate editorial editions, of which there are rather more.

Regional mornings These papers usually have a more serious-minded approach and consequent lower circulation, but with coverage spreading some way from the publishing centre. Editorially, they feature the business and political affairs of fairly wide areas in more detail than other newspapers.

Regional evenings These generally have more of a mass appeal, and consequently larger circulations than the morning papers. This larger circulation is usually concentrated on those who live and work near the publishing centre. Editorially, copies carry substantial amounts of local news and sports coverage, together with much classified advertising.

Regional Sundays Though few in number, these combine the benefits of local interest with the advantages of Sunday publication described earlier. Like the local mornings, regional Sundays also perform an area service with in-depth coverage of issues not duplicated by the national Sundays. With the launch of a number of new titles, such as *Scotland on Sunday*, circulation has grown by 45 per cent in the 1990s.

Local paid-for weeklies These 527 titles form a significant category. They tend to relate to smaller communities than those covered by evening newspapers, but are widely followed for details of local news and events, and for their local retail and classified advertising, including births, marriages and deaths. Local weeklies are likely to have a longer life, being kept a full week for reference.

Free newspapers Some newspapers (and magazines or directories) are issued free of charge, either distributed door-to-door or given away at important central points (such as hotels, or stations where they are handed to people on their way to work). This type of free circulation must be distinguished from the controlled-circulation publications described below, which are distributed through the post.

It is worth noting a similarity between both types of free publication (household/central distribution and postal delivery). Most conventional publishers have two sources of revenue: sale of copies and sale of advertising space. Free and controlled-circulation publications have both foregone cover-price revenue in the belief that they can make greater profit through increased advertisement revenue, by the promise of 100 per cent coverage of the advertiser's target market.

Free newspapers have been published in England for more than 100 years, but the modern upsurge started in the United States and then spread to the UK in the late 1960s. The growth was stimulated by a boom in classified advertising, later extended to most display advertising categories, and the inability of the conventional press to handle it.

A high proportion of companies which publish conventional regional newspapers are also involved in the publication of free ones – a major change since the early days when free publications were seen as a threat and some conventional publishers banned from their columns anyone who advertised in free newspapers! There are now more than 800 titles. Most free newspapers carry a degree of editorial, although the advertising/editorial ratio tends to be higher (eg 9:1) than with paid-for titles. In some areas, free publications have entirely supplanted the paid-for newspapers.

The majority of free newspapers are received by household delivery on a weekly basis, and VFD (Verified Free Distribution, described in Chapter 5) has procedures to confirm that distribution is carried out systematically, consistently and professionally. This official verification is important: a major problem in the development of free newspapers was providing proof of their most important advantage: ability to deliver total coverage of a given area. In the early days it was sometimes said that free newspaper distribution was a dumping operation, and there were apocryphal stories of delivery boys throwing them away by the bundle! Hence the importance of official verification, since a good free newspaper is often just what the advertiser wants: it ensures full coverage of the community. The established paid-for newspaper might be more thoroughly read by people with their roots in the area, but if it offers low household penetration, advertisers may seek more comprehensive coverage.

There are now very few areas of the country which do not have a free newspaper delivered, and in many cases advertisers use both free and paid-for newspapers to provide comprehensive press coverage within geographically-defined target areas. Some free newspapers can also be used to distribute leaflets as loose inserts (see Association of Household Distributors, described in Chapter 5).

Series and groups, and media organisations

A factor that sometimes deters media-planners from using local media is the sheer physical labour of sending individual orders and advertising material and subsequently correcting individual proofs and paying individual invoices, which becomes increasingly burdensome the more local papers are used. A number of developments are, however, overcoming these administrative problems.

Many of the 1,433 regional newspapers share common ownership, and combine into series or groups which make planning and buying much easier. The fact that most regional newspapers have London offices, or are represented by national sales houses, further facilitates planning and buying 'packages' of titles. There are indeed standard regional packages covering ITV areas (some sold together with local television) or providing national coverage, and even facilities for placing orders on a one order/one advertisement basis. For Regional Dailies, the Regional Daily Advertising Council provide a service branded *'The Word'*, which enables a national advertiser to advertise in 81 regional dailies with just one purchase order. To ease production, the RDAC require only six different masters to provide copy for a full page, or equivalent size in broadsheets. The Newspaper Society's marketing services, described in Chapter 5, include a central production facility. On receipt of master copies of each advertisement, the Society sends material to each newspaper on the schedule. Some 95 per cent of regional and local titles subscribe to this service.

Co-operative advertising

Setting aside the order/production chores just mentioned, another factor which sometimes deters advertisers from using local media is that joint manufacturer/dealer promotions involve companies in the considerable task of contacting an extensive distribution network to determine individual stockists' participation in co-operative advertising. The Newspaper Society's services are also important in this respect.

These various developments make it far easier from the administrative point of view to use local media, thus enabling regional newspapers to make their particular contribution to effective advertising schedules.

Magazines

Magazines, as newspapers, afford you an opportunity to deliver a detailed message. The exact manner of delivery can vary widely for there is great variety in magazine format, size, number of pages, printing quality, colour availability, and advertising facilities. Space is usually sold by the page and in fractions thereof and a variety of special positions, eg inside front cover or facing matter may be available.

One of the main reasons which leads advertisers to select magazines is mood – the reader's state of mind when your advertising message is delivered. This aspect of magazine media is frequently linked with another point in their favour, in that a finer degree of audience selection is often possible, since readership is usually in more clearly defined groups than the broad coverage of newspapers. These two points together give you considerable advertising advantages, since you reach a clearly defined group of prospects when they are likely to be receptive to your message.

A point which may count against magazines on the other hand is that of timing, since magazines are not precision instruments capable of delivering your message on a selected day, as can newspapers. The physical life of magazines is far longer, and your advertising message may be delivered at any time during this period. Indeed, cases are known where advertisers have received replies to magazine advertisements years after the cover date. Another aspect of timing is long copy dates, which may count against use of magazines by advertisers seeking to make swift announcements, or whose advertising content is subject to sudden and unexpected changes. Marketing considerations will determine which of the two contrasting points is more important to you: lack of precise timing, or the far longer life of magazine advertisements discussed later. Technological changes are having their effect here, however, as copy dates, whilst still longer than newspapers, are shortening, and some proprietors use new media such as CD Rom and Internet to distribute their magazines.

This preamble has, of course contained generalisations and it would be unrealistic to group all magazines together and view them as one homogenous media group. They can be divided into three main categories: consumer (usually sub-divided into general and specialist); business and professional (which include controlled circulation and trade magazines); finally, miscellaneous magazines (which contains the growing area of 'courtesy' or customer magazines).

General Consumer Magazines These appeal to the broad mass of men or women or both, but there is increasing segmentation by lifestyle. There is usually scope for a finer degree of audience selection, as readers tend to have more clearly defined characteristics than for newspapers. Advertisers know their audience characteristics, because most general magazines are included in the National Readership Surveys described in Chapter 5. Accordingly, total readership can be sub-divided into the various categories of age, gender and socio-economic group, or by specific characteristics such as ownership of appliances, and this makes precise audience selection much easier. This fine degree of selectivity is coupled with the other media factor of a receptive audience.

Specialist Consumer Magazines These, as the name implies, appeal to groups having a special interest in common, but can be further sub-divided into different categories according to the nature of that interest, which may be a hobby, sport or other specialist activity. British Rate and Data (BRAD) lists 182 different specialities ranging from aeroplanes to woodworking.

Business and Professional Magazines These magazines provide people with information relevant to their working lives and are categorised separately by BRAD which lists 227 categories ranging from accountancy to the wine and spirit trade.

When considering publications where the focus is a business or professional one, you should bear in mind the difference between 'vertical' and 'horizontal' media. The former cover a single trade or occupation at all management levels from top to bottom, whereas the circulation of horizontal media implies coverage of readers occupying similar positions but spread across a wide range of industries, for example accountants. (See also 'Points in Common' below.) The full range of business-to-business media was discussed in depth in Martyn Davis' other book, *Business-to-Business Marketing and Promotion* (Century Business).

Trade Magazines These are in fact also business publications, but are singled out for separate attention since advertisers use them in a particular way. In using consumer or business magazines, you try to persuade readers to buy in their own right, as consumers of your merchandise. Only a few advertisers, selling such things as shop fittings, use the trade press to promote their merchandise direct. Most advertisers use the trade press to contact retailers in their vital role as intermediaries between the manufacturer and the public. Accordingly, trade press advertising messages usually urge 'Be ready for the demand that public advertising will stimulate – stock up, display and make a profit!' rather than 'Buy for your own use'. Trade press advertisements, therefore, tend to feature incentives such as details of coming consumer advertising, display material available, and profit to be gained.

Consumer, Business and Trade Magazines: points in common

Despite the major differences in the way in which the media groups are used, they have certain characteristics in common, relating to the number and type of readers. With general magazines, you usually have circulation and readership figures to evaluate, but with special interest, business and trade magazines it is sometimes impossible for you to form a considered opinion in the same way. Circulation figures are usually available, but not always. Furthermore, where circulation is known, this frequently reveals that the publication does not fully cover the group in question. A counter argument to incomplete market coverage is that the proportion reached are the enthusiasts and 'trend setters', and that those who do not read the publication cannot have the same degree of interest as those who do. This, however, only highlights another point sometimes made against these magazines: that sometimes all you know about coverage is what is implied by the magazine's title. When considering a trade or special interest magazine, you need to know where the readers are located within the country, whether they are large or small buyers, traditional or modern in outlook, and so on. In some cases an 'ABC Profile' or for an international magazine an audit by BPA (see Chapter 5) may be issued, but in others, however, no readership information is provided and you are left to deduce what you can by common sense, from the title and contents of the magazine and, if available, publishers' own surveys.

In short, the specialist and trade press may reach only a proportion of your total market, and you know little or nothing about the characteristics of the proportion you do reach. This is perhaps a harsh statement, but it accurately summarises the problem you face when attempting to evaluate some of these media. Instead of hard data, you often have little choice but to rely on old-fashioned criteria like editorial 'feel' and your own personal knowledge of what is read and respected in the industries of your customers. The fact that there may be several publications competing for the same market makes this in-depth study of the actual magazines all the more important.

Controlled-Circulation Distribution The incomplete market coverage and lack of readership information just mentioned have led to an interesting development, namely controlled-circulation publications sent to individuals in certain defined categories. The magazine is not sold but distributed free of charge, through the post, in the same way as subscription copies. Controlled circulation magazines are important business-to-business media, with most publishers having worked hard to develop effective circulation databases. Conventional publishers have argued that readers are unlikely to value anything they do not pay for, but the counter-argument is that the cost of many special interest publications is borne by employers: the actual readers are unaware of the source of the copy that arrives on their desks, and value it according to the subject matter.

The benefits of a controlled-circulation publication depend on its distribution, which overcomes the two main drawbacks to conventional publications: incomplete coverage and lack of readership information. Controlled-circulation journals fully cover the market chosen by the publisher as his target market, and readership information is automatically available simply through analysis of the mailing list to which the journal is sent. Thus, in theory, the medium is near perfect. Any medium has its drawbacks, however, and those of controlled circulation arise from the credibility of the journal's mailing list.

Controlled circulation gives you full coverage of the market only if your market matches precisely the publication's market. Should the controlled-circulation journal's definition be wider or narrower than yours, this must mean either waste circulation or incomplete coverage. Further, there is the vital question of how the mailing list was compiled. One aspect of particular interest to advertisers is whether the magazine was individually requested, company requested or not requested. Giving a definition is one thing, but obtaining a list of all those coming within this definition is another. This problem is further complicated by the normal difficulty of keeping any mailing list up-to-date. The Audit Bureau of Circulations described in a later chapter provides data on controlled-circulation journals, but some media planners undertake additional 'spot checks' on reader attitudes and mailing-list accuracy by telephoning individuals who should be on the mailing list to ask if they receive copies, and their opinion of them.

Miscellaneous Magazines Another interesting variation in distribution method is for magazines to be given away free. This could be by door-to-door distribution in selected areas, or by handing copies to people on their way to work, or by mailing customers of companies with databases, or by making copies available through hotels or on aircraft etc. Such free magazines cover a wide spectrum and range from those that contain nothing but advertising to those with 30 per cent or more editorial as well as glossy magazines boasting carefully selected distribution and the up-market title of 'Courtesy publications' or customer magazines. This last category covers those magazines produced on behalf of companies to improve the image of the company and its brands, generate goodwill and secure customer loyalty. About 50 per cent of the titles in this sector are accounted for by in-flight and financial service industry titles. VFD (Verified Free Distribution) described in Chapter 5 is highly relevant in this respect.

Added Value Facilities

Some magazines provide a wide range of added value facilities (described in Chapter 7) to help advertisers communicate with their target markets. Advertorials are advertisements written and designed in the editorial style of the magazine and guidelines covering them have been published by the Periodical Publishers Association (PPA). Recent years have seen a growth in sponsored editorial–titled advertisement feature, but more commonly called 'advertorial' within the industry. There has been remarkable growth in the number of pages devoted to advertorials in women's, fashion and home interest titles. One interesting example of this technique was demonstrated by the PPA (described in Chapter 5) when it used advertorials in the advertising business press to promote advertorials!

Another interesting opportunity is the ability to negotiate 'cover mounts', the placing of free product samples on magazine covers. This technique benefits the magazine by attracting more readers, as well as benefiting the advertiser.

Other added value services include seasonal features (particularly for holidays, gardening and Christmas), gatefolds (extra pages folded inside the magazine which can be perforated for easy detaching and used for competition entry, as reply device or as a reminder of the advertiser's branch addresses), loose or bound-in inserts, gummed or 'tipped-in' cards (particularly useful for reply-cards), run-ons or pre-prints (particularly useful for mailing to the retail trade), point-of-sale material (for example: as advertised in . . .), 'scratch 'n' sniff' scent strips and sequential numbering (which enables advertisers to run lottery promotions).

Additionally, A/B copy splits (where two or more ads are alternated in the same edition of the magazine), regional copy splits and even geo-demographic profiling (using Acorn or Mosaic described in Chapter 12) are possible. The ever increasing range of added-value facilities is now an important media consideration.

The press medium overall

Before turning to other media, it is important to see the press media in context. What was formerly a relatively static marketplace is now a fast-moving and dynamic one, quite apart from changes in printing technology. Publishers compete for the same markets, adapt existing publications and launch new titles.

TELEVISION

In terms of overall advertising expenditure, television should be the next medium to cover. The many recent changes, those now taking place (such as satellite and cable) and other changes in the pipeline (such as digital and widescreen) mean the situation is so complex that it calls for separate attention in the next chapter. This chapter, therefore, now turns to the next largest medium in terms of share of overall advertising expenditure – direct mail.

DIRECT MAIL

Among the advantages of using postal services to deliver advertising messages is selectivity, since your mailing can be directed to a selected list of individuals. Further advantages are complete coverage of your market and the absence of wastage, since the mailing covers and is restricted to those within the defined market. All depends, of course, on the accuracy of your mailing list. This can be obtained in a number of ways, and in some cases you can build up a mailing list from your own records. Where internal records are not suitable, external sources can be consulted. Published reference books can provide much information, but this source suffers from two drawbacks. One is that frequently there is more than one reference book and the task of cross-checking one against the other is unavoidable, for clearly there is no point in mailing the same individual more than once. Removal of duplicate names, sometimes called 'merge and purge', is straightforward in comparison with the problem raised when two sources show different names for the holder of a given job. Only one can be correct, and the discrepancy no doubt stems from the fact that one reference source went to press later than the other and staff changes took place in the meantime.

Such changes highlight the second drawback of using published sources – the problem of keeping any list up-to-date. This involves carefully checking relevant publications regularly for news of staff changes, and this is no small task. For these reasons many firms turn to direct mail houses or list brokers, relying on them to provide mailing lists that are both comprehensive and up-to-date. External lists fall into two main groups – general consumer, and business-to-business or special interest. There are usually many lists available in the latter categories (industrial/occupational/professional/trade/technical, or alternatively, specialist activities/hobbies/sports or other interests) and your task is not so much obtaining lists but choosing between them. General consumer lists, on the other hand, once presented a major problem.

If you could not build your own list from customer enquiries and responses to earlier advertising, where could you go to get one? The population census was insufficiently selective and often very dated, and the same criticisms applied to telephone directories which, additionally, gave incomplete coverage. The situation changed dramatically, however, with the introduction of *geo-demographic* classifications. One such system is ACORN (A Classification of Residential Neighbourhoods) which, as its title implies, analyses where you live in terms of type of neighbourhood or residence. To give a simple example of its application, there is little point in your sending direct mail about lawn-mowers or garden furniture to someone who lives in a house without a garden! There are a number of geo-demographic classifications, described later, which can help you target your direct mail accurately.

Use of direct mail as a medium brings other advantages, such as personalisation. Direct mail letters can be run off in bulk, but with the name and address of each recipient 'matched in' at the head of each letter to give the appearance of individual word-processing, and your signature realistically reproduced to give the effect of a personal letter. Indeed, many direct mail letters are individually word-processed and personally signed for greater authenticity.

Further benefits stem from direct mail's flexibility, which permits sending different messages to different target groups and, for overseas markets, addressing them in their own language. Another benefit is that distance is no object, whereas a representative's visit would be most costly.

Flexibility is a major benefit even within the UK, and has become even more feasible as direct mail has become computer based. Mailing lists can be segmented, and sophisticated retrieval systems can send relevant letters to buyers of different products, or adopt other variations – different letters to those who have bought within the last month or stated multiples thereof, for instance. The computer can even signal those who have not responded within, for example, the last year, thereby making it possible for you to clean your list by removing 'dead' names and addresses. (The use of databases for direct mail purposes is discussed in more detail later.)

You can, if you wish, test different promotional messages, creative formats, mailing lists or other campaign aspects, before your main campaign. Pre-testing – a difficult task with other media – is relatively simple with direct mail.

Direct mail's flexibility also permits you to 'turn the tap' on and off with ease. This could be important if, for example, production restraints or salesforce capacity calls for a limited number of enquiries, or for controlled flow over time.

Timing is another advantage of direct mail, since you can select the most suitable dates and frequency for delivery of your advertising message and need not be restricted by any media-owner's publication dates.

Yet another advantage of direct mail is that inclusion of reply-paid postcards or envelopes can stimulate replies. Certainly you can include reply-paid folders or freepost coupons in press advertisements, but this takes up costly space and is often unattractive. With such press advertisements you cannot be so selective and your prospective customer must still write his name and address, while with direct mail you can enter the recipient's particulars on the card beforehand, so that all he need do is post it. Such direct response makes evaluation of results and control of your campaign that much easier.

Direct mail shots can also include leaflets, booklets, or even samples. In short, there is no limit to the information you can include. Some direct mail shots in fact amount to reference books and are kept by recipients as useful sources of information.

The attention factor of direct mail is somewhat controversial. Many claim that some people receive so much direct mail that they pay no attention to mailings, but throw them straight into the waste-paper basket. No doubt some people do receive a large number of mailings, but this is perhaps a creative rather than a media problem. Research from the Direct Mail Information Service (DMIS, described in Chapter 5) indicates that 83 per cent of consumer direct mail is opened and 68 per cent is read. No doubt some people do receive a large number of mailings and their opening and reading levels may be slightly lower. However, the mailing *did* receive attention and the problem is a creative one of devising a mailing that retains attention. I do not accept the generalisation that 90 per cent of direct mail is wasted: junk mail is *bad* mail and 100 per cent of it likely to be thrown away. Most *good* direct mail successfully reaches the intended target and is carefully studied, indeed, recipients may not even consider it to be a direct mail shot.

Direct mail houses can help here, and their services can be considered under three broad headings: provision of mailing lists, physical handling of the mailing, and creative advice on the type of direct mail campaign to be mounted. Also highly relevant in this context are the DMIS and the Royal Mail's Direct Marketing Department, described in Chapter 5.

The main drawback to direct mail is its cost. Though often low in total outlay, direct mail can be very expensive when considered on a cost per contact basis, though a well-planned campaign often gives a low ratio of cost per enquiry, or even cost per sale. The advantages, however, are many, and as always your task is to assess the benefits against cost. In this respect, this formerly static medium has in recent years undergone major changes in the light of new technology: computerisation of mailing lists, and new printing methods. These developments are of great importance, bearing in mind the rapid increase in direct marketing (discussed in Chapter 9) in which direct mail plays so vital a role: expenditure on direct mail increased from £530m in 1988 to £1,050m in 1994.

POSTER AND TRANSPORT

Facilities exist for poster displays in most urban areas in Great Britain. Perhaps the most traditional form of advertising, the poster industry is divided into 'roadside' and 'transport' sections, with Advertising Association statistics showing an expenditure ratio of just under 2:1.

Poster sizes

Poster size terminology is historical, and 'sheets' referred to the number of sheets of paper that had to be pasted (or *posted*) up on the hoarding. The standard poster sizes are:

4-sheet	1.524 × 1.016 metres
6-sheet	1.676 × 1.219 metres
48-sheet	3.048 × 6.096 metres
96-sheet	3.048 × 12.192 metres

In addition to these standard size panels, there are a number of other options available including 16, 32 and 64 sheet. The number of poster-panels available in these sizes is relatively small and they are frequently used by local advertisers. Of the total UK universe of 117,000 roadside panels, there are some 70,000 4-sheet and 6-sheet panels (in towns, shopping precincts and bus stops), 38,000 48-sheet sites and more than 3,000 96-sheet supersite panels and special displays. These supersite panels and special displays are normally on main roads and can be hand painted with three dimensional displays if required.

Within the transport section of the industry, there is a wide variety of sizes and sites (too many to list here – think how many different types you pass on your way to work!) on buses, trains and stations.

Poster research

The great majority of roadside sites (some 95 per cent of the total) are owned by poster contractors in membership of the Outdoor Advertising Association, and an independent measurement of audience delivery is available through POSTAR, the poster audience research described later. Within the transport section, audience statistics are not so widely available, although TDI BUSADS and TRAC (the Tube Research Audience Classification) described in Chapter 5 provide much useful information about sites on London's transport system.

The advantages of poster advertising

Posters, whether on roadside hoardings or transport sites, offer you the full benefit of colour. This can be of particular advantage since printing the posters rests within your own control, and high quality can thus be assured. With other media you must accept the colour quality uniformly available to all, but with posters you can if you wish achieve a quality often unobtainable in press media, simply by printing in more than the standard four colours. Some sites feature electronic displays, whilst a growing proportion provide 'Ultravision' panels with slats that rotate electronically to form three different faces. An increasing number of panels are illuminated, including backlit 4/6-sheets and front lit 48 and 96-sheet panels. Supersite advertisers have sometimes achieved spectacular effects with three-dimensional constructions (one adhesive manufacturer even stuck a car to his hoarding!). The majority of poster advertisers, however, achieve highly effective communications without this additional expense, through standard printing.

The poster medium offers many additional advantages. You control the area of coverage and can localise your campaign to a street, a town, an area, a region, or alternatively mount a nationwide campaign. You can in fact book sites in exactly those areas where you most need advertising support.

A further advantage is that you achieve almost complete coverage of the active population within the selected area, together with a high repetition factor (depending on the number of sites booked) for nearly everybody goes out and does so frequently, and therefore has the opportunity to see outdoor advertising. The greater the number of sites booked, the faster will maximum coverage of the population of the target area be achieved, and the greater will be the repetition factor.

For these reasons, posters are regarded by many as the ideal reminder medium. This view is reinforced by the fact that posters are usually read at a glance, and thus well suited to a brief message. When the factors of high coverage and repetition, colour and reminder close to the point of sale in selected areas are considered together, it becomes clear why a large number of manufacturers place great faith in poster advertising.

Poster advertising need not always be restricted to a brief message: on a number of occasions, particularly where the audience is captive as in railways and buses, there is an excellent opportunity for you to convey a more detailed message.

The drawbacks of the outdoor medium

The many advantages of the poster medium are almost self-evident but there are, of course, drawbacks. People are exposed to posters but often have difficulty in recalling campaigns, unless prompted. Another drawback is defacement – by weather or vandals. Defacement can be identified by employing an inspection service, which provides photographic proof that a panel has been posted. The industry does make efforts to reduce the impact of this disadvantage, and one contractor usually repairs damage within 24–48 hours of notification. Some former disadvantages of the medium – shortage of good sites due to the T/C (till countermanded) bookings described below, and lack of research data – have now largely been overcome by the overhauling of the industry, and by the new POSTAR system described in Chapter 5.

Buying poster advertising

Advertising rates vary according to site, but are subject to discounts for six-month or twelve-month orders. Sites can be bought individually (a method of purchase known as *site-by-site* or *line-by-line*), by pre-selected campaigns, or by selected packages. At one time, poster availability was a problem in that many good sites were tied up in 'till countermanded' contracts, but the proportion on T/C bookings is now less than 10 per cent.

Restructuring of the poster medium has made campaign planning and buying much easier, and the 1990s have seen the emergence of three national poster contractors for the sizes most in demand – 4/6 sheets, 48 and 96 sheet panels. Additionally, there are specialist poster agencies which can put together complete poster campaigns bought site-by-site, using the POSTAR system.

Other forms of outdoor advertising

A final point is that the term 'outdoor advertising' is sometimes extended to embrace other media not yet mentioned. British Rate &

Data, the standard reference work described later, features a wide spectrum of outdoor media including: aerial (banners, hot air, helium and tethered balloons, fireworks), mobile posters (with electronic changing messages, ultravision or 48/96 sheet posters), taxis (with advertising inside, outside or overall livery), eggverts (printed on eggs or egg boxes), supermarket trolleys, hospital waiting areas, livestock sales rings, sports grounds and arenas, exhibition halls, ports and airports, pubs, restaurants, motorway service stations and on golf courses. What are now termed 'Ambient media' are discussed further below.

RADIO

As the number of radio stations has grown over the last few years, accompanied by a doubling in radio's share of advertising spend to 4 per cent, coupled with forthcoming technological changes radio merits a chapter on its own (Chapter 3). This chapter now focuses on the next largest medium: cinema.

CINEMA

Since the mid-1980s cinema has enjoyed a sustained revival in popularity. 1994 saw admissions climb for the tenth successive year to reach 124m – the highest annual total since 1978.

There are now more than 1,900 cinema screens in the UK available for advertising, representing about 99 per cent of all cinemas. At the end of 1994, the number of screens operating in the UK was the highest since the mid-1960s.

This growth has been fuelled by investment in quality films as well as new and refurbished cinemas. The most significant development has been that of 'multiplex' cinemas offering up to 14 different screens, comfortable seating, quality sound and free parking. They are often located within new entertainment complexes which include shopping, discotheque, restaurants, bars, bowling and other facilities. Indeed, the 666 screens in multiplexes account for just over a third of all screens and 45 per cent of all visits.

Cinema advertising offers you the advantages of colour, stereo sound and movement, giving creative scope to demonstrate your product in full colour and with high technical quality on the large screen, to show people enjoying its use, and with music and the human voice heightening the effect. Other creative approaches such as animation and computer graphics are also possible. In addition, your message is screened to what is descriptively termed a 'captive' audience, sitting facing the screen in a darkened auditorium – contrast this with television viewing. The main cinema audience is a distinct one, composed largely of young adults with freely disposable purchasing power, at a point in their lives when they make many important decisions, thus providing a market of considerable attraction to many advertisers. There are two secondary audiences. Firstly, children, usually accompanied by a parent, who visit the cinema during the 18 non-school weeks. The other audience is the older, more up-market profile of those who visit 'art' cinemas, primarily showing continental or Asian films.

Coverage build-up is slow in comparison with TV and full penetration of your target groups is by no means complete. However, cinema is useful for extending multi-media campaigns at a low cost and for reaching light TV viewers.

There are two 'sales houses' to contact when booking cinema campaigns: Cinema Media, with 83 per cent of the audiences, and Pearl and Dean, who account for the remaining 17 per cent. Together, they provide three main ways to buy cinema campaigns.

1. Screen-by-screen Each cinema screen has individual weekly rates linked to admission levels, and advertising can be purchased on a weekly basis. The advertiser has total control over the localisation of the campaign to a town, an area, a region. This buying route is particularly effective if you wish to advertise in selected towns or sites close to retail outlets. The benefit to the local trader is obvious – he can appeal to his local audience and attract enquiries by featuring his name and address on the cinema screen. Other advertisers with broader distribution can follow the same principle by building a schedule based on cinemas that match their particular geographical requirements and, after demonstrating their product in the opening part of the film, conclude with the name and address of the local dealer, perhaps on a shared-cost basis.

2. Packages For advertisers whose needs are more general, there are a number of special packages. Advertisers can buy regional or town-based packages as well as buying into individual films taking advantage perhaps of any creative link between film and product. The commercial can be shown in an environment helpful to the product, or the advertiser can take advantage of the audience patterns created by different film certificates.

There are also packages targeting the secondary audiences of children and visitors to Art screens.

3. Audience Guarantee Plan (AGP) This enables effective mass coverage of the cinema audience and many major advertisers take advantage of the AGP by booking all the screens in at least one ISBA area. These areas are defined by the Incorporated Society of British Advertisers, the trade association for advertisers described in Chapter 9. AGP is costed using a seasonally weighted admission base and a fixed cost per thousand admissions.

Cinema advertising commercials are shown within one reel which is screened at all performances (except children's matinees) with the house lights down, prior to the main feature film. You can buy screen time in this reel on the basis of standard timelengths of 10, 15, 20 seconds, etc to the nearest 5 seconds.

A final point to make is that additional advertising opportunities are available such as foyer promotions, leafleting, sampling and advertising on TV monitors and video walls in some multiplexes.

OTHER ADVERTISING MEDIA

Exhibitions

Exhibitions, one of the oldest advertising media, originated with the mediaeval trade fairs. Exhibitions range from those of general consumer interest to those appealing to special interest groups or trades, with many intermediate categories. Some exhibitions may be considered in more than one category, as when entrance is restricted to the trade for the first few days, after which the exhibition opens to the public. In the course of time, exhibitions may perhaps shift their position in the scale, as when a special interest exhibition arouses such general interest that public attendance generally outnumbers special interest visitors. Cutting across the scale of special interest and general exhibitions are geographical variations, since exhibitions may be local, national or even international in their coverage.

According to the Exhibition Industry Federation (EIF) described in Chapter 5 there are up to 700 exhibitions a year in the 46 exhibition venues of over 2,000 square metres. Of these, over 300 are for the trade, over 200 are public and over 150 cater for both trade and public. One major location is the National Exhibition Centre (NEC), Birmingham, which has 12 halls, an hotel, railway station and airport. There are many other smaller venues that host events, as well as conference centres that host conference-associated exhibitions.

Whilst there are exhibitions of mass appeal, the majority of exhibitions provide a focus on specialised interests and attract tightly targeted or niche audiences. A drawback that the medium shares with the specialist consumer or business press is that sometimes all you know about the exhibition's coverage is what you can deduce by common sense from its title. Often there is little or no information about where visitors come from, the type of firm they represent, their position in the organisation, and so on. The Audit Bureau of Circulations, described later, independently certifies attendances at about 20 per cent of exhibitions and issues a Certificate of Attendance. The Association of Exhibition Organisers makes it a condition of membership that its members audit their exhibitions. The position is thus improving, but in many cases there is still a serious lack of information.

The advantages this medium offers really speak for themselves. Exhibitions afford you the double benefit of demonstration combined with personal contact. You can demonstrate your product (a tremendous advantage when it is too bulky to take around) and can do so under ideal conditions, in settings specially designed for the purpose. Prospective buyers can see and handle your product, try it for themselves and ask questions. As an exhibitor you can for your part answer their queries, distribute samples or literature, obtain names and addresses to follow up for subsequent action, or take orders on the spot.

An additional benefit with many special interest exhibitions is that they represent the one opportunity in the year when you can contact virtually all your prospective customers, since the opportunity to view all the current models ensures a consistently high attendance. Exhibitions can also provide an opportunity to express appreciation of support given during the year, with your company's sales director and other senior staff using the stand as a basis for dispensing hospitality and greeting those they cannot call on regularly themselves. Admittedly, this is sometimes abused, with exhibits being reduced to the role of free bars and buyers making the rounds of the stands. Accordingly, the main advantages of exhibitions – demonstration and personal contact – should always be kept to the fore.

A further benefit of exhibitions arises from the descriptive entry you contribute to the catalogue, which visitors frequently keep for reference. In addition, there is always the possibility, for a fortunate few, of valuable editorial publicity: most exhibitions merit considerable comment in the press and other media, and those with revolutionary products or striking stands may be the subject of many editorial features.

Other than the lack of audience statistics already mentioned, the main drawback to exhibitions is their high cost. They are often very much more expensive than would appear at first sight, for the cost of designing and constructing your stand can far outweigh the site costs, particularly where advertisers compete for visitors' attention by the lavishness of their exhibits. In addition, there are many running costs: electricity, telephone, literature and samples, direct mail shots inviting people to your stand, advertisements in the catalogue, hospitality, insurance and staff. On top of the expense of hired demonstrators are the hidden costs of your own staff, who must be present to deal with those questions temporary staff cannot answer: there may also be hotel and other expenses. The longer the exhibition's duration, the higher the costs of stand construction and running costs.

There can also be practical problems, and the small print on the contract should be checked carefully: regulations may restrict what exhibitors are allowed to do on their stands. The practicalities of exhibiting should also be considered – if the product is a bulky or heavy one, it may be too big to get through the exhibition hall's doors, and are there any special Health and Safety restrictions?

Furthermore, most exhibitions permit only a once-a-year stimulus. Where repetition/continuity is achieved by participation in a series of exhibitions, expenses rise proportionately. Frequently, too, exhibitions occupy far more top management time, before and during the exhibition, than is customary with other media. The attention paid by management shows, however, that although exhibitions may be costly, the benefits clearly outweigh the drawbacks, where personal contact and demonstration are of major importance.

Other forms of demonstration Formal exhibitions are not the only medium to offer you facilities for demonstration and personal contact. Some advertisers mount private exhibitions, either on their own premises or by using a portable display which they erect in premises hired for the occasion. This type of exhibition can often be combined with an invited audience film show. Some advertisers, in preference to portable exhibition stands, construct mobile exhibitions in special trailers, buses or railway carriages which they then send round the country.

The very extreme of personal contact and demonstration is, of course, salesmanship. Rather than use conventional advertising media, your company's representatives may demonstrate the product. Even here, however, the range of media includes activities which can assist you in your marketing operation. Demonstrators can be hired to promote your product in retail outlets, shopping precincts or railway stations and distribute samples; demonstrations can also be achieved by distributing samples from door to door. Sales aids such as lap-top computers or portable video units are provided to sales representatives to assist their selling task and many organisations produce their own promotional videos and organise hospitality events at which to show them. These are examples which show that personal selling by representatives and indirect selling through advertising are not separate activities but overlap considerably.

Point-of-sale material

Display material can serve as a vital reminder at the very point of purchase, delivering your advertising message at the time and place most likely to result in sales. The range of display material is too wide to cover fully here, and extends from showcards of various shapes and sizes, through window stickers and crowners, in-store video units, and other display pieces to dispenser units which both sell and display your product.

Adequate display at the place of purchase can make or mar the success of your marketing campaign, and point-of-sale material is therefore of great importance. As a medium, however, it differs markedly from others. It has been said, with some justification, that 90 per cent of all display material is wasted. Usually, the reason is failure to realise why point-of-sale is a unique medium. With other media, you pay the media-owner and have the assurance that he will deliver your advertising message: with display material, however, this depends entirely on the retailer who selects, from the vast amount of material available to him, the few display units he will use.

The high wastage of display material arises usually from one or both of two basic faults – production of poor material, and failure to merchandise this material. And in this context poor material means not only that which is inferior in quality but also high-quality material that does not suit the retailer's needs. Much display material is alas based on what the advertiser would like, and ignores the hard fact that only the material that the retailer wants is put on display. And even when you have produced exactly the right display material, you must still devise a complete selling programme to ensure its effective use at point of sale. Sending out a showcard with your merchandise, to be unpacked in the warehouse and thrown away, its existence unknown to the display manager, illustrates lack of attention to this point. There are many ways of ensuring the dealer's co-operation in display (see Part 3); all have the common aim of making the dealer confident your product will sell, and eager to use your display material to promote it to best advantage.

Miscellaneous advertising media

The range of advertising media is considerable and within this chapter it has been possible to review only the major ones. This is not to detract from the growing importance of miscellaneous media. Indeed, the growing range of new outdoor facilities has been categorised 'Ambient media' and includes: painted buses and taxis, airships, shopping and airport trolleys, golf holes and tees, TV screens on buses and ads on vertical 'step risers' on Underground stations. Other examples of diverse and original ambient media are ads on petrol pump handles, talking devices on supermarket aisles, ads on train departure boards, coloured trains and the projection of ads onto famous buildings.

There are also 'new media' opportunities associated with the other media described in this book. With target audiences becoming ever more segmented, so too are media options (or, so the cynics would have us believe, becoming more fragmented).

Historically media plans relied on two or three of the main media (typically, television supported by magazines and roadside posters) to reach their targets. Now, media plans are increasing the range of media used to reach their targets with new media contributing to reaching targets interactively in the right environment.

INTERNATIONAL MEDIA

To cover international media properly would call for a separate book. However, most media types described in this book and the principles governing their use are the same. Thus if you are concerned with planning, buying and evaluating media on an international basis, the basic questions are the same as for domestic media discussed later.

There are some important variances, however, which are outlined below.

Media Diversity and Importance

Whilst most, if not all, of the various media may exist in other countries, their relative importance may vary considerably. For instance, the UK is distinctive in having a strong National press. In countries spread over wider geographic areas or with wide cultural differences (such as France, Spain and the USA), regional media are considerably more important than they are in the UK.

Radio can be more important in countries where economic pressures preclude customer purchase of other media. For instance, in Eastern Europe and many parts of Africa, radio is a more important medium than television and consumer magazines.

Posters can be more important in some countries such as Spain, where control over planning of urban areas is not as strong as in the UK. In Poland, there is an excellent computer mapping system controlling the way that posters are bought, whereas in Russia there is little control of poster contractors and competition between contractors can be detrimental to an advertising campaign.

Cinema is an important medium in many countries, where mobile cinemas travel between villages and are seen by the whole community.

Television is relatively new in some countries. As a result, other media such as press are more important, for instance in Germany. Conversely, television in Greece takes a far higher proportion of advertising spend than in the UK.

The structure of television spot advertising varies between different countries. Those who have visited the USA are sometimes surprised by the frequency and amount of commercials, arising from the difference in the time allowed for commercials. In the UK seven minutes per hour (seven and a half in peak time) is the limit, whereas in America eleven minutes is permitted. In some countries innumerable commercials are screened consecutively, whereas the UK norm is to have under three minutes of commercials at any one time.

Media Buying

Different policies in regard to buying apply in different countries. For instance, in Germany prices are just starting to be negotiated, whereas negotiation is a central part of the UK buying process. In some countries such as Spain, discounts can reach high levels, whereas in France a recent law (the 'Loi Sapin') restricts discounting. Conversely, in Greece extensive debate over the level of control imposed meant that a similar law was postponed.

Media Research

Subsequent chapters of this book discuss the wide range of media research vehicles available in the UK. Some countries do not have such a wide range. For instance the 'people meter' television monitoring system exists in only 48 countries, and the Star TV Network described below can be measured in only 17 of the 53 countries in which it can be viewed. There are various countries in Europe that use meters, whilst the PETAR Pan-European study described in Chapter 5 still uses a Diary system which does not measure second sets nor guests in the home. In each European country, the meter system varies slightly. In German, it is run by GfK, in Denmark by Gallup and in Holland by Infomart.

Individual countries do not always have independent research. The historic basis of most media research in this country is the 'JIC' (Joint Industry Committee) whereby the three elements of the industry – advertiser, agency and media-owner – jointly co-ordinate the research. This improves impartiality and reduces the possible bias of media-owners' own research. In some countries advertisers have only media-produced research to rely on.

There are other examples of the need to apply local knowledge. For instance, being aware that politics may play a role in research in certain countries. There are also countries where, whilst literacy in a local language may be high, the cachet attached to English may increase readership per copy of an English language publication, particularly if a village shares one copy. This can give the paper a greater importance than suggested by its circulation.

International Media

Balancing these problems, is a widening availability of international media. Television channels broadcast by satellite can be viewed in many countries. For instance the 'Star' satellite network mentioned above can already be seen in 53 million homes in 53 countries stretching from Lebanon to Japan, and plans to extend coverage to Australia.

This is just one indication of the trend towards the globalisation of media ownership, which will affect the practicalities of advertising. For instance, global advertising can already be purchased on the CNN television channel. As other television channels expand internationally they too may offer global agencies the opportunity to negotiate with one central sales point. Advertisers who take advantage of these global opportunities will need to allow for local issues to be considered, when implementing their creative and media tactics.

Some newspapers are printed in a number of countries. The *Financial Times* is printed simultaneously in eight different locations throughout the world and circulates in 140 countries. It is possible to change advertising copy, so that different messages can be directed towards Pacific Rim readers as compared with those based in Europe.

Many magazines, particularly those appealing also to the business community, are also printed and circulated internationally. Some general interest and women's interest magazines are similarly published in various countries. The editorial content usually varies and is printed in the local language. International advertisers can negotiate deals, however, with different copy appearing in various editions, co-ordinated centrally.

The Internet is, of course, available throughout the world, so that your pages, or advertisements on another location's pages, can be seen internationally.

Increasingly, advertisers are appreciating the benefits that can accrue from a Pan-European or even global media campaign. The vexed question of who pays is discussed in Chapter 15.

Chapter 2

Television Media

Television merits a separate chapter because of its complexity, rather than because of the amount spent on TV advertising – Advertising Association statistics show that in 1994 press media accounted for 55.1 per cent of all advertising expenditure, compared with television's 28.3 per cent.

The public body responsible for licensing our commercial television channels is the Independent Television Commission. The ITC regulates all non-BBC transmissions, including Channel 3 (the ITV regional network and our national breakfast channel), Channel 4 and Channel 5 – which can all be grouped together under the heading of terrestrial broadcasting. It also regulates satellite and cable transmissions, and 'additional services' such as teletext, carried on the spare capacity of the television signal.

This chapter therefore reviews television media under similar main headings of terrestrial broadcasting, satellite transmissions, and cable, together with one further category: non-broadcast source. Before discussing these various types of television, it is important to recognise the evolution of the medium over the last decade, and that it continues to be in the throes of change.

For many years, most viewers were restricted to three television channels. This choice was then widened by the introduction of Channel 4 and then later by breakfast TV, satellite and cable. Soon, it will be broadened even further by the launch of Channel 5 and the introduction of Digital Television, broadcast both terrestrially and by satellite. The ITV network delivered mass regional audiences at predictable times but, as this chapter makes clear, these continuing developments have changed that pattern: the mass regional audiences of past years have been whittled away by viewers switching to other channels, which may in turn cover smaller niche audiences or larger geographic areas.

Furthermore, TV audiences are no longer viewing at predictable times, since many viewers now 'time-shift' using video-recorders.

THE STRUCTURE OF TELEVISION

The ITC replaced the Independent Broadcasting Authority (IBA) and the Cable Authority in 1991, and is concerned with television services only. (Commercial radio services, formerly also regulated by the IBA, are now the responsibility of the Radio Authority described in the next chapter.)

The 1990 Broadcasting Act provided the framework for a new style of regulation. The ITC has the duty to ensure that:

- '. . . [a] *wide range of television services is available throughout the UK and that, taken as a whole, they are of high quality and appeal to a variety of tastes and interests.*'
- '*[there is] fair and effective competition in the provision of such services.*'

The ITC ensures that each Channel 3 licensee provides a suitable balance of programmes, of proper quality. While advertisers are not *directly* interested in programmes as such, the size and composition of the audiences they attract are of immediate concern. BBC1 and BBC2 programmes are of equal importance – the BBC does not carry advertising but, if audiences watch their channels, they cannot watch independent television at the same time. Both BBC and ITC channels must also ensure their programmes satisfy the government watchdog, the Broadcasting Standards Council (which monitors standards of taste and decency) and Broadcasting Complaints Commission (which covers complaints about unfair treatment and infringement of privacy). The Broadcasting Bill (currently under debate) calls for these bodies to be merged to form the Broadcasting Standards Commission.

Unlike the IBA, the ITC does not build, own, or operate transmitters. The IBA's former Engineering Division became National Transcommunications Ltd (NTL) which has since been privatised. The company transmits both ITV and Channel 4 (and S4C in Wales) as well as serving various satellite channels and all the major commercial radio stations. The company is involved in developing the terrestrial digital technology described later in this chapter.

The following pages cover spot advertising, sponsorship and teletext, all of which are available to varying degrees on terrestrial, satellite and cable television, all discussed below.

Any commentary on television media runs the risk of becoming quickly outdated – new developments are being announced day by day.

Advertising on Television

The great impact of television comes from its ability to demonstrate your product's benefits to an audience at home in a relaxed atmosphere, and with the additional benefits of sound and colour. Other creative approaches, such as animation and computer graphics, are also possible.

Television as a medium is flexible by time and day as well as area. It is possible, by making appropriate bookings, to stimulate the market on a date and at a time of your choice. Control of timing is, however, increasingly affected by video-recorders, discussed below.

Advertising time is sold usually in standard metric units of 10, 20, 30, 40, 50 and 60 seconds duration, booked into different time segments with advertising rates appropriate to the size and composition of the audience you are likely to reach. Subject to availability, longer spots may also be booked.

The frequency, amount and nature of the advertisements must be in accordance with the Broadcasting Act and the extensive rules and principles laid down under it by the ITC. There must be total distinction between programmes and advertisements, and advertising is limited to seven minutes an hour averaged over the day's programmes. A maximum of seven and a half minutes per hour is permitted during peak viewing hours (ie, 0700–0900 and 1800–2300) as long as the preceding averaging rule is adhered to. The Broadcasting Act provides for the insertion of advertisements not only at the beginning or end of a programme but also 'in the natural breaks therein'. There are also opportunities for sponsorship, discussed below.

Television differs from other advertising media in that it is almost a commodity market: rate cards are structured to extract whatever advertising revenue the market will bear. The supply of airtime is fixed so price is determined by demand – contrast this with press media where a media-owner selling many pages of advertising can simply print thicker issues.

Supply and demand of television airtime are balanced by omitting less profitable advertising. Spots booked at a relatively inexpensive 'broad spot advertisement rate' may be pre-empted (or displaced) by spots sold to other advertisers at a higher cost, such as bookings made at a first-level 'pre-emptible fixed spot' rate. These fixed spots, may, however, be pre-empted by spots sold at various higher level pre-empt rates. These higher-rate pre-empt spots may in their turn be pre-empted by spots sold to other advertisers at the very highest rate – that for non-pre-emptible fixed spots, which are the only ones certain to appear. This is a straightforward matter of supply and demand for the media-owners, but for the advertiser and agency it makes the already difficult problem of planning and buying a television campaign more complex.

Television rate cards thus call for detailed study, and television schedules – under such circumstances – demand constant attention, review and adjustment. The volatile nature of television can be contrasted with other media where advertising is usually a 'one-off' operation in which you plan and book your schedule and then wait for your advertisements to appear. With television advertising, schedule adjustment is more important than the original basic plan, and most spots are repeatedly shifted as information about programmes is released, and new audience data becomes available. The advent of many new channels, discussed below, makes television schedules even more volatile.

Television rate cards are frequently more complex than those for other media and, in addition to the different categories of spot rates already mentioned, may include a wide range of other facilities – support spots you can book on a 'run-of-day', 'run-of-week', 'run-of-campaign' or 'seasonal' basis – all of which may have separate rates for peak and off-peak screening. Rate cards may also include a wide variety of different discount rates as well as other advertising packages (such as the Guaranteed Home Impressions, described in a later chapter) by which television programme contractors attempt to balance supply and demand for television airtime.

Rate cards (or separate brochures) may feature further facilities. As well as transmitting your advertising message, most television contractors also offer a number of additional added-value services to advertisers, including production of commercials and a wide range of other facilities. (These are described in Chapter 8.)

Sponsorship

In addition to spot advertising, television also offers sponsorship opportunities. A programme is deemed to be sponsored if '*any part of its costs of production or transmission is met by an organisation or person other than a broadcaster or television producer, with a view to promoting its own or another's name, trademark, image, activities, products, or other direct or indirect commercial interests.*'

The ITC's *Code of Programme Sponsorship* effectively allows any programme – except pure news and current affairs – to be sponsored, and two forms of sponsorship have emerged.

Programme sponsorship provides the sponsor with a 15 second on-screen credit at the beginning and end of each programme. A 'bumper' is allowed at the beginning and end of each commercial break. Programme trailers can mention the sponsor, who can have no influence over programme content or scheduling. There are rules restricting the involvement of any sponsor whose product relates to the editorial content of the programme. As an example, a food brand is not allowed to sponsor a cookery programme. However, a sponsor can include a registered trade mark which may, in some instances, remind viewers of and reinforce television commercials. There have been a number of successful programme sponsorships where the programme image has reflected positively on that of the brand, whereas others have achieved little impact on awareness levels or image.

The other type of sponsorship is *advertiser supplied programming*. This provides 10 second on-screen credits at the beginning and end of the programme, but no bumpers during the breaks. There are, however, opportunities to influence the editorial. There have been examples of detergent manufacturers funding C4 and ITV programmes (the original meaning of the phrase 'soap opera' was that the programme was funded by soap companies!). Other advertisers, such as soft drink and lager companies, are now funding programmes on Channel 4.

Sponsorship is likely to expand, if not to the American extent, then at least more than previously envisaged. The reasons are that viewers are feared to be more selective in their viewing, reducing the effectiveness of traditional spot advertisements. As viewers increasingly take on the role of programme controller, watching only those programmes they wish to view, the pressure from advertisers to become involved in programming could increase.

Teletext

The ITC is also responsible for telecommunications services provided on the 'spare' capacity of a television signal, ie those lines not used for transmitting the picture itself. These include the Teletext services provided on ITV and Channel 4 which, like the BBC's 'Ceefax', provide news, entertainment and information (and also programme sub-titling) whenever the services are on air. The licence holder for Teletext on both ITV and Channel 4 is Teletext Ltd which also sells advertising space. It must be considered from two standpoints – as an advertising medium in its own right, and as a supplement (or alternative?) to conventional viewing. Advertisers purchase advertising pages, sometimes supported by 'signposts' (a strip along the bottom of other pages to direct viewers to the advertising page). As examples: a signpost for a margarine advertiser appeared on a recipe page, and a building society signpost appeared on a Family Finance page. Space is available regionally or nationally. Teletext is a leading provider of holiday advertising, with overseas holiday pages viewed by more than 3 million people every week.

Teletext, transmitted over the television broadcasting network, should be distinguished from *Viewdata* services transmitted over phone lines. Teletext and Viewdata are collectively called *Videotext*, the generic term for data and graphics presented on a television screen.

Penetration of teletext sets stands at 57 per cent, and the main brake on sales is the rate at which people replace their sets – they do not get a new TV set before the old one breaks down. Penetration of teletext sets is increasing, however, and could be accelerated by the rental market.

The Television Audience Reached

The regular flow of research information about the size and composition of television audiences (described in Chapter 5) enables you to gauge the audience you are likely to reach. To some, particularly the less experienced in television advertising, this wealth of information causes some embarrassment, especially when taking into account additional research information provided by programme contractors. In passing, this view highlights the two ends of the complaints scale about media research: with some advertising media, practitioners complain about lack of information, while with others they complain there is too much!

TERRESTRIAL BROADCASTING

Channel 3

Channel 3 is a regional system of broadcasting in which 15 ITC-appointed licensees provide programme services in 14 separate areas of the country (London is served by two contractors on a split-week basis), together with one national breakfast-time service and one teletext service broadcast over the same network. See chart opposite.

Licensees have responsibility for ensuring that their programme services comply with the Broadcasting Act and the ITC codes and guidelines. The ITC has a range of sanctions and financial penalties for licensees who fail to comply with their licence conditions. It monitors compliance through its headquarters and regional staff, with the assistance of regional Viewer Consultative Councils.

ITV areas seem to present convenient regional advertising facilities but transmitters do not recognise lines on a map and, although television coverage is almost at saturation level, there are still a minimal number of households within areas which cannot receive signals, and other households which are in overlap areas.

CHANNEL 3 – THE ITV REGIONAL NETWORK

Area	Contractor	% share of net ITV homes[1]
London weekdays	Carlton Television	19.30
weekends	London Weekend Television (LWT)	
East, West and South Midlands	Central Independent Television	15.46
North-West England	Granada Television	11.79
Yorkshire	Yorkshire Television	9.99
South and South-East England	Meridian Broadcasting	9.26
Channel Islands	Channel Television[2]	-
Wales and West of England	Harlech Television (HTV)	7.63
East of England	Anglia Television	6.57
Central Scotland	Scottish Television (STV)	6.35
North-East England	Tyne-Tees Television	5.09
South-West England	Westcountry Television	2.93
Northern Ireland	Ulster Television	2.31
North Scotland	Grampian Television	2.14
Borders and The Isle of Man	Border Television	1.18
		100.00
National breakfast-time licence	GMTV	
Teletext	Teletext Ltd	

Notes:
1 *Source*: BARB June 1995
2 Currently sold by the S and SE England licensee

Programme contractors' areas are larger than those served by essentially local media. For this reason many advertisers regard television as a regional medium rather than a local one. This has led a number of advertisers, who place great reliance on television, to revise their marketing areas to match ITV transmission areas, thus reversing the original practice of seeking a medium whose coverage coincided with an advertiser's sales area.

ITV, though regional in structure, gives you the benefit of an impact on the audience equivalent to that of a national medium. Viewers think of ITV as a medium of national importance, and many advertisers value it for that reason.

The ITV network

New ten-year franchises came into force in January 1993 for the companies listed above. Licences were awarded (amid some controversy) 'by competitive tender', subject to the licence applicant passing a 'quality threshold' and satisfying the ITC that it was able to sustain a quality service over the full licence term.

From the very first day of their new licences, the programme companies faced Channel 4 selling its own airtime in direct competition, as described below, and ITV's monopoly had thus been broken.

Since the granting of the Channel 3 licences, there have been changes to the ownership of the licence-holding companies. After the licences were awarded, pressure mounted for ownership rules to be relaxed so that one organisation could own two companies holding a licence.

During the period 1993-95, changes in the ownership of major licence holders, through merger or takeover, led to the emergence of three major television sales houses which handle the selling of airtime for their parent company and, in two instances, other licence holders as below:

Carlton UK Sales:	Carlton and Central
Laser:	Granada, LWT, Yorkshire-Tyne Tees and Border
TSMS:	Anglia, Meridian, Westcountry, HTV, Ulster, Scottish, Grampian and S4C

Ownership rules continue to evolve and the new Broadcasting Bill envisages a further relaxation so that companies will be allowed to own more than two television stations as long as they do not exceed more than 15 per cent of the total television audience. At the time of writing, this led to stock market activity involving major television contractors and major newspaper groups.

Breakfast Television

The programme contractor holding the breakfast-time licence (GMTV) differs from the other 15 in having a national franchise, which permits the company to broadcast from 6.00 to 9.25 am seven days a week throughout the year, to all areas of the United Kingdom. The service is available to the public on Channel 3 and thus offers advertisers the same coverage potential.

The programme company sells its own airtime, and makes this

available as both packages and spots which precede or follow the programme units. Advertisers can book national advertising from a single source, rather than having to negotiate separately with several sales houses. Moreover, the service provides the opportunity to advertise simultaneously throughout the United Kingdom. However, as GMTV transmits on the same network as ITV it could, if it so wished, sell advertising time on a regional (or perhaps macro-region) basis.

One advantage of breakfast-time programming is that it reaches a high proportion of housewives (and housewives with children), and advertisers and agencies are therefore able to target this important audience before they go shopping. A large proportion of breakfast-time advertisement revenue is contributed by manufacturers of food and household products whose principal markets comprise these important target groups. Other products which account for a significant proportion of advertisement revenue are toys, confectionery, retailers, and cosmetics/toiletries.

The company holding the early morning franchise does not have a monopoly of breakfast-time advertising, however, as Channel 4 is also on air at that time. It also competes for audiences with BBC1 and BBC2.

Channel 4

The Channel Four Television Corporation was established by the 1990 Broadcasting Act to continue to provide the Channel 4 TV service. The Corporation holds the licence until 2002 to provide a national service except for Wales, which is covered by S4C (Sianel 4 Cymru), a separate broadcasting authority with its own network.

When Channel 4 first began broadcasting it was intended that 'the new service will cater for special interests and concerns for which television has until now lacked adequate time, and also foster new and experimental programme ideas'.

Channel 4 does not seek to compete with the mass channels for a major share of viewing at all times but nevertheless does attract large audiences at some points in the week, with popular programmes as well as documentaries and arts programmes. This range of programmes helps balance the smaller more targeted audiences the channel serves at other times. In interpreting its remit, the channel makes provision for multi-cultural programming to reflect the diversity of modern Britain, as well as serving youth audiences.

Advertising on Channel 4

Although Channel 4 can be a mass as well as a selective medium, it does not deliver conventional mass audiences. Cumulative cover builds up by a mix of audience sizes, ranging from the specialist to the large, allowing advertisers to buy whatever audiences they want. It provides the following advertising opportunities:

- *Strong up-market coverage* – particularly of the AB socio-economic groups, who traditionally are 'light viewers'.

- *Special-interest groups* – selected by considering programme content rather than standard demographic research data.

- *Coverage build-up* – the 4th channel, over time, delivers conventional audiences in large cumulative numbers, regardless of whether or not more specialist groups are also reached.

- *Better balanced schedules against any target audience* – providing additional opportunities-to-see for any group inadequately covered by the ITV schedule.

Regular TV advertisers use Channel 4 in parallel with ITV to increase their total coverage, and to give better balance to their schedules. Advertisers new to television use the channel to reach specialist target audiences, either nationally or regionally. Channel 4 is also used by advertisers seeking more general audiences, whose advertising budgets are insufficient to provide an acceptable weight of advertising on ITV.

When Channel 4 was instructed to sell its own airtime under the 1990 Broadcasting Act, a funding formula provided a safety net to meet fears that it would not be able to attract sufficient commercial revenue while fulfilling its public service remit.

This funding formula provided that if the channel attracts less than 14 per cent of total terrestrial advertising and sponsorship revenue the ITV companies would make up the shortfall to a maximum of 2 per cent of total revenue. However, if Channel 4 attracts more than 14 per cent of total terrestrial revenue, any surplus will be divided with 50 per cent going to the ITV companies, 25 per cent into reserve to finance any future shortfall, leaving 25 per cent for the channel to spend.

During the first years of its independence, Channel 4 thrived commercially. The channel has achieved in excess of 20 per cent of total terrestrial revenue and, in line with the formula, has handed over £169m to ITV, now effectively its commercial rival. Thus a formula intended to protect the channel is actually curbing its ability to invest and compete.

Channel 4 launched a campaign against this funding formula. In their view, not only is the safety net redundant, but the costs to Channel 4 are onerous. The Broadcasting Bill, under debate in parliament at the time of writing, provides for an amendment to this formula, so that a greater proportion of Channel 4's revenue can be retained for investment in programming.

Channel 4 sells most of its airtime on a national basis, but also offers airtime on a regional basis: an advertiser can buy airtime on one or more of six macro-regions (London, South, Midlands, North, Scotland and Ulster). Alternatively airtime can be bought nationally and different commercials can be used in each macro-region.

Like other channels, Channel 4 provides a range of options in its rate card. These include 10 per cent discount to larger 'contract' advertisers, 10 per cent surcharge for specified position in break, increased rates for 'specials' which attract higher audiences and themed packages which provide for commercials to appear in specified programmes or genre of programmes.

Channel 5

The ITC (after various delays and failing to issue a licence in 1992) re-advertised a single licence for Channel 5 in 1995. The 1990 Broadcasting Act requires the channel to carry news and current affairs, children's and religious programmes and to appeal to a wide variety of tastes.

Following the same competitive procedure as Channel 3, the licence was awarded for ten years to Channel 5 Broadcasting Ltd (C5BL). After a judicial review, C5BL has been confirmed as licence holder and transmission will commence early in 1997.

The Channel 5 licence is for a service which initially covers 60 per cent of Britain's homes, although it is envisaged that coverage will increase rapidly.

The cost of establishing the new service, including installation of the transmission system, must be met by the licensee on top of the costs of providing the programme service. One big drawback for Channel 5 is responsibility for retuning video-recorders or other equipment which may experience interference from C5 transmissions. In areas such as London, Birmingham, Leeds/Bradford, Glasgow, Bristol and Cardiff, Channel 5 has undertaken to call at every home to offer a free retuning service. Another drawback is that many viewers will need to install a new aerial to receive the new channel.

There is great interest in the first terrestrial station to be launched in today's multi-channel world. Demand from advertisers for airtime is moving inexorably higher and following Channel 4's financial success, media commentators envisage that Channel 5 could generate substantial advertising support. To help in this task, airtime will be sold by a dedicated advertising sales team.

Some commentators, however, doubt whether the advertising revenue will be sufficient to pay the high set-up costs. The question is whether viewers, who for a little more money could obtain an even wider choice from satellite or cable, will watch Channel 5 in sufficient numbers. Without these numbers and quality of audience, Channel 5 would have great difficulty in obtaining sufficient advertising revenue to make the channel profitable within the life of its licence.

SATELLITE TRANSMISSIONS

Terrestrial broadcasting has been supplemented in two ways. One is geo-stationary communication satellites which 'bounce' TV (and radio) signals back to earth, either to individual homes – *direct* broadcasting by domestic satellite (DBS) – or to community reception stations, from where the final link to the home is through the second supplement to traditional broadcasting: cable TV.

Satellite transmissions differ from terrestrial broadcasting in that coverage is national (or rather international). The reception areas are known as 'footprints' or 'groundprints' and, to give an idea of their size, UK transmissions overlap Northern France, while France's groundprint reaches into the UK not far short of Scotland. The net effect is a web of overlapping transmission areas, which become even larger if the signals are then spread further by cable.

Although discussed separately for ease of analysis, the two supplements to traditional broadcasting are clearly inter-related. Both are the ITC's responsibility.

Direct Broadcasting by Domestic Satellites

The first direct broadcasting by domestic satellite to the UK was undertaken by Sky Television in February 1989 using the Astra satellite. In 1990, Sky merged with British Satellite Broadcasting (BSB), which had been broadcasting from a separate satellite, Marco Polo, using a different technology. Together, they formed BSkyB, which now broadcasts solely from Astra. Viewers with BSB 'Squarials' were offered free dishes and installation to facilitate Astra reception.

There are now four Astra satellites (Astra 1A to D) broadcasting to the UK. Marco Polo has ceased broadcasting.

BSkyB has expanded from its original five channel package and, together with other broadcasters also using Astra, there are over 40 channels broadcasting in English to the UK and an additional 35 European language channels. Some channels are only available for a limited number of hours each day, and share a transponder with another channel.

Free Channels

K Some English language channels are provided free, including:

Cartoon Network:	Children's cartoons
CNN International:	News from an American base
Eurosport:	A range of different sports
NBC Super Channel:	24 hour American entertainment
Playboy:	Adult programming
Quantum:	Home shopping
Sell-a-Vision:	Home shopping
Television X:	Adult programming
The Christian Channel:	Religious programming
The Adult Channel:	Adult programming
The Racing Channel:	Racing programmes
TNT:	Movie channel

There are also a number of stations broadcasting free to ethnic communities in the UK. These include:

CNE:	Chinese News Channel
JSTV:	Japanese entertainment
The Chinese Channel:	Entertainment in various languages
Zee TV:	Entertainment in Asian languages

Subscription Television

To receive 'scrambled' programmes, viewers need a decoding device and must pay a monthly subscription. Satellite broadcasting differs from terrestrial broadcasting in having this source of revenue, additional to their income from spot advertising and sponsorship. Indeed, around 80 per cent of BSkyB's revenue comes from subscription, reducing its reliance on advertising revenue. In comparison, terrestrial channels are virtually totally reliant on advertising as a source of revenue. There may, of course, be revenue from the sale of programmes, but our interest within this book focuses on advertising aspects.

Subscriptions vary according to the type of channel to be viewed. At the time of writing, there were four cost levels. For a basic subscription, viewers can receive the basic 'multi-channel' package, comprising around 20 channels which can be categorised as:

Music:	MTV (pop videos), VH1 (music for 25–49s), CMTV (Country Music)
Documentary:	Discovery Channel, Sky Travel, History

	Channel, TLC (The Learning Channel)
News:	Sky News, EBN (European Business News)
Children:	Nickelodeon, TCC (The Children's Channel)
Entertainment:	Sky One, Sky Soaps, UK Gold (BBC and Thames TV archive), UK Living (women's programmes), The Sci-Fi Channel, Bravo (cult, mainly B&W programmes), The Family Channel, The Paramount Channel (archive and original programming)
Home Shopping:	QVC (Quality, Value, Convenience)

The remaining channels calling for higher subscriptions are categorised as either Premium or Premium Bonus channels.

The Premium channels are Sky Movies, The Movie Channel and Sky Sports.

The Premium Bonus channels are Sky Movies Gold and Disney Channel (available when subscribing to both Sky Movies and The Movie Channel) as well as Sky Sports 2 and Sky Sports Gold (available to subscribers of Sky Sports).

At its inception, viewers of BSkyB were not required to pay a subscription for any channel: viewers paid only for the purchase or rental of satellite equipment. When BSkyB first introduced subscriptions, it was thought that many viewers would not be prepared to pay. Certainly there was a 'churn' effect whereby, in 1995, around 11 per cent of viewers ceased viewing BSkyB. However, churn is now at its lowest point, considerably reduced from its historic height of 30 per cent in 1992.

BSkyB's success in attracting new, and retaining existing, subscribers has been achieved through provision of 'niche' channels, particularly those providing sports and children programming. At time of writing, the total number of homes subscribing to BSkyB is estimated at around 4.5 million, representing nearly 20 per cent of UK homes. Projections indicate that satellite penetration of UK homes will increase, as will the provision of even more choice in terms of new channel options.

Satellite Advertising

As with terrestrial television, there are three ways to advertise on satellite: spots, sponsorship and teletext.

BARB (described below) data suggests that people in satellite homes do not watch more television, but are more selective in what they view. BSkyB argue that, having reached 20 per cent penetration of UK homes, it is not a question of whether satellite should be added to a media schedule but rather at what level, to reach the niche audiences attracted to satellite programmes.

More than 20 satellite programmes have been sponsored, partially because ITC regulations for satellite sponsorship are more flexible allowing, for instance, title sponsorship with no restrictions on length of credits.

The BSkyB teletext service 'Fastext' attracts 2.4m users each week. Additionally, the BSkyB 'Intertext' service allows viewers to access a range of information and games using their existing teletext television and a touch tone telephone. Viewers can, for instance, book ferry crossings, event tickets, check bank accounts, etc.

Many commentators are concerned that advertising on satellite, and cable (described below) is sold on as practicable a basis as possible. They want television time to be as flexible and simple as possible to plan and buy. There is concern that, whilst ITV has merged the number of their sales points to three major sales houses, there has been a proliferation of sales points for satellite television with relatively small stations selling their own advertising time.

ITV 3 put vendre

The future may thus see the formation of sales houses, nationally for satellite and regionally for cable on similar lines to those for Channel 3 and commercial radio (described in the next chapter).

CABLE TELEVISION

A cable system is primarily just another means of delivering television and other added value services to the home. The television channels carried by cable systems include those from a number of satellites, as well as from other sources. The major value added service provided by cable is that of 'telephony': the provision of telephone services. The lower cost of cable telephone services has attracted more than a million customers and has been an important factor in the growth of cable during the mid 90s. Apart from this service, however, cable has not yet realised its full potential as an interactive communication vehicle. There are various additional interactive multimedia services that cable could provide. These include security services, education, music videos, home banking, home shopping, computer games and 'video on demand'. Their provision is being tested by British Telecom (BT) in Colchester and Ipswich in the UK as well as at various locations in America. The 'BT Interactive TV' test is described in more detail below. Because cable connection avoids the need for individual viewers to have satellite dishes, receivers and decoders, it provides an easy and cost-effective way of delivering the new television choices now developing.

Cable franchise holders usually cover local council areas (such as Windsor or Coventry) and each one is at a different stage of development. Some have not started construction, others are busily laying fibre optic cable (as many readers may be personally aware!) and a small number have completed construction of their cable network. A particular problem for cable companies has been the high cost of construction, physically passing people's homes, and the limited uptake once a home is passed.

At the time of writing, 131 licences have been issued by the ITC, of which 99 have started constructing a cable service. Only 77 cable franchise holders have more than 2,500 subscribers.

More than 5.5 million homes are currently passed by Broadband cable (described below) and 20 per cent of these – 1.1 million – are connected to cable. 34 per cent of these homes have two or more decoders, giving access to cable TV in different rooms in the home.

There has been a growth of 'Multiple Systems Operators' (MSOs), organisations which manage more than one licence. The top ten MSOs each pass more than 100,000 homes and the largest, Telewest, passes 1.7m homes with 356,000 connected.

There are different kinds of cable systems, including narrowband, broadband, SMATV, and local delivery.

Narrowband Cable Just over 50 old narrowband cable systems in various parts of the country presently provide new television programmes. Most systems have only four channels, though some of them cover relatively large areas.

Broadband Cable These are the multi-channel and interactive systems that are the focus of this section. The systems can carry between 30 and 45 television channels, although some can carry more. They also have a facility to control which channels are delivered to specific premises, allowing viewers to subscribe to some channels but not others. Broadband cable systems are permitted to provide a full range of television, telecommunication and interactive services.

SMATV A growing number of new 'Satellite Master Antenna Television' systems are being installed. These are smaller systems, often serving blocks of flats, which deliver a range of satellite television channels to the homes connected to them. No ITC licence is needed for any SMATV system covering fewer than 1,000 homes. Several SMATV systems operating on a joint basis could, however, require a Local Delivery licence.

Local Delivery Any system providing television services in an area of more than 1,000 homes will require a Local Delivery licence. This differs technologically from a purely cable franchise, in that the service may be delivered not only by broadband cable but could also utilise one or more SMATV systems, or even microwave video distribution systems

(MVDS). The latter technique has not yet been used in the UK, but is nevertheless undergoing development.

Programme channels

Programme licences, as distinct from cable franchises, are issued on demand for any programme service which conforms to the 'consumer protection' requirements of the ITC's Codes on Programmes, Advertising and Sponsorship. A licence lasts for ten years. Separate arrangements apply to the DBS broadcasting channels allocated for UK use, which are awarded by competitive tender.

Each cable franchise holder provides a mix of channels relevant to the needs of its audience. Typically, there will be around 40 channels including the terrestrial channels, a selection of satellite channels, and channels dedicated only to cable. Sky One is the satellite channel available in the largest number of cable homes at 1.2m, whereas Sky Travel is available only in 400,000 homes.

There are some channels, not broadcast on satellite, which can only be viewed on cable. These include:

The Parliamentary Channel:	Relay of proceedings in the Houses of Commons and Lords
Channel One:	News in the style of the Evening Standard
HVC: (Home Video Channel)	Features action films
Live TV:	24 hour TV owned by the Daily Mirror
Landscape:	Classical music videos
Performance:	Arts programming such as opera, dance and classical music
SelecTV:	General entertainment such as 'Birds of a Feather'

Additionally, various foreign language programmes may be provided. In Westminster, for instance, the cable franchise holder provides: Rai UNO (Italian), TVE (Spanish), TV Asia (Indian and Asian), Dubai TV (Arabic) and TV5 (French).

Many broadband cable franchise holders provide a local channel with news, information and advertising of local interest. On Westminster Cable, this channel is branded *Metrovision* and offers both video and text advertising. The terrestrial and satellite channels carry the same commercials on cable as elsewhere, except for satellite channels such as UK Gold, Discovery, CNN and TNT which provide for local ads to be inserted at specified times. Some cable channels, such as Live TV and Channel One, also provide for local advertising. The technology exists for this local advertising to be highly targeted with different commercials for different groups of homes according to socio-economic status or other advertiser needs.

As with satellite transmissions, unless the MSOs work together (in a similar way perhaps to local radio stations, with an advertising 'marketing' board and sales houses to promote their airtime), the cumbersome mechanics of booking may well limit advertising opportunities on cable.

Cable Audience Research

The ITC publishes quarterly reports about cable audiences and the latest (December 1995) indicates that terrestrial channels remain the most popular with cable viewers. The third most popular after ITV and BBC1 is The Movie Channel with 5.8 per cent of viewing. Some other channels have such low viewing figures that their viewing is shown as 'less than 0.5 per cent'. In cable homes, however, cable and satellite viewing accounts for over half of children's total television viewing. Traditionally there has been a heavy slant of cable and satellite viewing towards the DE grades, this although appears to be less marked than in previous reports. Light viewers (those in higher socio-economic groups) are increasing their viewing of cable and satellite channels, and favour Sky One, Sky Sports and Nickelodeon.

NON-BROADCAST SOURCES

Britain now has one of the highest penetration levels of video-cassette recorders in the world (76 per cent of households have one) and the trend is for penetration to increase. With such a high 'ownership' (many VCRs are rented) it is not surprising that more and more people make use of them, reducing their use of TV sets for conventional viewing.

The main advantage of VCRs is to enable viewers to declare their independence of the programme schedulers and 'time-shift', that is watch broadcast programmes when it suits them rather than the schedulers. VCR owners also have the ability to record a programme whilst viewing another channel or when they are not able to view at all. They can also view the wide range of pre-recorded videos available for purchase or rental. Advertising can be purchased on these videos, and research (see Chapter 5) suggests that 70 per cent of video viewers watch the commercials. Very popular pre-recorded videos can achieve ratings equivalent to a peak spot on ITV.

An important implication of VCRs is that viewers may edit out commercials by use of the 'pause' button if present when the recording is made. Alternatively, if the recording is made during the viewer's absence, commercials may be 'zipped' – avoided by use of the fast-forward button – during subsequent screenings. Finally, a new generation of VCRs have built-in technology that can eliminate commercials from the recordings, by editing out the high quality stereo signals commonly used to carry advertising.

Other sources of non-broadcast material include the computer and BT. The computer uses either disc or CD-Rom based software but, unlike videos, cannot be used to make recordings, being a replay medium only. They do, however, provide sponsorship opportunities as illustrated by a Bank's sponsorship of a computer game, reproducing a bank statement with the bank logo. Certain types of television set double-up as computer monitors and if the screen is used for computing purposes, it cannot be used for conventional viewing.

As mentioned above, in 1995 BT commenced testing 'BT Interactive TV' with 2,500 customers in Colchester and Ipswich. The test utilises existing copper cable telephone lines to provide a range of interactive multimedia services into the home. One service, branded 'Adland', allows 20 advertisers to use interactive commercials to promote goods on-screen. The customer uses a remote control unit to obtain more information or to purchase goods. Although only a small scale test, this is an interesting pointer to the future potential for advertisers to utilise unique, measurable screen-based advertising opportunities.

NEW TECHNOLOGY

New developments within television necessitate a rethink of the marketing concept and the way in which television advertising is used. These developments involve changes to the television signal itself offering high definition pictures and digital stereo sound or even wide-screen TV.

During 1996, Parliament is considering a new Broadcasting Bill designed to allow development of Digital Terrestrial Broadcasting for both television and radio. This will provide better quality television, available in wide-screen format and with CD quality sound, as well as more channels. It will also provide a limited degree of interactivity through a telephone return path. Its introduction will have a fundamental effect on broadcasting.

The Bill calls for six 'Multiplexes' each with capacity for three channels of fast moving action (such as adventure movies) or seven of less movement (such as studio interviews). This could lead to between eighteen to forty-two channels replacing the current five (two BBC and three commercial channels including Channel 5). The new arrangements would provide for each of the existing 'analogue' channels to 'simulcast' (broadcast current channels on digital at the same time).

- The BBC will be awarded the multiplex with the widest geographic coverage, for BBC1 and BBC2 to be 'simulcast'. Additional channels, such as wide-screen broadcasts, a news channel, increased parliamentary and sports coverage could be licence-fee funded, or provided on a subscription basis.
- Channels 3 and 4 will share the second multiplex.
- Channel 5 will be offered half of the third multiplex alongside another multiplex operator.

There would be various restrictions over control of multiplexes. For instance, one multiplex operator would be able to control only up to three of the six multiplexes.

As far as digital satellite transmissions are concerned, BSkyB has announced plans to broadcast from 14 transponders on an Astra satellite to be launched in 1997, providing up to 500 channels. If launched to schedule BSkyB could become operational a year before Digital Terrestrial Television (DTT).

Various unresolved issues will influence the introduction of digital broadcasting:

- If costs reach the envisaged level of £500m, will broadcasters be prepared to invest in it?
- How long will the current 'analogue' transmissions continue? The Secretary of State for National Heritage has indicated that once 50 per cent of UK households can receive DTT, or after five years, she will review the switch-off date.
- Will viewers be prepared to invest in new sets or the set-top 'black box' necessary to de-code signals? 'All-digital' wide-screen TV sets could cost more than £1,000 and decoders between £300 and £500. The Government envisages that prices will come down (as they did for colour TV, CD players and microwave ovens) but this could take many years.
- Which set-top box will dominate the market? The Government envisages development of a single decoder to receive both terrestrial and satellite digital broadcasts. If viewers have invested in a digital satellite decoder, will they be prepared to invest in an additional terrestrial box? Or would they wait until a combined box is available?

Digital has important implications for advertisers. Subscription may become an increasingly important method of funding television, possibly matching, or perhaps exceeding, advertising. There are already a small number of satellite channels which do not accept advertising and in the future, more channels may rely solely on subscriptions for their funding.

As viewers watch 'pay per view' television, inevitably they will watch fewer commercials and advertisers will find it more difficult to reach these viewers, using the television medium.

Media Ownership The new Broadcasting Bill calls for removal of the current two licence limit on control of ITV licences. This would be replaced by an ownership limit of 15 per cent share of the total television audience. The result could be further mergers/takeovers by the current 'big three' Channel 3 contractors of another TV licence holder, bringing their total share to the 15 per cent mark. This possibility has been illustrated by an increase in the share prices of licence holders such as Scottish and Yorkshire/Tyne Tees.

The implication for advertisers lies in the possibility of Channel 3 no longer acting as a fully regional network. It raises, yet again, the spectre of 'conditional selling', whereby a large sales house might sell airtime in all of its stations as a composite package, rather than individually.

CONSEQUENCES OF INCREASED PROGRAMME PROVISION

Penetration of TV sets is at saturation level, and so it follows logically that the TV audience cannot increase in proportion to the ever-increasing programme output which will arise from additional channels transmitting, supplemented by the trend towards 24-hour broadcasting. There might, however, be a marginal increase arising from new programmes which attract those who otherwise would not wish to view. A further increase could result from the growing incidence of two (and three or more) set households, which permits individual members of the family to view separate programmes rather than losing the argument about which to watch! 37 per cent of households already have two TV sets, while 17 per cent have three.

Fragmentation and Selectivity Increased programme-provision, but a total audience of only marginally increased size, necessarily means that this audience will be fragmented. The greater the fragmentation, the greater, in theory, the possibility of audience selectivity. There will be alternative inroads into mass regional audiences.

Segmented audiences One alternative to mass regional audiences is niche viewing groups as the increasing range of channels segment the total audience into smaller and more selective viewing groups. Wider choice will lead to diversity rather than uniformity, allowing advertisers to pinpoint markets with greater accuracy. This could be by cable TV's community-size areas or alternatively by programme interests and audience types. There will be great opportunity for advertisers who think in terms of 'narrowcasting' rather than broadcasting.

Cable TV could take narrowcasting even further as, in theory, broadband cable systems have the capacity to transmit different commercials to different market segments: imagine delivering AB commercials to AB homes, C1 commercials to C1 homes, and so on, or a range of commercials specifically tailored to the various geo-demographic groupings – or perhaps even individual personalised messages. The technology is there!

Transcast audiences The other alternative to mass regional viewing is 'transcasting' to even larger audiences: direct broadcasting by satellite means a single channel covers all 14 ITV regions, while Channel 5 will cover most of the UK, and some satellite/cable channels overlap international boundaries to give pan-European coverage.

Time-shift audiences TV no longer delivers mass audiences at predictable times: increasing VCR usage will spread message delivery over time.

Volatile audiences The more programme choice is increased, the greater the likelihood of viewers switching from one programme to another. This is for three reasons:

1.   Natural curiosity to find out what is available on other channels. This curiosity could be encouraged by technology which enables viewers to call up on their screen a multitude of miniature pictures to facilitate programme selection.

2.   Greater physical facility for switching programmes, through remote control units. Now that the vast majority of households (84 per cent at the time of writing) have remote control units, people's viewing habits have changed. Remote control allows the viewer to edit their programmes either by 'zapping' one channel to view another, or by 'zipping', moving fast forward on a tape to avoid viewing commercials.

3.   Greater choice through pre-recorded videos, which viewers might prefer to the broadcast provision, and which represent an advertising medium in their own right. Viewers might, alternatively, choose to view a programme recorded earlier. Ready availability, at a low cost, of both blank and pre-recorded tapes mean that many viewers are building extensive video-tape libraries, aided by the bar-coding and VideoPlus code numbering of programmes, devices for pre-setting VCR timings, which make recording that much easier. Furthermore, some VCRs have a two-tape capacity, which permits viewers to watch one tape while

recording another, thereby increasing the VCR's facility to make (and store) permanent copies, leading to even further inroads into conventional mass audiences.

Interactive facilities The BT Interactive TV test described above is a first step in the provision of interactive multimedia facilities. New opportunities will arise, far broader than existing teletext or direct response commercials which merely give phone or fax numbers for viewers to place orders by means of credit cards. Interactive services make direct purchasing easier and enable direct marketing to penetrate the television screen even further.

There could be interactive facilities in shopping precincts or within retail outlets to enable people to shop by cable. There is already a small chain of 'cafes' which provide interactive facilities on the Internet reaching ever wider audiences. These interactive audiences could themselves be increased by means of interactive quiz and game shows which offer prizes to those viewing, as well as to the studio audience. (The offer of a small cash prize on conventional television recently generated a record response of one and a quarter million phone calls in five minutes!)

Inroads into conventional mass audiences will present opportunities as well as problems to the TV contractors, who could sell to the new media – to cable and satellite TV (in overseas markets just as much as in the UK) and to the world-wide pre-recorded video market. The appetite for material in countries with limited production facilities could be voracious. Furthermore, production of minority (and thus usually commercially unviable) programmes could be most profitable when sold to multiple minority markets on a world-wide basis.

TELEVISION – THE FUTURE

This chapter started by stressing that television is in the throes of change, and the many new developments just discussed show this to be more than a slight understatement! Nevertheless, the future structure of the medium is clear in outline, even if there will be numerous changes in detail. Should you find these many new developments insufficient in scope, there are further possibilities to consider.

1.   Internet Computers with modems can use telephone networks to communicate with each other. The most widely used system is the World Wide Web (WWW) whereby an organisation can deliver a message to anyone with a modem, anywhere in the world. It is estimated that 20m people world-wide regularly use the Web. Advertisers can utilise the

Web in two ways: firstly by constructing their own Web site and second-ly by advertising on another Web site.

Technically, the construction of a web site is not advertising as there is no cost connected with buying space – it is purely a matter of production and handling costs.

It is, however, screen based communication and as such potentially both complementary and competitive to television advertising. Internet is complementary in the sense that some advertisers feature a WWW address on their television commercials and direct viewers to find out more about their products through the Internet.

As the number of people able to communicate through the Internet increases (and providing the technology can cope with the volume) it could become a communication medium competitive to television and other traditional media.

The alternative options, for buying advertising space on someone else's web site are similar to those in many other media: an advertiser either buys a traditional advertisement or alternatively negotiates a co-operative deal.

There are various Web sites where advertising is available, most frequently newspapers (such as the *Electronic Telegraph* and *The Times*) or magazines (such as *GQ on-line*, *Top Gear* or *New Scientist*). It is still too early, however, to tell whether these electronic publications will be financially viable.

Co-operative deals are between advertisers with Web sites seeking mutually beneficial partnerships.

More users must invest in Internet link equipment and there must be more investment in research before the value of the Web can be more fully assessed.

The growth of both Web sites and users has been one of the most remarkable phenomena of the mid-90s. If the next generation obtains information from such screen-based databases, it is important for advertisers to appreciate their potential. As people use the Internet more, they may place less value on traditional information sources such as advertising.

2.   Direct Marketing Television is increasingly used for direct marketing purposes targeted towards niche audiences. More commercials now feature telephone numbers and there is a growing science in planning the timing of commercials to enable telemarketing units to handle the response. One advertiser was able to answer only 1,200 telephone calls, leaving 54,000 calls unanswered. This example demonstrates the importance of both experience and technology.

Rather than the usual 30 second peak spot, direct marketing campaigns use longer 'informercials' (90 seconds in the afternoon seems to be the norm for charity campaigns) supported by 10 second spots reminding viewers of the phone number to ring.

These transmissions form part of an overall campaign, also using direct mail, timed to integrate with other advertising activity.

So a suitable adage on which to finish this chapter might well be:

DO NOT ADJUST YOUR MIND – THE FAULT IS IN REALITY!

The next largest medium after television, in terms of percentage of total advertising expenditure, is in fact Direct Mail: this and other advertising media were, however, covered in the preceding chapter.

The one remaining medium is Commercial Radio, discussed in the next chapter.

Chapter 3

Commercial Radio

Radio merits a separate chapter because of its complexity as well as its growing importance, reflected in the amount of money spent on radio advertising. There has been dramatic growth in the number and type of radio stations, whilst the proportion of advertising money spent on radio has doubled to 4 per cent of the total, representing an increase in expenditure to £243m.

Radio as an advertising medium is available in three layers. The original and largest layer is the extensive network of Commercial Local Radio (CLR) stations. The second layer is a growing number of Commercial Regional Radio (CRR) stations. On the top of these two layers is the small number of Commercial National Radio (CNR) stations.

Before discussing radio advertising, it is important to review the way it is supervised by the Radio Authority (RA), which has three main tasks:

- assign frequencies
- appoint licensees with a view to widening listener choice
- regulate programming and advertising

When the 1990 Broadcasting Act came into force, the RA was one of two bodies which took over control from the Independent Broadcasting Authority. The other body is the Independent Television Commission, described earlier. The RA licenses and regulates all commercial radio services. These comprise national, regional, local, cable, satellite and restricted services. The latter category includes all short term services (for example, 'special events' radio) and highly localised permanent services (for example student and hospital radio).

CLR/CRR licences are awarded to applicants whose proposals would, in the opinion of the Authority, best cater for the needs and interests of listeners in the area/region. CNR licences are awarded to those who submit the highest cash bid and adhere to the other requirements of the Broadcasting Act 1990. The Act specifies that one CNR service must be a 'non-pop' FM service, whilst the other two are AM services. One of these latter two must be predominantly speech based.

As well as satisfying the RA's programme codes, licence-holders must also ensure that they meet the requirements of its advertising and sponsorship codes. Under the IBA, there was a maximum of nine minutes advertising per hour. This requirement has been removed, and the amount carried is now left to the discretion of individual radio stations. All programmes, with the exception of the news, can now be sponsored.

The Authority can apply sanctions to any licensee who breaks either programming or advertising rules. These require that advertising must be clearly separated from programmes and obvious for what it is. As with other media, advertising created for radio should be compatible with the medium that carries it, and there is evidence of growing awareness of the special needs of radio: the Authority's controls have not inhibited advertisers from creating entertaining, informative and interesting commercials which make a special contribution to the sound of commercial radio.

From time to time you may hear of 'pirate' radio stations (so called because they originally transmitted without licence, from ships moored outside British territorial waters). Tighter anti-piracy provisions in British law and in international regulations usually succeed in driving these illegal radio advertisers off the air. These preventative measures are reinforced by the fact that it is now illegal to advertise on such stations.

ADVERTISING ON COMMERCIAL RADIO

Advertising on commercial radio is sold in two formats: spots or sponsorship. Spots are sold in standard metric units of 10, 20, 30, 40, 50, 60 seconds or longer. A programme is sponsored, according to the Radio Authority, if it is broadcast in return for payment or other valuable consideration.

Each sponsorship is subject to individual negotiation and sponsorship on commercial radio has seen considerable growth and success. Radio sponsorship generates a similar amount of financial support to that given to sponsorship on television, representing a dramatically higher proportional commitment to radio sponsorship rather than television sponsorship. There are three forms of radio sponsorship.

Firstly there are Network Sponsorships such as the *Network Chart Show*, which is transmitted every Sunday afternoon on 65 CLR stations, covering 94 per cent of the population.

The second form are 'short' promotions, often tactical two to eight week promotions integrated into the fabric of a programme, such as sponsorship of breakfast games.

The third, more regular, form of sponsorship typically lasts six to twelve months and includes sponsorship of particular programme strands, the 'Flying Eye' or a community action programme.

Radio allows the advertiser to target distinctive groups, as people listen in the car, on the beach, in the park, at home and at work. It reaches them at different times and in different moods from other media. Indeed, the composition of the radio audience varies between different periods of the day, and selective timing can deliver the advertising message to various target groups, eg: business executives (at 'drive time'), housewives, teenagers and young adults.

The pattern of listening naturally differs according to each station's programming. However, the typical pattern for radio listening peaks in the morning and gradually tails off during the day (in contrast with the typical television viewing pattern which starts slowly in the morning and builds up to a peak in the evening).

One great advantage of radio as an advertising medium is its ability to communicate your advertising message at very short notice. A commercial can be scripted, recorded and transmitted in a matter of hours. As discussed later, however, certain categories of advertising, such as for medical items, must be 'cleared' to ensure that they comply with the RA's codes and with the many UK laws which impinge on advertising.

This operational flexibility means that radio executives can accept and transmit your advertising messages at short notice and therefore meet urgent needs for swift transmission when marketing conditions call for this. Examples of advertisers which this flexibility can benefit include charities facing urgent needs resulting from a disaster, and users of 'thermal' packs such as ice cream manufacturers who could broadcast as external temperatures reach 'trigger' levels. Frequent market stimulation is also possible, simply through repeat transmissions.

A further advantage of radio is that it can be relatively inexpensive to use. Both spots and sponsorship are considerably cheaper on radio than on television. Radio commercials are also cheaper to make than television commercials. An investment in sound effects can enhance the effectiveness of a radio campaign for a relatively small sum. Advertisers frequently take advantage of the opportunity to build a 'sonic identity', with background sounds and music from a television commercial creating a memory of the commercial: a type of 'audio pack shot'. In this way, radio advertising can help to maintain awareness and recall levels created by a television advertising campaign.

Although there are many radio production companies, all radio stations can make your commercials as well as transmitting them. Thus for advertisers seeking a low-cost medium, radio advertising is often extremely attractive.

Radio is frequently a 'companion' to its listeners, so your advertising message is received in an intimate and personal atmosphere. Successful advertising requires an appreciation of radio's one-to-one relationship between listener and broadcaster. The medium is a transient one, and your message is received through one sense only: that of hearing. Messages should usually be brief and make maximum effective use of words. Their delivery and the supporting sound effects or music are equally important.

Commercial Local Radio

As CLR is a local medium, many broadcasters speak with an intimate knowledge of their local community, so establishing a link with their audience. It can serve the advertising needs of local firms and equally give 'area boosts' where necessary for national advertisers.

As well as being flexible by time and day, radio is also flexible by area, as airtime can be booked with individual stations. The Radio Authority's most recent 'Pocket Book' lists over 160 Commercial Local Radio services and this number will increase.

There are various options available to the local radio advertiser: split broadcasting on AM and FM frequencies as well as the different types of local radio station described below.

At one time radio programme contractors transmitted the same service over both AM and FM frequencies. What was once termed 'simulcasting' has in most cases been replaced by split broadcasting, whereby two services are now provided instead of one. As an example, London's single Capital Radio service has been replaced by Capital FM and Capital Gold (AM). Most CLR stations now provide two programme services.

Typically, an FM station provides current chart music, with recent 'oldies' targeting people aged 14–44. Whereas AM stations feature music from the 60s, 70s and 80s aimed at people aged 35–54.

Consequently, these two types provide opportunities for advertisers to target different age groups and lifestyles.

At one time, the plan was for local radio stations to be provided on a 'one station per area' basis. Under the 1990 Broadcasting Act, however, additional licences are being granted by the RA to provide new radio services within existing CLR areas. Indeed, the RA is currently issuing two CLR licences per month. It intends to adopt a new policy of awarding more small scale local licences.

Currently, in London, there is a choice of 18 competing AM and FM stations. These stations can be analysed under five headings:

1. Specialist music (eg: Melody and Kiss, providing a range of musical styles from easy listening to dance music)

2. Ethnic interests (eg: Sunrise, LGR, Choice and Spectrum, which broadcast for the Asian, Greek, Afro-Caribbean and other ethnic communities)

3. Specialist interests (eg: Premier and Viva which feature items of interest to Christians and women)

4. Speech Radio (eg: London News)

5. Specific communities (eg: RTM which provides a specialist music, community, ethnic and news service specifically for Thamesmead)

The RA intended to provide an additional 33 radio licences from Autumn 1995, provided the new services do not duplicate existing provision. To date, it has not been difficult to provide a wide range in London, but time will tell whether there is sufficient advertiser demand to support some of the specialist interest stations.

Each CLR station is awarded a licence lasting eight years and there has been a continuous stream of new licences to fill in the 'white spaces' on the map where there is still no local commercial radio.

Commercial Regional Radio

The most recent addition to the range of radio media is the Commercial Regional Radio Station. At the time of writing there were five stations broadcasting:

Central Scotland – Scot FM: speech and adult contemporary music
North East – Century: music and speech
North West – JFM: jazz, blues, soul music
Severn Estuary – Galaxy: classic and contemporary music
West Midlands – Heart: soft adult contemporary music

Plans have been announced for a further four regional stations in East Anglia, East Midlands, Solent and Yorkshire

Commercial National Radio

There are four commercial radio stations that broadcast nationally.

Three of them are licensed by the Radio Authority:

Classic FM – classical music
Virgin AM – rock and pop music
Talk Radio UK – popular speech and talkback radio

The other station, Atlantic 252, holds an Irish Republic rather than RA licence, and has a particularly strong coverage of the North of England through its specialisation in 'Hot adult contemporary' music.

National buying can also be achieved by using one of the following: the Network Chart Show, Newslink and National Network Radio.

As described earlier, the Network Chart Show allows advertisers to reach a youth audience. More than 3m listeners tune in each Sunday.

Newslink offers the opportunity to advertise on 120 stations following the Independent Radio News broadcast on the hour. The commercials are broadcast in the mornings at the time of highest audience volume, between 7 am and 10 am on weekdays and up to 12 midday at weekends. As the news broadcasts attract high audiences and high attention, this is an attractive way of using radio.

National Network radio is a range of packages available from the sales houses listed below

- Network Frequency packages which offer the same weight of exposure across each station
- Network Sports package which facilitates advertising on all the Saturday afternoon sports programmes
- Gold network packages which deliver the 35–54 age group

Booking Commercial Radio

Airtime can be booked direct with each CLR station by local advertisers. Regional and national advertisers book time through national sales houses, responsible for maintaining contact with these advertisers and their advertising agencies.

The National Sales Houses are:

Katz Radio Sales (KRS), No 1 Carriage Row, 163 Eversholt Street, London NW1 1BU

Media Sales and Marketing (MSM), 365 Euston Road, London NW1 3AR
Scottish and Irish Radio Sales (SIRS), 55 Bondway, London SW8 1SJ

Whilst MSM is by far the largest sales house, each represents a unique combination of stations and provides regional groupings to mirror ITV regions. Thus an advertiser can, with one booking, reach 60 per cent of all adults in the North West region with their radio commercial carried by eight different stations.

All three sales houses sell time on National Network Radio which, as described above, is designed to attract national advertisers, who might otherwise not advertise on radio.

Some stations have their own 'in-house' sales teams. These include the national stations such as Atlantic 252, Talk UK, Classic FM and Virgin as well as Capital, Melody, Choice and JFM (sold by Golden Rose).

Radio Advertising Bureau

The radio industry mounted a new marketing initiative with the formation of the Radio Advertising Bureau (RAB) to act as the central marketing department for the medium, promoting radio generically, totally independent of the Sales Houses.

The RAB's mission is to 'contribute to the achievement of significant market share growth by the radio industry in total, by actively managing the development of an improved climate of familiarity and favourability for radio as an advertising medium amongst advertisers, their creative and media intermediaries alike'.

Without doubt the RAB has been a success, having increased radio's share of total ad spend from its historic base of the '2 per cent medium' to more than 4 per cent.

To assist in its task, the RAB has two 'frontline' customer contact departments: Sound Planning and The Brand Team.

The Sound Planning Service aims to assist media planners in planning radio strategies, on a confidential basis.

The Brand Team is designed to go beyond the core media and research information provided by Sound Planning, going deeper into the strategic needs of the advertiser. They aim to work closely with advertisers and agencies on in-depth projects to further knowledge of how radio really works best.

Radio – the future

The future structure of the medium is clear, with a growing number of smaller local radio stations overlayed by a growing number of regional stations and three National RA stations.

Overall, commercial radio has been successful in increasing its proportion of listening hours to more than 50 per cent. Indeed, in London, where the choice of commercial stations is widest, this figure has grown to over 60 per cent. Radio can thus be expected to continue to grow its audience as the provision of new stations increases choice.

For the major television advertiser, however, radio can seem complex and difficult to buy. There are more buying points and less detailed media research information (for instance: BARB, described later, analyses minute by minute viewing whereas RAJAR, also described later, only provides quarter-hour listening, four times a year). The radio industry is addressing the need to improve the perception of its accountability.

The next major change will be the introduction of Digital Audio Broadcasting (DAB), which like Digital Television is featured in the 1996 Broadcasting Bill. The implications of DAB for radio are:

- *Potential changes of ownership.* At present, ownership of licences is limited by the Radio Authority points system. This restricts the number of licences an organisation can hold, according to the points value of the licence, based on the number of people served by each station. There is an overall limit on the number of licences at 35 local licences and various limits within that. For instance, an organisation cannot hold more than 15 per cent of all points allocated for local services. This is currently 99 points and there are three major radio groups close to this limit: EMAP plc with 98.32 points, GWR Group plc with 80.83 and Capital Radio plc with 64.92 points.

  The system will evolve as the new Broadcasting Bill allows greater cross media ownership between newspapers, television and radio stations. For instance local newspapers with between 20 per cent and 50 per cent of the local newspaper circulation will be able to acquire up to 50 per cent of the local radio points in their area.

- *DAB provides CD quality sound.* Seven digital radio multiplexes would each have capacity for at least six stations. One multiplex would be allocated to the BBC, another to CNR and the remainder to regional and local radio stations.

- *Need for lengthy changeover period.* Small 'chip' sets suitable for receiving DAB are under development for use, for instance, in new cars. It is envisaged that programmes will be 'simulcast' on existing wavebands for many years before the majority of sets are able to receive DAB. To encourage existing stations to 'simulcast' their current analogue broadcasts on digital radio, stations would be able to renew their licences for a further eight years if they take up their allocated digital slot.

Having discussed the full range of *advertising* media, it is important to see them in context and recognise that there are alternative means of contacting your target markets, reviewed in the next chapter.

Chapter 4

Other Media

This book concentrates on the effective use of *advertising* media, defined earlier as 'the use of paid-for media space or time'. However, if your advertising is to achieve maximum results, it should be supplemented by, and synergistic with, other forms of promotion. These other forms demand far more attention than can be given in a book about advertising. The purpose of this chapter is simply to alert you to their importance.

1. THE EDITORIAL ROUTE

As Chapter 8 makes clear, advertising is not the reason for existence of most media, but only a means of helping them exist. Newspapers and magazines are read for their editorial content, and television watched for news and entertainment. The radio audience, too, tunes in for news and entertainment. Never forget that your *new* product is 'news' and could feature in the editorial just as much as the advertising, hence the importance of effective media relations.

2. CREATED MEDIA

Although there are numerous media which enable you to contact your target markets, through both advertising and editorial, you may find that even this wide range does not fully meet your company's communication needs, and you must therefore create new media.

There is literally no limit to the range of created media, which could include advisory bureaux, annual reports, audio-visual devices, awards and prizes, competitions, conferences, demonstrations, facility visits, films, incentives, gifts, house journals, newsletters, open days, printed material, provision of equipment or samples, seminars, speakers panels, videos, and many more.

Created media present a paradox because many executives forget that, as well as creating a medium, they must also create an audience for it. This, however, raises matters in illogical order, since nobody should ever create a medium without first having a specific target audience in mind. Equally, you should decide in advance how to deliver the created medium to this created target market. Booklets, leaflets, or videos – however well created – cannot deliver their message from inside a cupboard! Contrast this with the use of advertising and editorial, when you know from readership, viewership or listenership data precisely who you will reach, and also how your message will reach them.

A further point is that those who create media become media-owners in their own right. Many house journals are subsidised by the sale of advertising space. Other companies' created media may present you with both advertising and editorial opportunities, and your own may present such opportunities to others. When considering other organisations' created media as promotional vehicles, they should be evaluated in exactly the same way as other media, described in Chapter 7.

3. OTHER MESSAGE SOURCES

Marketing communications should also be considered in terms of message sources, and how existing and potential customers receive information about your organisation and its products. Those involved in marketing planning often categorise their activities under the headings of The Four Ps – Product, Price, Place and Promotion.

This review has so far considered only Promotion, but the other three Ps have equally important marketing communications implications.

Your product (or service) itself delivers a marketing communications message through its name, design, presentation and packaging.

Price also has marketing communications implications – lower price does not necessarily result in increased sales. Prospective purchasers often equate price with quality, and may suspect that low prices mean cheap and unreliable merchandise rather than price-advantageous products.

Place is important too – consider products widely available through any outlet which wishes to sell them irrespective of facilities and expertise, and – by way of contrast – merchandise available only direct from the manufacturer or appointed dealers, carefully selected for their ability to provide expert advice and effective after-sales service.

PROMOTIONAL PLANNING

When planning your company's overall promotional campaigns, as discussed in later chapters, you should therefore consider communicating through the full range of promotional media – editorial as well as advertising and, if necessary, creating additional media – against the background of the other three Ps and indeed all your target market's message sources.

It is equally important for these campaign components to re-inforce each other to maximum effect: there is little point in planning an effective media schedule if the advertising message it delivers conflicts with, or is undermined by, messages delivered by other media. On the contrary, all parts of the plan should reinforce each other, thereby multiplying their individual effects.

Chapter 5

Media Research and Services

Having reviewed in general terms the media you can use to communicate your advertising message, the next step is to examine what we know about them: the quantitative or qualitative data available which permit you to evaluate properly the various media and make comparisons. To quote current facts would be of very limited value as such information goes out-of-date all too quickly: for example, any statistics about circulation, costs, readership or viewing habits would be invalid by the time this book was published. In any event, some figures are already 6–12 months old before new data is published. This chapter therefore reviews the data sources available, rather than giving actual figures. Mention is also made of various services that may facilitate your effective use of advertising media.

Since various sources cover more than one medium, they will be reviewed by title rather than by media. The following brief cross-reference will, however, facilitate your locating those data sources relevant to the media that interest you:

All Media:	BRAD, MediaTel, Nielsen Register-MEAL
Cinema:	CAA, CAVIAR, NRS, TGI
Direct Mail:	DMIS, Royal Mail
Door to Door:	AHD, Stepcheck
Exhibitions:	ABC, EIF, Exhibiting Value Analysis
Outdoor:	Media Audits, POSTAR, TGI, TDI BUSADS, TDI TRAC
Press:	ABC, AHD, BPA International, CAVIAR, EBRS, EMS, JICREG, Media Audits, MMS, NRS, OPMA, PES, PPA, TGI, VFD
Radio:	CAVIAR, CRCA, Media Audits, NRS, RAJAR, TGI
Television:	BARB, CAVIAR, EMS, ITC, Media Audits, MMS, NRS, PETAR, TGI
Video:	BARB, CAVIAR, Videotrak
International:	BPA, EBRS, EMS, OPMA, PES, PETAR

70

These various sources are discussed in more detail below, in alphabetical order. This chapter necessarily has a 'list' format, and it is suggested that initially you read through it rapidly to acquaint yourself with the range of information available, and then return to the chapter for more detailed study later, *together with actual copies of the data sources mentioned.*

ABC (AUDIT BUREAU OF CIRCULATIONS)
(Black Prince Yard, 207–209 High Street, Berkhampsted, Herts HP4 1AD) (www.abc.org.uk)

ABC is a non-profit company, limited by guarantee, controlled by a tripartite council of advertisers, agencies and media-owners, the latter representing the Bureau's four categories of publishing members – national newspapers, regional newspapers, consumer magazines, and business magazines. This tripartite structure is reflected throughout the working parties that regularly review the different categories' audit rules and procedures, to ensure that they meet the needs of both publishers and advertisers.

ABC's primary function is the protection of advertisers against false claims. It provides certification of circulation figures and attendance at exhibitions, by independent professional auditors for consumer titles and ABC staff auditors for both business titles and overseas members, using standard audit rules and procedures for each ABC membership category. The independent auditors are usually the members' financial auditors. The ABC maintains regular liaison with a working committee representing the financial institutes and accounting professions, to ensure a consistent standard of audit procedures.

The Audit Bureau employs staff inspectors to conduct random inspections of the methods and procedures of the independent auditors. Should such inspection reveal errors, then the certificate will be re-issued and the auditor's professional body informed if there is evidence of malpractice.

CIRCULATION AUDITS

ABC's four categories of membership have differing requirements. Before reviewing these, some general points must be considered, as certain copies cannot be included in audited circulation figures. These vary according to readership categories but in all cases returned, unsold or undelivered copies must be excluded.

There is also provision for certain issues to be excluded at the request of the publisher, when an industrial dispute, mechanical failure, etc beyond the publisher's control results in loss of distribution of a publication.

All audit periods must be continuous, and a publisher may not choose to omit an audit return. Publishers failing to make a return without good cause are expelled from ABC membership.

Unless otherwise stated below, net sales are the only audit category: these are copies bought by individuals either from the retail point or by direct subscription, and represent the audited primary paid readership of a newspaper or magazine. With some publications, however, specified types of free circulation are also audited.

National Newspapers

These have monthly audit periods, and the Bureau also publishes six-month rolling averages.

Regional Newspapers

These have six-month audit periods.

Consumer Magazines

These divide into two separate categories:

General: these may have three-month, six-month or 12-month audit periods.

Specialist: these magazines share the same audit periods but may include, in addition to paid circulation, an element of free circulation as discussed below.

Business and Professional Journals

These have six-month or 12-month audit periods, and are primarily free distribution as discussed below.

All audit periods must be within a calendar year.

FREE DISTRIBUTION

The rule for free distribution is that each copy must be auditable down to the individual recipient. In the main, therefore, only postal distribution can be included. The ABC recognises three main types of free circulation, as follows.

Controlled circulation

This category comprises single copies sent free to individuals who fit the 'Terms of Control'. This control must define the individual commercial or professional classification, together with job specification, a reader must have to qualify for receipt of the journal. Terms of control must not be published within the publication. Controlled circulation is further sub-divided into the following seven categories:

1. Paid but subscriber matches 'Terms of Control'
2. Individually requested in writing
3. Individually requested by telephone
4. Company requested in writing
5. Company requested by telephone

Circulation within these five categories must be supported by an auditable source document – a signed and dated application form or a telephone request form agreed with ABC, valid for the current audit period, ie not more than three years old. The two further categories are:

6. Non-requested by name
7. Non-requested by job title or function

Circulation within these two categories covers non-requested copies which nevertheless meet the terms of control, and may include copies previously recorded as controlled circulation, after their expiration.

Society/Association free circulation

The second main type of free circulation recognised by the ABC relates to societies or associations, and divides into four categories:

1. Paid single copies where subscriber has option to pay additional to association membership.
2. Unpaid single copies requested in writing
3. Unpaid single copies requested by telephone
4. Non-optional single copies.

Society/Association journals sent to non-members must not appear in this section of the ABC return, but can be included within the controlled section provided they are supported by a valid source document: otherwise they must appear in the non-controlled section.

Non-controlled circulation

This type of free circulation normally comprises copies sent to advertisers and agencies, as well as exchange copies, which do not satisfy the rules for controlled circulation.

ABC PROFILES

The ABC Profile provides a demographic analysis of subscribers to a publication. Audited by an ABC staff auditor, it is an optional extension to the standard ABC Certificate and is available for both predominantly paid and predominantly free circulation titles.

The mandatory features of the profile are:

- The ABC Standard Certificate forms the first two pages of each Profile.
- Geographical analysis by UK regions and the world.
- Job title/function analysis using breakdowns specified by the publisher.
- Company activity breakdown, preferably using Standard Industry Classifications.
- Circulation additions and deletions analysing how many addresses are added to and removed from the mailing list. This is optional for the first profile.
- Sources and ages of records supporting free distribution copies. These identify the sources of the list and measure how up to date it is.

Optional data can include any other demographic analysis if that data is auditable. Examples include company size, purchasing responsibility or market specific data.

EXHIBITION AUDITS

Exhibition attendance is administered through the ABC's Exhibition Division. A working party representing the interests of the industry has developed rules and procedures for the Certificate of Attendance (COA), the industry standard for exhibition attendance data.

The COA verifies the total attendance at an exhibition and the demographic data held for attendees.

Attendance Data

This gives the total number of visitors admitted during the run of the exhibition, reported under the following categories:

- *Registered Attendance (Free)* Attendance may be claimed if the organisers can provide auditable proof of the attendee's name and address through an exhibition registration form.
- *Registered Attendance (Paid)* An attendee can be claimed if the organiser can provide auditable proof as with free attendance, plus proof of payment.
- *Other Paid Attendance* This gives the number of other visitors who gained entry by paying an admission fee.

Attendance data may also include visitors who transfer between exhibitions held at the same location, those who register during a previous exhibition and multiple pre-registrations.

Demographic Data

As a minimum, the COA analyses registered attendance into the following categories:

- Geographic location
- Job title
- Company activity

Any demographic analyses, if auditable, can be included within the COA, eg: company turnover, number of employees, buying responsibilities, etc.

The COA also identifies the organiser; sponsor (if applicable); date and venue of show; the number of stands and stand space occupied; the date and venue of the next show; Association membership (if applicable); target audience and the products/services exhibited.

Note: The information given here on ABC procedures is a summary and should not be used as a 'rule book' for ABC procedures. Furthermore, ABC's working parties continually review its rules and procedures, to ensure all aspects of an audit are considered. For further details, contact the Audit Bureau.

AHD (ASSOCIATION OF HOUSEHOLD DISTRIBUTORS)
(36 Frogmore Street, Tring, Hert, HP23 5AU)

The AHD promotes the medium of door-to-door distribution: unaddressed leaflets, brochures, coupons and samples reaching consumers in their homes.

AHD members offer three distribution techniques: solus (where an item is delivered on its own); shareplan (sharing costs with up to four other items); and – more relevant to our discussions – distribution with free newspapers.

All free newspapers are required to have Verified Free Distribution certification (discussed below) and many also have VFD's additional Leaflet Verification Certificate.

AHD publishes the Annual *Letterbox Marketing Handbook* which details all AHD members and the areas to which they deliver, to postcode sector level.

AHD also undertakes research on the medium and a recent survey demonstrates that 85 per cent of the sample researched had read or glanced through leaflets that came through their doors; 43 per cent keep leaflets for at least a few days (71 per cent for coupons). Up to 65 per cent claimed to have been stimulated by a door-to-door item.

BARB (BROADCASTERS' AUDIENCE RESEARCH BOARD LIMITED)
(Glenthorne House, Hammersmith Grove, London W6 0ND)

Since 1981, BARB has provided a single system for TV audience research, replacing the separate research once operated by the BBC and ITV. BARB's Board of Directors includes representatives of both the BBC and the ITV Association, who are joint holders of BARB shares, as well as the main subscriber groups. These are the Institute of Practitioners in Advertising (IPA), Channel 4 and BSkyB (representing satellite broadcasters). The Board meets under an independent chairman. BARB itself employs only a few staff, and provides information using professional research suppliers to conduct and report on audience research.

BARB operates through a committee system, related to its two main areas of research – audience measurement and audience appreciation – with separate Management Committees and Technical Sub-Committees controlling each of these two activities. Various interested parties join the partner organisations on these committees. On the measurement side, the IPA represents advertising agencies, and the Incorporated Society of British Advertisers (ISBA) represents advertisers. Both organisations, as users of television advertising, have a direct interest in how audiences are measured, and have an equal voice with shareholder committee members. The ITC is also represented on the audience appreciation committee, having an equal voice with the shareholders. BARB subscribers are represented on the appropriate committees.

Audience measurement

Unlike many surveys, BARB does not use personal interviews to measure the size of television audiences, but relies on electronic meters fixed to television sets in a representative sample of homes throughout the UK.

The first step in selecting the sample of homes to have these meters is the Establishment Survey, based on a random sample of more than 40,000 interviews conducted continuously throughout the year. The results of this Survey, together with Government census data, are used to select a sample of homes fully representative in terms of demographics and family composition, TV equipment ownership and viewing habits, to participate in the audience measurement panel. Panel members receive a nominal incentive for their services.

BARB's audience measurement panel comprises 4,435 homes, and the Establishment Survey provides a pool of households to replace those which, for some reason or other, drop out. A sufficient reserve of homes is maintained to provide a weekly panel balanced to be representative of the ITV and BBC network. Within this total are net balanced panels in each ITV area, each representative of its own area.

The electronic 'people meters' linked to all the television sets in a panel household register when each set is switched on or off and to which channel it is tuned. In addition each household has the equivalent of a remote control unit with numbered buttons. Each member of the household has their own number, and presses the appropriate button when they start to view, and 'off' when they stop. Should panel members forget, a signal on the meter flashes if the television set is on but no buttons have been pressed. Guest viewers are allocated special buttons, with a facility for registering their age and sex.

The use of video recorders for viewing programmes previously recorded at home significantly affects audience measurement, so a separate meter is fitted to the VCR, with the same button-press serving to register individual viewers for both the VCR and the TV set.

If a programme is recorded, this registers on the VCR meter which imprints an electronic code (channel, date and time) on the video tape. When the tape is played back the TV meter 'reads' this code, and 'time-shift' viewing can be reported separately or added to 'live' viewing information. The contents and viewing of hired, borrowed or purchased pre-recorded tapes is registered only as 'Other playback' (see Videotrak, described below.)

The electronic equipment can collect data from almost any number of television sets, VCRs and satellite receivers in any one home. All information is recorded by the electronic meter, retrieved overnight over the telephone line, and data automatically fed into a central computer. The meter results are then combined with details of programmes and commercial broadcasts, and the computer makes a series of calculations to arrive at estimates of audience sizes.

The data collected is compiled into a form required by BARB subscribers. The basic format comprises computer input data from the meters for those subscribers who wish to analyse it or, alternatively, calculated audience statistics showing the number or percentages watching particular programmes or commercials.

In the past, several bulky weekly reports were issued, but these have dwindled with the use of more efficient computer facilities. Three specialist reports are issued:

1. *The Network Report.* This shows summary information for those primarily concerned with advertising usage of research data. It summarises live and time-shift viewing figures for each of the main channels, and analyses audiences for both programmes and time segments.
2. *The Astra Report.* This summarises viewing statistics for those homes which receive Astra Channels, either by cable or by dish. This information is clearly of special interest to satellite broadcasters, as well as agencies and advertisers. (Satellite data is included, but in less detail, in both the Network Report just mentioned and the BBC Report described below.)
3. *The BBC Report.* As its name suggests, this is tailored to the BBC's somewhat different needs. Although the BBC carries no advertising and most of its output is networked rather than regional, the Corporation is nevertheless interested in both live and time-shift information about programme audiences, in the performance of other channels, and in regional variations.

BARB issues a weekly press release giving the hours of viewing to each channel and listing the audiences to the most popular programmes of each channel.

Audience measurement data is currently collected by two research companies contracted by BARB for this purpose: Audits of Great Britain (AGB) and RSMB Television Research Ltd, each company controlling separate aspects of the research operation. The contract comes up for renewal on a regular basis, and tenders are then invited from research organisations with the necessary interest and facilities.

Audience Appreciation

BARB manages an audience appreciation service which is totally confidential to the subscribing broadcasters (BBC, Channel 4 and the ITV companies).

Research Services Ltd (RSL) run the current service which comprises a national panel of 3,000 adults. Regional boost panels are also available to subscribers, as is a children's panel of 1,000 children aged 4–15. The adult panel operates weekly, whilst the regional boosts and children's panel cover one week in every four. Panellists are asked to complete two booklets:

1. *Programme Diary.* This covers a week's viewing and asks panellists to rate each programme they watch on a scale of 0–10. The data is used to produce an Appreciation Index for each programme expressed as a mark out of 100.
2. *Viewpoint.* The second booklet comprises questions asked by broadcasters about any aspect of a particular programme on a particular day. A broadcaster might wish to know, for example, what viewers think about a presenter or programme or whether a quiz game is exciting. More general questions about series or serials are also asked. Any questions can be asked about any programme, but the results remain confidential to the broadcaster asking the question.

BPA INTERNATIONAL
(35 Picadilly, London W1V 9PB)

BPA is an American-based organisation whose primary function is to provide independent verification of circulation data for business and special interest consumer magazines. Circulations may be all-paid, all controlled or any combination.

Like the British ABC, BPA is an independent non-profit organisation supported by publishers, advertisers and agencies.

A BPA circulation statement is recognised internationally and intended to help evaluate and select publications. BPA audits nearly 1,600 magazines for six-monthly periods ending 30 June and 31 December. Around 100 UK-based publications are audited by BPA, primarily those with international circulations.

There are a wide variety of special audits which allow a publication to provide advertisers with detailed profiles of its circulation, including:

- analysis of the buying influences of recipients
- the number of locations reached by the publication. Sites can be analysed by area, type of business, products manufactured, volume

of sales and number of employees
- duplication audits and pass-along receivership showing the additional recipients of a publication.

BRAD (BRITISH RATE AND DATA)
(EMAP Business Communications, 33–39 Bowling Green Lane, London EC1R 0DA)

BRAD provides a comprehensive listing of all media which carry advertising. It is published monthly in two separate volumes.

The main volume of BRAD features media in four main sections:

- Consumer Press
- Business Press
- Broadcast Media
- Posters and Outdoor Media

The supplementary volume, BRAD Newspapers, features all national and regional newspapers.

The topicality of BRAD is demonstrated by the fact that every month there are over 2,000 changes to the rates and data featured for 11,000 advertising media.

BRAD features the key facts and figures relevant to choosing and using advertising media. A typical listing for a newspaper will feature descriptive information such as contact addresses, frequency of publication, cover price, etc. Subsequent sections include:

- ABC circulation data
- NRS/JICREG (described below) Readership data
- Advertising rates
- Production specifications

Magazines are organised by market sector and each entry follows a similar structure to the newspaper listing described above. Magazine entries feature NRS data where available and include a short description of the editorial profile and the target readership.

Broadcast media listings feature individual spot rates analysed by the different day parts to which they apply. Packages are summarised. Data from RAJAR (described below) is provided for radio stations.

The listings for the remaining media differ considerably, reflecting the peculiarities of the markets they serve.

BRADbase

The entire BRAD database can also be held within subscribers' own PC or computer networks, and up-dated daily using BRAD's e-mail service.

One strength of the BRADbase system lies in its media selection capability. Users can specify an area of media interest (based on, for example, data classification, minimum circulation, frequency, or rate category) and from this produce a media list displaying comparative data on page rates, circulation and costs per thousand.

Overseas Media

Parallel volumes to BRAD are available for other countries, including Australia, Belgium, Canada, China, France, Germany, Holland, Italy, Scandinavia, South Africa, Spain, Switzerland and the United States.

BRAD Publishing Companies Portfolio

Published each Spring, this annual guide to corporate structure in print media comprises two main sections. One gives details of Publishing Companies (an alphabetical listing of UK companies and their subsidiaries with business interests in print media), while the second provides a Publication/Company Index (listing alphabetically all publications appearing in the Portfolio, cross-referenced to their publishing company and the page on which it appears in the preceding main section).

BRAD Agencies and Advertisers

This publication, updated six times each year, contains information about leading advertising agencies – who and where they are, their billings, recognition and status, key executives, IPA membership, and which clients and brands they handle. Similar information is given about the top national advertisers – their products or services and brands, who to contact, how much and in which media they spend, and their advertising agencies. The List also gives details of all main trade associations involved with the advertising industry.

BRAD Direct Marketing Lists, Rates & Data

This annual publication features direct marketing lists covering consumer and business markets, as well as the public sector (all categorised under 'Interest' headings) giving source, profile, previous use and 'cleaning' against the Mailing Preference Service, address type (whether individuals can be mailed at home or business), rental costs and conditions. In addition, it gives the names and addresses of owners and list brokers, and also provides information about the supply and services side of the industry.

In conclusion, it is worth mentioning that BRAD not only provides an information service but is also an advertising medium in its own right, used by those whose target market is those personnel whose judgement affects media decisions.

CAA (CINEMA ADVERTISING ASSOCIATION)
(127 Wardour Street, London W1V 4NL)

The CAA is the trade association of cinema advertising contractors in the UK and as such is devoted to developing and maintaining high standards of practice and presentation within the medium.

Its role is partly that of watchdog, acting to ensure that professional standards are maintained by the cinema advertising industry. One aspect of this work is that it is responsible for conducting regular checks to ensure that cinema advertising bookings are screened as scheduled and under optimum conditions, ie prior to the main feature film, and with the house lights down. Another aspect of its watchdog role is vetting all commercials prior to screening – a matter discussed in more detail in Chapter 17.

The other major purpose of the CAA – hence its inclusion in this chapter – is to educate and inform, and in this role it aims to provide advertisers and agencies with up-to-date information about the cinema medium and the advertising advantages it has to offer.

Information published by the CAA:

Admissions Monitor Gallup conducts a continuous weekly admissions audit covering all cinemas accepting advertising in the UK. Weekly figures are collected from all major circuits and a panel of independent cinemas. This data helps administer the Audience Guarantee Plan described earlier.

Screens Data on each screen is analysed by ISBA area, conurbation area, circuit and seating capacity. A complete master list of all screens by county is also available.

Cinema Audience The CAA provides information based on questions in NRS (described below) regarding the cinema audience: composition, penetration and coverage and frequency obtained by typical cinema campaigns. The CAA's Coverage and Frequency Guide based on NRS figures is published annually.

TGI (described below) provide index figures giving a quantitative measure of purchasers of individual products or services in terms of their cinema-going frequency. For example, an index of 130 means that cinema-goers are 1.30 times as likely to use a product as the average person. Five index figures are available for each product group: all cinema-goers (those who ever go to the cinema), heavy cinema-goers (go more than once a month), medium cinema-goers (go once a month or every two or three months), light cinema-goers (go less than once in three months) and non cinema-goers (those who never go to the cinema).

CAVIAR (CINEMA AND VIDEO INDUSTRY AUDIENCE RESEARCH COMMITTEE)
(Cinema Advertising Association, 127 Wardour Street, London W1V 4NL)

To provide advertisers with more detailed audience information than that provided by NRS or TGI, the CAA commissioned a series of in-depth audience studies. These were the forerunners of CAVIAR, an annual survey which researches the entire film market, from cinema to video tapes, both rented and bought, and contains information on television, satellite and cable watching as well as newspaper and magazine readership. It is funded by the CAA and a consortium of leading organisations in the cinema and video industries.
The survey has been conducted by BMRB since 1992 and takes place between October and November each year. Around 3,000 face-to-face interviews are carried out using Computer Assisted Personal Interviewing (CAPI) in people's homes among a representative quota sample of individuals aged seven plus throughout Great Britain. Younger age groups are heavily weighted within the sample reflecting the importance of young people to both the cinema and video markets.
CAVIAR is developed on a constant basis to reflect current developments and the interests of the consortium. The twelfth CAVIAR study, carried out in 1994, was the most comprehensive survey yet and covered the following:

Cinema Respondents are asked about cinema-going frequency and how recently they went to the cinema.

Cinema-goers are asked about all visits in the last two months. Information is recorded about the film seen, name and location of cinema, where they heard about the film they saw, who/how many they went with, how they got there, etc.

Each annual survey analyses 48 top films on general release over the year, to give their total viewership and audience profile. In addition, the audiences of 12 selected 'art' films are measured separately. CAVIAR has developed a classification system to identify more than 50 types of film.

Cinema information is now supplemented by the *Film Monitor* studies described below.

Video Similar information to the cinema section is obtained on hired and purchased videos, where they were hired/bought from, who they were bought for, who they watched with, where they heard about them, etc.

Each annual survey analyses 36 top pre-recorded video releases over the year, to provide their total viewership and audience profiles. Data is also analysed by CAVIAR's classification codes, to provide audience profiles for specific film categories. Rented and purchased tapes are considered together when determining the audiences for specific titles.

Other Media This section covers ownership of TVs and VCRs and other hardware such as CDi, video games systems, home computers, etc. Weight of radio listening and TV viewing, including satellite and cable is also covered along with readership of newspapers and selected magazines. Specialist film magazines are covered in some detail.

Report Format Subscribers receive reports in both written and tabular form. The tabular reports contain tables with extensive cross-analyses detailing age, gender, and social grade (certain tables contain expanded sub-groups such as frequency of cinema-going, ownership of satellite, frequency of watching hired films, and type of video bought). The written report contains pertinent trend data in addition to the survey results.

Special interest tables are also included, with analysis by:

- age, gender and social grade
- family size, siblings, marital status, age of mother/children
- terminal educational age, school/work status
- TV area
- electronic equipment in home
- length of VCR ownership
- accommodation type
- weight of media usage (TV, cinema and video)

PC analysis of the data is also available to subscribers via the main computer bureaux, such as those listed under the TGI section later.

CAVIAR Film Monitor Each quarter, this provides viewership and profile data on individual cinema releases more frequently than the main study. Interviewing is conducted jointly by Carrick James Market Research and National Opinion Polls with a combined sample size of more than 4,000 individuals.

Each quarterly survey covers 24 films, classified by CAVIAR codes, with audience analysed by age, gender and social grade.

Advertising Recall studies The CAA has conducted several advertising recall studies to test awareness of cinema commercials as opposed to television and demonstrate the communication abilities of the medium.

CONFERENCES & EXHIBITIONS DIARY
(Themetree Ltd, 2 Prebendal Court, Oxford Road, Aylesbury, Bucks HP19 3EY) (see also Exhibition Industry Federation below)

This Diary is published quarterly and is categorised in 42 comprehensive sections. Within each, events are listed by country (the Diary now includes European events) in date order, with title, venue and location, and the address and telephone number of the organisers.

CRCA (COMMERCIAL RADIO COMPANIES ASSOCIATION)
(Radio House, 46 Westbourne Grove, London W2 5SH)

CRCA is the trade association for companies holding Commercial Radio licences awarded by the Radio Authority. It represents these radio companies in their dealings with Government, the Radio Authority, copyright societies and other organisations concerned with radio. CRCA provides a forum for industry discussion, is a source of advice to members on all aspects of radio and acts as a clearing house for radio information.

The CRCA jointly owns RAJAR (Radio Joint Audience Research Ltd discussed below) with the BBC. The CRCA also owns the *Network Chart Show* mentioned earlier.

DMIS (DIRECT MAIL INFORMATION SERVICE)
(5 Carlisle Street, London W1V 6JX)

The Direct Mail Information Service is the source of official statistics on direct mail: it also provides regular reports and updates on major trends and relevant issues within the industry.

Each year DMIS undertakes several new research projects, as well as continuing its on-going programme. The work may range from gauging the volume of direct mail to more complex projects dealing with specific issues affecting the industry. Some of the most important research provides information on both consumer and business opinions and their treatment of direct mail. More recently, DMIS has completed research into consumer attitudes towards different creative treatments and the techniques used in direct mail. Recent publications include the following:

Direct Mail Trends Survey The 1994 report examines levels of opening and reading, response to direct mail and satisfaction with purchases made through the medium.

Users, Non-Users and Potential Users This survey investigates usage and non-usage of direct mail, the function of marketing databases and use of information. The report also explores users' and rejectors' personal, strategic and marketing views of direct mail. A separate report, taken from this survey, **Mailers and Rejectors**, covers methods of evaluating direct mail, its integration with other media and the factors affecting the decisions to use it. A third extract: **Size, Success and Direct Mail**, examines direct mail in the business context.

The Users Survey examines how and why companies use direct mail based on interviews with senior business executives in 400 companies.

Open for Business This qualitative study examines the motivations behind the actions of direct mail users.

Business to Business Catalogues Research sets out to establish the size and value of the business mail order market.

Response Rates This report on over 600 direct mail campaigns analyses response rates by sector, response method, offer made and by list type.

Between Enjoyment and Junk A consumer survey which covers attitudes to a wide range of issues. An extract, titled **The Medium and the Message** covers how attitudes affect behaviour.

Consumers Responding Direct investigates reasons for using post or telephone response methods.

The Letter Box Factfile is a top line summary of information on Direct Mail.

DMIS also provides assistance with the planning, execution and evaluation of direct mail campaigns.

EBRS (EUROPEAN BUSINESS READERSHIP SURVEY)
(The Economist, 25 St James Street, London SW1A 1HG)

EBRS is a survey of 283 national and international newspapers and magazines read by 9,500 senior executives in 17 European countries.

The survey is sponsored by 28 titles and 8 advertising agencies, with research undertaken by Research Services Limited using postal self completion questionnaires. Typical data provided includes:

- business newspapers and magazines which respondents read and the languages they read at work
- responsibilities of respondents, particularly their involvement in international business and their business purchasing/leasing decisions
- respondents' use of electronics, air travel, hotels and car hire

Respondents to this survey work in establishments with over 250 employees (150 for Head Offices of large companies) or work in corporate, business and financial companies. EBRS is widely used for planning corporate business and financial campaigns aimed at influencing senior executives in leading companies.

EMS (EUROPEAN MEDIA AND MARKETING SURVEY)
(Massons, 1 Maybury Court, Marylebone Street, London W1M 7PP)

EMS is designed to measure press readership and television viewing in 17 European countries. Based on a survey of 467 national and international press titles and 67 national and international television channels, it measures overlap readership/viewership from neighbouring countries, so providing an analysis of a medium's penetration across Europe. The sample is 18,000 main income earners in a household with income double the average for their country of residence.

The survey is undertaken using random telephone dialling which produces a true probability sample of households. Computer Assisted Telephone Interviewing (CATI) from a single base in Amsterdam helps achieve consistent quality of interview and also assists in minimising problems with pronunciation and prompting. A 16 page self-completion questionnaire sent to respondents obtains additional information.

The first Report was issued in spring 1996 and purchase commitment had been made by 34 advertisers, media and agencies. These include Time, Readers' Digest and The Economist, as well as CNN International, NBC Superchannel and EBN TV channels.

87

Reports will be available on computer tape every six months showing 12 months data on a rolling basis. Typical data to be provided includes:

- *Press* read in last 12 months, recency of reading, frequency of reading and time spent reading.
- *Television* ownership and frequency of viewing. Pattern of viewing during last 12 months, recency of viewing, frequency of viewing and place of viewing.
- *Corporate Image Tracking* allowing advertisers and agencies to track awareness and image, giving insights into advertising effectiveness.
- *Marketing Database* providing a wide variety of demographics and classifications including ownership and consumption of products and services, attitudes and personal interests, business responsibilities and travel habits.

EIF (EXHIBITION INDUSTRY FEDERATION)
(115 Hartington Road, London SW8 2HB)

The activities of this Federation are best illustrated by its seventh research report – *The UK Exhibition Industry: The Facts* – published to assist present and potential users of exhibitions in planning their marketing programmes, and to give reliable data to those who stage or service exhibitions.

The report's key findings cover visitor and exhibitor attendance data together with a listing of all exhibitions and hall space occupied. The data is cross analysed by industry sectors. Included in the appendices is a list of venues which submit data to the Clearing House for Certified Data on Exhibitions (CCDE). The appendices also show trends in exhibition sizes between 1989 and 1994. Finally, there is a summary of exhibitor spend, cross analysed by sector, cost (for stand, staff and promotion), usage (shell or free-build) and exhibitor size.

The Effectiveness Survey The EIF also produced this survey to identify the marketing opportunities presented by exhibitions compared with other media.

Although mainly limited to three industry sectors (engineering, computers and food) it demonstrates how marketing decision-makers view the interdependence of exhibitions with other communication tools such as advertising, direct mail and personal selling.

It includes tables analysing the following:

- exhibitor objectives
- allocation of budget by communication tool

- proportion spent on exhibitions
- effectiveness rating of each tool
- importance of tools and various media for exhibitors
- methods used to record stand contacts
- average costs
- perception of exhibitions as 'worthwhile'

British Conference Market Survey This 1994 survey monitors trends and levels of activity in the UK conference industry focussing on conferences involving 15 or more people that occur for six or more hours.

Respondents, who complete a monthly questionnaire, are drawn from a wide variety of venue type and location including:

- Residential Conference Centres
- Purpose-built Conference Centres
- Municipal Multi-purpose venues
- Universities
- Hotels, of various types
- Unusual venues such as historic houses, libraries, and tourist attractions

The data provided by this report includes:

- Volume of activity
- Type of conference
- Revenue from each delegate
- Conference size
- Conferences within exhibitions
- Length of conference and start days
- Method of booking reservations

EXHIBITING VALUE ANALYSIS
(Exhibition Surveys Ltd, PO Box 7, 22 Digby Drive, Melton Mowbray LE13 0RQ)

Exhibiting Value Analysis (EVA) is a research service for exhibitors. The information results from a twin survey of each exhibition and the performance of individual stands.

Private Stand Performance Report This confidential report is tailored to meet each exhibitor's special needs, analysing each stand's performance in detail.

Shared Audience Profile This comprehensive analysis of audience quality shows visitor interest in *each* exhibitor's products and services as well as intention to buy.

EVA studies exhibiting effectiveness under four headings:

- Strengths and weaknesses of the exhibition from the exhibitor's viewpoint
- Specific questions of policy or performance that must/should be addressed if effectiveness is to be improved.
- Competitor stand achievements compared with the exhibitor's stand.
- Information specific to the exhibitor's needs and requirements.

ITC (THE INDEPENDENT TELEVISION COMMISSION)
(33 Foley Street, London W1P 7LB)

The ITC publishes quarterly bulletins which state the number of operating cable franchises, and also gives the number of Broadband homes passed and connected, together with average penetration.

The bulletins also give 'Pay/basic ratios' which are a measure of the number of subscriptions to the pay channels (Sky Movies, The Movie Channel, Sky Sports and Home Video Channel) as a percentage of total subscribers. For example, if all cable homes subscribed to just one pay channel and neither of the other three, the pay/basic ratio would be 100 per cent; if to all four, the ratio would be 400 per cent.

The bulletins also detail the number of franchises providing telephony, the number of telephone lines installed and whether residential or business. Finally the bulletin quantifies all cable homes passed and connected, and penetration data.

Similar figures for homes passed/connected and penetration, together with pay/basic ratios, are also given for individual Broadband franchises with more than 2,500 subscribers. Totals are provided for the main Multiple Service Operators (described earlier).

The bulletins also give overall numbers for cabled homes receiving the various available channels, but do not cover the DBS dish audiences for them.

The ITC also publishes an annual Cable study. Undertaken by Continental Research over a two week period in October, it is based on diaries completed by 653 respondents aged two years old and over in 39 cable franchises. The key data includes:

- share of viewing in Broadband cable homes
- share by adults (weekday and weekend)
- children's viewing (weekday and weekend)

- satellite TV channels' weekly reach within homes receiving each channel.

ITC cable statistics are based on returns made by every licensed cable operator, and some SMATV operators.

JICNARS (JOINT INDUSTRY COMMITTEE FOR NATIONAL READERSHIP SURVEYS)
(See NRS below)

JICPAR (JOINT INDUSTRY COMMITTEE FOR POSTER AUDIENCE RESEARCH)
(c/o The Outdoor Advertising Association, 77 Newman Street, London W1A 1DX)

JICPAR comprises representatives of the Outdoor Advertising Association (OAA) of Great Britain, the Incorporated Society of British Advertisers, the Institute of Practitioners in Advertising, and the Council of Outdoor Specialists (COS).

JICPAR supervises the development of the poster medium's audience measurement: POSTAR (described below under the heading of OAA). Future POSTAR developments will be jointly funded by the OAA and COS/IPA.

JICREG (JOINT INDUSTRY COMMITTEE FOR REGIONAL PRESS RESEARCH)
(Bloomsbury House, 74–77 Great Russell Street, London WC1B 3DA)

The Newspaper Society launched JICREG in 1990 to provide readership information on the majority of regional and local newspapers with area flexibility, establishing the performance of papers or schedules within any marketing or catchment area.

JICREG's board includes representatives from the Institute of Practitioners in Advertising, the Incorporated Society for British Advertisers, the Association of Media and Communication Specialists and a number of regional publishers.

Many regional newspapers undertake regular readership research on their own behalf, but any database that merely held this information centrally would have large gaps caused by titles without research. It was therefore decided, after much technical debate, to see if these gaps could be filled by mathematically modelling readership figures from circulation and demographic data. The modelled data would then be merged with the researched information, to construct a comprehensive database for the regional press. Rigorous examination proved the modelled figures generally matched actual figures extremely closely, within the 95 per cent confidence levels generally acceptable as an industry standard. New JICREG models were introduced in 1995 based on findings from more than 200 readership surveys. As more readership surveys are submitted, so the models will be further refined.

JICREG provides readership information for 98 per cent of eligible titles, covering morning, evening and Sunday newspapers, and paid-for and free weeklies. There is, of course, nothing to prevent individual newspapers from commissioning research to demonstrate their particular merits, and indeed JICREG encourages this and has provision to incorporate the results within its own database. Such independent research must however be in accordance with JICREG's Survey Guidelines (which specify carefully prepared sampling procedures and precisely drafted questionnaires) to ensure it is statistically valid.

Regional and local press schedules can now be analysed against JICREG data to show reach and frequency (both discussed in Chapter 7) within any geographic area, by any combination of titles. The database is held at the Newspaper Society. JICREG can be accessed in five ways:

1. Hard copy reports from the database
2. Computer analysis from JICREG or one of two authorised computer bureaux (Telmar and IMS). (See TGI section below)
3. Mediatel discussed below (selected information)
4. JIC-in-a-box PC system held by agencies, publishers, advertisers, sales houses and others
5. Internet using the Adweb service (http://www.adweb.co.uk)

JICREG is used by agencies to plan and buy advertising, and by publishers and their sales houses to prepare sales presentations about regional press.

MEAL (MEDIA EXPENDITURE ANALYSIS LTD)
(see **Nielsen Register-MEAL** below)

MEDIA AUDITS LTD
(16 Dufours Place, London W1V 1FE)

This company provides consultancy services in the measurement and use of advertising media. Media Audits neither buys nor sells space or time, but advises subscribers on how to maximise the value they obtain from media. The company works primarily for advertisers evaluating their usage of major consumer media.

For television, advertisers provide Media Audits with their media strategy and plan, together with a detailed campaign schedule and actual costs paid. Media Audits, as a BARB subscriber, validates the audience data and places the information into data pools – mainly differentiated by the target audience purchased eg: adults, shoppers, men. In return, advertisers receive an evaluation of how their individual campaign compares to the price and quality achievements of the data-pool. In addition, advertisers receive advice across a range of media issues including:

- strategic media choices/forward planning
- centralised media pitches
- incentive schemes on agency performance.

Media Audits operates this service for TV, press, outdoor and radio in the UK. It also provides a data-pool service to advertisers in France, Netherlands, Spain and Ireland as well as offering multinational clients advice on achieving best practice in other markets.

In addition to reviewing media performance, Media Audits provides advice and analysis of advertising effectiveness, linking levels of advertising awareness, image and response to the delivery of messages to individual consumers. This service allows advertisers to judge the effectiveness of their advertising delivery and improve their media schedules and targeting.

THE MEDIA REGISTER
(see **Nielsen Register-MEAL** *below)*

MEDIATEL
(52 Poland Street, London W1V 4LQ)
(http://www.mediatel.co.uk)

MediaTel is an on-line media news and information database accessed daily by most UK advertising agencies, media independents and media owners. MediaTel is a privately owned company, not affiliated to any particular medium or industry body, and offers a subscription-only service which is updated every working day, available seven days a week.

MediaTel's database covers all the cost and audience details normally used as a basis for media planning. Data available covers the following main media markets (each sub-divided): national newspapers, magazines (consumer and business), television, outdoor, cinema, radio, regional media and sponsorship. The *Newsline* service reports media events as they happen, and is the most heavily accessed section of the database. *Encyclomedia* compiles useful media statistics on expenditure and revenues. The *Miscellaneous* section includes, among other items, a useful 'Minefield' warning (a chronological list by month of irregular events that may affect audience deliveries).

Various standard media calculations (cost/coverage ranking for press, and a coverage and frequency guide for radio, as examples) can be performed on MediaTel's interactive services.

MediaTel is transferring its databases to allow access through the World Wide Web (see Web-site address location above) on the Internet. This opens the way for a range of new facilities, some accessible by anyone 'surfing the net', others restricted to MediaTel subscribers. MediaTel also offers media-owners the opportunity to set up and edit their own 'web sites' within the overall database. In this way, media-owners can make available to MediaTel subscribers the latest research or marketing data about their own medium. MediaTel also serves as an advertising medium in its own right, with solus advertising space.

News Search Five years of media stories can be searched by key words. The media opportunities in any town, for example, can be accessed by keying in the name of the town, or information on a particular publication by keying in its title. This will soon be extended to postcode data and include geo-demographics.

Press Planner This facility extends and improves access to data held on newspapers and magazines. The database incorporates full rate-cards for more than 3,000 titles, including details of regional editions, inserts, and contacts. Rates data can be integrated with circulation and readership data to produce costs-per-thousand for any list of titles. In addition, more than 20 different reports, ranging from readership and circulation trends through to editorial assessments, can be viewed on screen or printed out.

Television Database During 1995, MediaTel introduced an interactive television database on its web site, covering up to ten years of viewing trends and profiles plus costs and revenue shares.

Regional Media Database This features regional media data by postcode sector, covering radio, outdoor, regional newspapers, cable and cinema plus demographics by postcode sector. There are future plans to introduce a facility which will create computer-generated maps using postcode data.

IPA Database This database is for the Institute of Practitioners in Advertising (IPA). It provides information on member agencies plus regular news bulletins and an advertising effectiveness database, legal information, media and marketing appraisals. Some information is available to IPA members only.

TDI Database This database has been created for TDI (described below) to include photographs of advertising opportunities across London buses and Underground, with text descriptions of coverage and costs.

MMS (MEDIA MONITORING SERVICES LTD)
(Madison House, High Street, Sunninghill, Ascot, Berkshire SL5 9NP)

This company monitors all types of media: television, radio, cinema and posters as well as more than a thousand press titles. These range from business-to-business press and consumer magazines through to Sunday and Daily newspapers. Over 8 million advertisements are recorded every year with a rate card value of £5 billion.

MMS's system is flexible, so each report covers individual subscribers' particular needs. Each client selects the media to be monitored and information is provided in magnetic tape, disc or printed form.

The database can provide reports on a one-off or regular basis, in the following media categories:

Business-to-Business Press

MMS monitors over 800 titles in more than 90 markets, and its reporting service encompasses display, recruitment and classified advertising.

Reported in volume and/or expenditure terms, MMS data provides everything from 'Management Summaries' down to detailed schedules of advertiser activity by product, publication and month.

Performances can be tracked by total market, product category, individual advertiser and defined geographical area, and new business opportunities for publications identified through 'Absent Advertiser' reports.

Printed reports can be complemented by a PC system which allows users to analyse data further in a variety of ways. The system can, in addition, create 'Prospect Lists' and includes an 'Address List' mailing facility.

Consumer Magazines and National Newspapers

MMS's *Medialog* Consumer Magazine database contains detailed advertising information across more than 150 publications and in excess of 36,000 products.

A PC system allows users to analyse raw data flexibly, to create customised reports and graphics, as well as detailed advertising schedules.

These analyses enable clients to track advertising within their defined magazine markets by product category, advertiser, agency, brand and publication.

MMS has extended its press media coverage into the national daily newspapers, thus offering a comprehensive national 'Print monitoring service'.

Recruitment

MMS measures all Recruitment Advertising across national newspapers and selected trade markets.

Detailed reports allow clients to track performance by job category and title and by individual advertiser, as well as identifying new business opportunities by reporting on 'absent advertisers' not using the client's publications.

Classified

MMS coverage of Classified Advertising allows detailed reporting down to category and advertiser level within national newspapers, consumer magazines and selected trade publications. Users can track performance in their total sector, by category within each sector, and by advertiser, as well as identify new business opportunities.

Editorial

MMS currently measures editorial content in more than 200 consumer magazines, in the national quality press and in a growing number of trade publications.

Editorial references are measured by category within each publication, with detailed reports available showing coverage volumes, editorial/advertising ratios, category breakdowns by publication, and profiles by category.

MultiMedia

Data from six media types (television, radio, cinema, poster, business and consumer press) are merged at brand and advertiser level, by each type of media and by month so that full cross analysis can be undertaken.

NEWSPAPER SOCIETY
(Bloomsbury House, 74–77 Great Russell Street, London WC1B 3DA)

The Newspaper Society represents and promotes the interests of Britain's regional and local press. Its marketing arm provides a range of services to improve the understanding and usage of regional press by advertisers and agencies.

Press-Ad, the Society's commercial arm, founded in 1988, is due to be re-launched in 1996 as part of a new marketing strategy. At the time of writing, the range of services provided was as follows:

The Regional Press Database

The largest of its kind in the world, this covers all regional titles, giving rates, production details, key staff etc, by title. It also contains details of subscribing titles' circulation areas, by some 8,900 postcode sectors. These sectors can then be used as building blocks to cover any larger geographical area, from villages and towns, through to store/dealer catchment areas, shopping centre 'drive time' areas, counties, or television areas. Coverage can be provided by population, household and other demographic data, or by geo-demographic systems. In many cases, resultant press lists or media schedules are then analysed against the JICREG readership data described earlier.

The database is available in printed and disc format, while other users access it by telephone or even on-line. For planning and presentation purposes, a computerised mapping service is available for advertisers, agencies and publishers.

Production services

The Society also offers facilities for advertisers or agencies who wish to centralise the task of advertisement production. On receipt of master copies of each advertisement, the Society then sends out correct-size material to each newspaper in the schedule.

Co-operative advertising

Co-operation with distributors is a major component of many campaigns: co-operative advertising is a multi-million pound business, almost all of which appears in the regional press. The Society works with manufacturers and suppliers in facilitating effective joint manufacturer/dealer schemes, by helping advertisers contact their local outlets. The Society has worked with or instigated co-operative advertising schemes in 40 different categories, ranging from motors to photography and carpets to holidays. Its *Feature Link* service provides promotional platforms for national events and campaigns (such as crime prevention) as well as product/brand promotions with competitions, features and other ideas.

Publications

A 200 page reference guide to Britain's regional and local press: *Reaching the Regions*, was published by the Society in 1995. It features maps and tables pinpointing every regional newspaper in the country by region.

The Society produces a range of other publications including *Headlines*, a bi-monthly magazine on regional press advertising issues.

NIELSEN REGISTER-MEAL
(7 Harewood Avenue, London NW1 6JB)

This organisation results from the merger of two formerly competing long-established services, namely MEAL (Media Expenditure Analysis Ltd) with The Media Register, and their acquisition by A C Nielsen.

Nielsen Register-MEAL provides a continuous monitor of advertising to assist advertisers and their agencies in monitoring competitors' advertising activities and expenditure.

The consumer media monitor is based on comprehensive coverage of display advertisements in National press, magazines, television, selected radio companies, cinema and outdoor. It also includes national and major regional advertising in regional dailies, Sundays and selected weekly newspapers. Classified advertising in all national newspapers is monitored by advertiser and for magazines in total.

Each month more than 750,000 advertisements are attributed to over 50,000 brands. These are then attributed to one of 483 product groups within 33 categories as below:

Agricultural
Business to Business
Charities
Clothing
Confectionery
Corporate
Cosmetics & Toiletries
Do It Yourself
Drink
Education
Entertainment
Financial
Food
Gardening
Government
Household Durables

Household Furnishings
Household Stores
Houseware
Industrial
Leisure Equipment
Luxury Goods
Mail Order
Motoring
Office Automation
Pharmaceutical
Publishing and Broadcasting
Retail
Small Electrical Appliances
Sport
Tobacco
Travel
Utilities

Expenditure is calculated as follows:

Television Details of all spots transmitted are extracted from the BARB weekly commercials tape, including the station, day of week, time transmitted, length of commercials and impacts (the total number of individuals exposed to each commercial).

Television advertising expenditure is notoriously difficult to estimate, so each month a panel of media buyers provide their estimates of the net revenue for ITV, C4, S4C, GMTV and BSkyB.

An average cost per thousand for 12 target audience categories (such as All Adults, Men, ABC1 Adults, Adults aged 16–24, Children aged 4–15) is calculated by dividing the estimated revenue for each contractor by the total number of impacts. Thus, expenditure estimates for a brand may be made by multiplying the total impacts achieved by the most appropriate cost per thousand.

This technique yields an expected expenditure for all TV advertised brands, although some brands will spend slightly more and some slightly less than this expectation, depending on market place factors.

Press No practical method has yet been developed to calculate actual press expenditure so Nielsen Register-MEAL applies published rate card costs to each advertisement. This includes premiums for special positions and colour but does not allow for series discounts. Details of page numbers and editorial environment are also recorded.

Radio Details of radio transmissions are obtained from participating radio stations. The RAJAR (described below) adult audience figures for each station are then divided into eight time segments. Expenditure by brand is calculated by multiplying the total audience achieved by the average cost of buying a 30 second spot across the network. This rate will vary, for instance, being £1.65 during the period Oct–Dec 1995 and £1.50 for the rest of the year.

Cinema Details of all cinema campaigns over £5,000 are provided by the two cinema contractors (Cinema Media and Pearl & Dean described in Chapter 1), expenditure being calculated at rate card cost.

Posters Brand expenditure by sheet size and region is provided by a consortium comprising the major poster buying specialists and major contractors and is based on average weekly cost per sheet size.

Nielsen Register-MEAL Reports Data is available as hard copy either as syndicated services described below or analyses tailor-made to client requirements. Nielsen Register-MEAL data can also be accessed on-line through Donovan Data Services (described in Chapter 12) or through a PC based system '*Dataview*', which is up-dated monthly by Nielsen Register-MEAL using disk or CD Rom.

Nielsen Register-MEAL provides access to other advertising expenditure monitoring companies owned by A C Nielsen, and can provide Pan-European advertising data.

Syndicated Services

- *Quarterly Summary of Brands and Advertisers* This gives total expenditure across all five media for brands within product groups spending over £150,000 per annum.
- *Annual Advertiser Digest* This gives expenditure by brand by medium for all advertisers spending over £1m.
- *Ten Year Trends* This gives total television and press expenditure for each product group over the last ten years.

NRS (NATIONAL READERSHIP SURVEYS)
(Garden Studios, 11–15 Betterton Street, Covent Garden, London WC2H 9BP)

NRS is published by National Readership Surveys Ltd. The twelve Directors represent the Newspaper Publishers Association, the Periodical Publishers Association and the Institute of Practitioners in Advertising. The Incorporated Society of British Advertisers is represented by a non-voting Director.

Currently, NRS publishes the results of 37,500 interviews a year, measuring average issue readership for around 280 titles including all national daily and Sunday newspapers and several hundred national magazines.

The fieldwork is undertaken on behalf of NRS by Research Services Ltd and the results are used by publishers to assist their selling efforts as well as by agencies to evaluate readership by target markets.

The data is collected by CAPI (Computer Assisted Personal Interviewing), using laptop computers which present the questions on a screen and guide the interviewer through the questions. As answers are down-loaded by telephone from the interviewer to Head Office, this speeds up the reporting process considerably.

Since the NRS research began (as long ago as 1956) there has been a consistent procedure for classifying informants into grades A, B, C1, C2, D and E. This system of social grading (explained in Chapter 7) has been widely adopted throughout the advertising industry. In addition to readership data, the NRS provides information on other matters, as follows.

Volume 1 This is based on fieldwork for the period July to the following June, and contains information on

- Average issue readership of all major publications analysed by gender (men, women and main shopper), age, six social grades, survey region and Incorporated Society of British Advertisers (ISBA) area.
- Profile tables showing the readership composition of each publication in terms of gender, age, social grade and region, and weight of ITV viewing.
- Tables showing Commercial Radio listening and cinema-going, analysed by gender, age, social grade and ISBA region.
- Readership of each publication by weight of ITV viewing and radio listening, and frequency of cinema-going.
- Readership of each publication among special interest groups such as housewives with children, members of car-owning households, owners of consumer durables, etc. There are also sections on readership by chief wage earners and housewives.
- Group readership figures.
- Frequency of reading each publication plus group probabilities for informants claiming each reading frequency. Cumulative readership tables are included.

The NRS incorporates ACORN (A Classification Of Residential Neighbourhoods, described in Chapter 7) as well as MOSAIC and Superprofiles (described in Chapter 13).

Volume 2 This further report has the same contents as Volume 1, but is based on the calendar year's fieldwork: January to December.

Volume 3 This contains duplication tables showing the extent to which readers of one publication also read other publications.

NRS Bulletins Subscribers to the NRS also receive various bulletins, including:
- Early monthly estimates of readership for national newspapers.
- Total readership figures in advance of the main reports.
- Additional information including early monthly estimates for some publications that have undergone major change or relaunch, or are newly launched.
- A regular quarterly bulletin giving results for the four quarters ending with the latest period, and for the four previous 12 months' moving averages, and the three latest six-month periods.

Additional services

Although the published reports contain several hundred tabulations, the amount of data stored on computer is very much larger, and facilities are provided for the extraction of the additional information as increasingly required by subscribers.

Computer Analysis Many subscribers use a computer bureau to cross-analyse the data. Alternatively, the data can be provided for analysis on a subscriber's own computer network.

Either way, the use of computers is highly developed (see Chapter 16) and software is available to analyse the raw data in four key ways:

1. Cost ranking.
2. Schedule analysis.
3. Schedule construction.
4. Cross tabulation.

OAA (OUTDOOR ADVERTISING ASSOCIATION)
(77 Newman Street, London W1A 1DX)

Among the principal activities of the Outdoor Advertising Association is the provision of poster audience research:

POSTAR (POSTer Audience Research) This outdoor advertising measurement system replaces OSCAR (the former Outdoor Site Classification and Audience Research), and provides agencies with the data to plan, target and evaluate audiences for roadside poster panels. It results from collaboration between 60 outdoor contractors, the IPA and the Council of Outdoor Specialists, representing specialist outdoor agencies.

Three different data sources are at the heart of POSTAR. First is a travel survey conducted over 18 months by NOP measuring the journeys taken by a sample of 7,400 respondents. This is used to build audience profiles of key demographic groups ranging from ABC1s to 16–24 year old women. Second are over 7,000 Local Authority traffic studies, and finally 9,000 pedestrian counts. These data sources are the basis of a computer model, using the latest neural network technology (based loosely on the operation of neural cells in the brain) which estimates the traffic passing the 73,000 roadside panels covered by POSTAR.

POSTAR uses a visibility experiment conducted at London University to provide a more realistic method than OSCAR for measuring outdoor advertising. This measures 'Visibility Adjusted Impacts', evaluating them in terms of respondents likely to *see* a poster site, not simply pass by.

POSTAR allows users to plan a poster campaign by conurbation or by television region analysed by any of the 240 demographic groups described above. It will estimate coverage, the percentage of audience with one or more opportunity to see a panel and provide pre and post campaign evaluation. Different size panels (6, 48 and 96 sheets) can be compared.

To ensure the data remains current, POSTAR will be up-dated with annual traffic estimates, and monthly site updates.

At the time of writing, PC-based POSTAR systems were under test and the launch of POSTAR planned for Summer 1996.

Competitive Data Reports Key Systems publish monthly reports, using data supplied by outdoor specialists and the OAA, listing the sectors/advertisers/brands that have used roadside advertising, and the number/sizes of panels used. A split by ISBA television areas is also available.

Media Monitoring Services (described earlier) publishes monthly brand expenditure estimates for outdoor advertising, both roadside and transport.

OPMA OVERSEAS MEDIA GUIDE
(OPMA, c/o John Fairfax (UK) Ltd, First Floor, 95 Fetter Lane, London EC4 1HE)

The Overseas Press and Media Association (OPMA) *Overseas Media Guide* is an authoritative UK source of information on overseas media.

It is published each year by OPMA, the professional organisation of UK advertisement managers and representatives of over 7,500 of the world's media.

The 28th edition lists each of the media represented by OPMA member companies. Under each publication's heading the Guide features the frequency of publication, the language of publication/ broadcast and details of the UK contact point.

The guide is presented in seven geographical areas:

- International
- Europe
- Middle East and North Africa
- Africa and Indian Ocean Islands
- The Americas
- Asia
- Australasia and Pacific Islands

OSCAR (OUTDOOR SITE CLASSIFICATION AUDIENCE RESEARCH)
*(see **OAA** above)*

PAN-EUROPEAN SURVEY (PES) 6
(The Economist, 25 St James Street, London SW1A 1HG)

This 1995 survey is the sixth in a series of cross-border media research studies of up-market Europeans, providing data for planning international business, consumer, travel and corporate campaigns. Based on a comprehensive survey which permits comparability of press media across national boundaries, it covers more than 300 national and international newspapers and magazines (including in-flight magazines) as well as television viewing.

PES 6 was sponsored by various international business publications including *The Economist* and the *Financial Times*. Fieldwork was undertaken by Research Services Limited and covered just under 7,500 people, aged 25 or over, working in 14 European countries in a professional or executive occupation, working 15 or more hours per week and qualifying by one of the following criteria:

- gross personal income of the stated minimum
- took six or more business trips in the last 12 months
- director of establishment with 25+ employees
- MA, MBA or other higher qualification

Each respondent participated in an extensive face-to-face interview, then completed a self-completion questionnaire in the presence of the interviewer. The survey included:

- demographics, income and employment benefits
- personal and business air travel and holidays
- industry, company size, occupation and area of responsibility
- business purchasing responsibility
- purchase of luxury products including drinks, tobacco, investments, insurance, car ownership and credit card usage.

PETAR (PAN-EUROPEAN TELEVISION AUDIENCE RESEARCH)
(MTV Europe, Hawley Crescent, London NW1 8TT)

PETAR is a single-source cross-border research on television audiences. The 8th PETAR study covered six European countries: Belgium (Flanders only), Denmark, Germany, Netherlands, Norway and Sweden. 2,312 individuals aged 4+ kept diaries over a four week period. Additional attitudinal data was obtained from 1,791 members of the sample. PETAR is available in hard copy or disc format.

People meter systems, such as BARB's described earlier, are increasingly replacing diaries in individual countries. Unfortunately, these people meter systems do not have agreed standards and each system measures slightly different aspects of viewing. For instance, whilst the UK system measures minute-by-minute viewing, some countries measure on a quarter-hour basis. In the absence of a harmonised Pan-European measurement system, the diary system remains the most effective way of collecting television viewing levels across Europe.

The PETAR research is now funded by the MTV channel, and not by joint industry involvement, as is the case with the UK's BARB system.

There is thus no independent single source of commercial television viewing patterns across Europe.

POSTAR
*(see **OAA** above)*

PPA (PERIODICAL PUBLISHERS ASSOCIATION)
(Queens House, 28 Kingsway, London WC2B 6JR)

The Periodical Publishers Association represents magazine publishers in the UK. Its members publish some 1,800 titles (ranging from mass-circulation consumer magazines to highly technical business and professional publications) and generate more than 80 per cent of all magazine advertising revenue.

The PPA implements separate generic campaigns to promote both consumer and business magazines. Business and professional magazines are promoted through the media and marketing press, interestingly using advertorials (described in Chapter 1) to promote advertorials! The *Business Magazine Week* promotion provides an annual focus for this drive.

Consumer magazines are promoted in a separate generic drive using advertising as above as well as presentations to advertisers.

Both types of media are supported by a range of published information, the most recent including:

How Magazine Advertising Works This report is a synthesis of the large body of existing research, which demonstrates how readers use magazines and how the advertising within them works.

The 62 sources for this report include 29 major research studies described in outline, including:

- Youth Facts 4: a study of 11–19 year olds
- Media Values Diary: a study of 250 magazine readers who recorded their readership over a two week period
- Ad Track 94: 10,000 interviews with women who read a magazine.

Hearts and Minds Advertising This report continues the international series of *Media Multiplier* studies. The basic premise is to strengthen long-term brand prosperity by increasing media expenditure in an integrated multi-media fashion. A number of case histories demonstrate new thinking on the integrated approach to media: planning across media and in particular, the effectiveness of using television and magazines together.

The Role of Business Magazines This major study, published in 1996, describes how Business and Professional magazines are read and used by highlighting the importance and authority of the media.

Magazine News

The publication *Magazine News* is circulated on a bi-monthly basis to selected individuals (including major advertisers and agencies, city analysts and publishers).

Magazine Handbook

The PPA has developed a comprehensive database to provide up-to-date information about the magazine industry's size, spread, development and readership. This data, published in 1996, is the focus of the fourth edition of the PPA *Magazine Handbook*. It traces the development of circulation, readership, main titles, advertising shares and volumes, looking also at magazines in Europe and overviewing magazine profitability.

Business Press

The Business Information Publishers Association, part of the PPA specifically promotes business and professional magazines. The booklet *An Introduction to Business Press Research* examines the various types of research available to the business press and their uses, showing how research can improve the quality of information available to advertisers.

PRESSAD
(see **Newspaper Society** *above)*

RAB (THE RADIO ADVERTISING BUREAU)
(74 Newman Street, London W1P 3LA)

The commercial radio industry formed the Radio Advertising Bureau as its 'marketing department'. The Bureau is separate from the Commercial Radio Companies Association (CRCA, described above) and, by promoting radio generically, it has played a major part in in radio's share of the advertising cake. The RAB was described in Chapter 3.

RAJAR (RADIO JOINT AUDIENCE RESEARCH LTD)
(Collier House, 163–169 Brompton Road, London SW3 1PY)

RAJAR was established in 1992 as the joint industry source of radio audience information. It is jointly owned by the BBC and the CRCA (described above) and also includes representation from the Institute of Practitioners in Advertising and the Incorporated Society of British Advertisers.

The RAJAR audience research system provides quarterly reports both on a national and local level and for commercial and BBC stations. Information is collected through a self-completion 7 day diary. Each day is broken into quarter-hour segments (half-hour segments between 12 midnight and 6 am).

Until 1995, stations available in a particular area were prelisted on each page of the diary. Given the rapid increase in radio stations, this is no longer practical and a revised approach (the Personal Prelist Diary – PPD) was adopted. This involves the use of labels containing station information; respondents select the stations they have listened to over the last four weeks, and create their own station lists across the top of the diary. Respondents may also record the name of any station not listed, or mark the 'any other station' box. They are also asked to provide information on place of listening.

Following the introduction of PPD, RAJAR recorded a reduction in listenership for some stations, which led to controversy within the industry and RAJAR decided to return to the original system until September 1998. It will develop a new measurement system to be introduced after this date. However, any new system must satisfy the different needs of commercial and BBC radio.

The annual sample of around 150,000 includes the boost surveys conducted in two quarters a year in order to satisfy local station requirements.

Detailed audience results for each commercial station, and for the BBC network radio stations include weekly reach, total hours and share, together with half-hour audience averages for weekdays, the average Saturday and average Sunday separately. In addition a model has been developed to make audience projections for four weeks and beyond.

Results are available both in printed report form and increasingly through computer bureaux.

ROYAL MAIL
(Direct Marketing Department, Streamline House, Sandy Lane West, Oxford OX4 5ZZ)

The Direct Marketing Department of the Royal Mail publishes a number of useful free booklets for the benefit of advertisers seeking advice on the direct mail medium.

The Royal Mail Direct Mail gives comprehensive guidance on how to use direct mail effectively.

Royal Mail Services gives details on the Royal Mail's range of services for high volume mailings, including:

- *Mailsort* discount service for mailings which have been pre-sorted by postcode.

- Response services such as *business reply* and *freepost* which enable respondents to reply without paying for postage.
- *Admail* (described in Chapter 19) which enables replies, orders or enquiries to advertising to be automatically re-directed to an alternative address.
- *Electronic post*, the printing, enveloping and despatch of personalised mail using electronic communications.

Royal Mail Door to Door Direct mail as defined (individually addressed and stamped material) does not include unaddressed letterbox deliveries. The Royal Mail nevertheless also offers a household delivery service, described in this booklet, which details the Royal Mail's services for unaddressed mail.

STEPCHECK LIMITED
(Leofric Court, Progress Way, Binley, Coventry CV3 2NT)

Stepcheck aims to provide a sound estimate of accurate delivery as well as effectiveness measurement of door-to-door distributions.

Both advertisers and distributors need delivery estimates and a common standard requires mutual involvement and agreement of details.

Stepcheck selects customers (or 'cells' of 50 targeted households) to represent the distribution area. A typical distribution of 2 million items would require 50 cells, providing a research sample of 2,500. The number of cells will increase or decrease in relation to the size of distribution.

Stepcheck gathers information from each household to determine their experience of the distribution in three core areas:

- was it received?
- was it recalled?
- what effect did it have?

The research report provides an area profile and a summary of the householders and their interest levels. Particular note is made of any hostility. Results are graded into three classes:

Class I: Households with above average recall.
Class II: Households with some recall, but below the average level. The information can be used to identify, road by road, cell by cell, an estimate of actual delivery
Class III: No recall among households in a cell: clear indication there has been no delivery.

Up to four closed-ended questions provide opportunity for cross-analysis individualised for each advertiser/distributor. Typical topics include:

- readership levels
- cross analysis by primary and secondary targets
- purchase intent

TDI BUSADS (BUS AUDIENCE DATA SYSTEM)

(TDI Advertising Limited, 10 Jamestown Road, Camden, London NW1 7BY)
(HTTP://WWW. tdi media.com)

London buses carry mobile advertisement sites throughout Greater London, reaching more than 200 shopping centres as well as all commercial areas. TDI BUSADS is based on an independent survey into the travel patterns of Londoners, to establish a database for measuring the effectiveness of bus advertising campaigns. The survey calculated:

- the audience for bus advertising campaigns in terms of net unduplicated audience coverage and repetition
- the audience profile by demographic variables
- the campaign audience in terms of campaign size, site type, duration and location.

The survey allows for updates to take account of changes in either the demographic profile of the Greater London population or changes to the bus service which carry the advertisements. Three databases were assembled as follows:

1. Bus Networks The network was recorded on detailed street maps covering all Greater London, on which the roads travelled by buses had been colour coded, in order to define the bus network as a series of links, each identified by its start and end. This information was then matched with data from the Home Interview Survey described below, to calculate campaign site encounters for each individual interviewed.

2. Home Interview Survey Interviewers recruited a sample of 1,000 individuals, representative of the Greater London population. Each respondent supplied details of all journeys made and their frequency, identified by time, purpose and mode(s) of transport, broken down into component stages. This information was then matched with the detailed maps used for the Bus Network Database, to establish the probability of each individual encountering a campaign advertisement.

3. Car Video Survey This calculated exposure to bus advertisements by car drivers and passengers. A survey car was equipped with a video camera mounted on a tripod over the front passenger seat, and driven over much of the bus network. The camera was positioned to obtain a driver's or passenger's view of the road ahead, and the car's location and travel time and distance on and off bus routes recorded. The recordings were then analysed for observations of each advertisement site, with different types separately logged. An average encounter per minute was then calculated for each site separately (broken down between Inner and Outer London) and matched to the Home Interview Survey to establish audience coverage and repetition amongst car drivers.

Sample research tables are published in TDI's bus brochure. This specifies expected pedestrian/vehicle encounters for different site types and campaign sizes, giving both coverage and frequency figures for all adults (men and women separately), housewives, 15–24 year olds). TDI's London BUSADS also offers a campaign planning facility, advising advertisers on how to buy a bus advertising campaign which delivers optimum coverage and frequency.

TDI BUSADS is available on-line at TDI's Internet site shown above.

TDI is extending the concept into TDI National BUSADS, a desktop planning facility to facilitate bus campaign planning at a national, ITV region and town level. It will produce data relating to the number of buses needed in any given area to achieve the coverage objectives against specific target audiences.

TDI TRAC (TUBE RESEARCH AUDIENCE CLASSIFICATION)
(TDI, 10 Jamestown Road, Camden, London NW1 7BY)
(HTTP://WWW. tdi media.com)

TRAC is an independent survey into the travel patterns of Underground users, which was set up to establish a database for measuring the audience coverage and frequency of advertising campaigns on the medium.

Nearly five thousand respondents, recruited at Underground stations throughout the system, supplied details of all the journeys they made during a period of four consecutive weeks. By breaking down the resultant journey patterns into their component 'locations', ie ticket hall, corridor, escalator and platform locations, TDI were able to calculate exposure to campaigns of different sizes and site types.

Sample tables of the research are published in TDI's Underground brochure which gives audience profiles and coverage of all adults (men and women), businessmen, 15–24 year olds.

TRAC also offers a Campaign Planning facility, advising advertisers on how to buy an Underground campaign which delivers the optimum coverage and frequency. TRAC is available on-line at TDI's Internet site.

⊚ TGI (TARGET GROUP INDEX)
(Hadley House, 79–81 Uxbridge Road, Ealing, London W5 5SU)

The Target Group Index is a national product and media survey produced by the BMRB (British Market Research Bureau) and available on subscription to advertisers, agencies and media-owners. The TGI is entirely owned by BMRB and, unlike the usual joint industry media surveys described in this chapter, there is no guaranteed long-term contract or indeed guaranteed income.

TGI findings are based on 24,000 self-completion questionnaires received from informants who have been previously contacted by random location methods in some 5,000 sampling points in Great Britain. There is a separate TGI survey covering Northern Ireland. TGI provides an up-to-date base directly relating media and product usage.

TGI identifies heavy, medium and light users as well as non-users in a vast range of product categories and sub-categories. A full range of demographics and media usage is reported for these groups. TGI tables can explain who these people are, what they are like and which media vehicles are best to reach them.

The TGI product group information provides the foundation for assessing individual markets' major or potential users and their characteristics and media habits. It similarly provides information about brand usage, listing solus users (users of the product group who use a brand exclusively), most frequent users (including 'solus' users and those who prefer it to another brand also used) and minor users (those who are more casual in their use). These definitions establish some element of brand loyalty and the degree of involvement that users have with a given brand.

TGI reports the users of thousands of brands. As with heavy to light users of product categories, demographics and media usage are reported for brand users. By using TGI, you know who your users are and what they read, watch and listen to. You also have the same information for your competitors.

For the appliance and durables category, TGI provides a further measurement – whether the respondent had a major or equal say in the purchase.

The TGI measures the following product and media habits of the population:

Products Heavy, medium and light usage/purchase by consumers of over 400 brands in more than 500 product fields are covered. Brands with more than a million claimed users are broken down demographically and by media.

Media Readership of around 200 newspapers and magazines; weight of viewing ITV, Channel 4 and GMTV, and half-hour viewing behaviour for television, satellite and cable viewing, weight of listening to commercial radio and exposure to outdoor media and the cinema. The TGI is designed to be complementary to NRS, the industry's readership survey. The levels of readership are, wherever possible, weighted to equal the NRS readership figures for the corresponding period of field work. Depending upon the relative importance of men or women in the readership, TGI readership levels may be weighted so as to reconcile with the NRS for men only, for women only, or for both. Since 1993, TGI has additionally reported on Male Housewives.

Fusion of the main TGI information with BARB data is also available. This enables media owners and agencies to directly link BARB's TV programme-viewing data with TGI's product and brand usage data.

Characteristics The full range of standard demographics including social grades, household income, together with special breakdowns such as terminal education age, working status, home ownership, size of household and marital status.

TGI was the first major survey to offer analysis by ACORN (A Classification of Residential Neighbourhoods) described in Chapter 7. It has kept pace with developments and offers also *Super Profiles* and *Mosaic*, described in Chapter 13.

In addition to factual data, TGI provides Lifestyle data. Respondents provide scaled responses to 200 attitudinal statements covering lifestyle aspects such as: motivations, status, diet, personal appearance and the environment.

TGI measures interest in specific television programmes as well as measuring 30 topics of interest for both newspapers and magazines.

As with all other parts of TGI, lifestyle data can be cross related with any part of the database.

The TGI reports

There are 34 separate TGI volumes summarising a vast amount of data. In outline, these cover:

Volumes	1–2	Demographics
	3–10	Food (virtually all packaged lines)
	11–14	Household goods
	15–16	Pharmaceuticals and chemist products
	17–20	Toiletries and cosmetics
	21–23	Drink (alcoholic and soft drinks)
	24–25	Confectionery
	26	Tobacco
	27	Motoring (cars and accessories)
	28–29	Clothing and shopping

30	Leisure
31	Holidays and travel
32	Financial services
33–34	Consumer durables and appliances

Premier TGI

The Premier TGI seeks to give a higher degree of detail than the main TGI within those areas of product purchasing and lifestyle especially relevant to heads of household/housewives in the high (AB) socio-demographic status households. It also provides this information based on significantly larger sample sizes than are found in the main survey.

The survey is based on a sample of 5,500 AB adults, entirely separate from those interviewed in the main TGI. Respondents are initially interviewed by telephone in order to collect classification data, and then sent a self-completion questionnaire.

Premier is of great value in measuring characteristics likely to be significantly different among ABs. The survey does not set out to provide data on food, but focuses on holidays and travel; sports and leisure; clothing; personal possessions, cosmetics and gifts; house, home and car; drink; and finance. Additional to the customary demographic analyses, Premier measures quality and volume of purchase. As part of the lifestyle section, Premier measures consumption of print and broadcast media and over 200 attitudinal questions, some unique to Premier. Finally, as Premier asks questions on occupation, it is possible to analyse business people separately.

Youth TGI

Youth TGI provides information on the purchasing, media consumption and attitudes of 7–10s, 11–14s and 15–19s, using separate questionnaires for each group.

The annual sample is 6,000, with quotas set by sex, social grade and age breaks. To build their confidence, those selected have parents who have taken part in other BMRB surveys. All key product fields targeted at children and teenagers are covered, including food and drink, music, clothes and games. One extra section is 'concerns', which deals with the issues facing today's youth.

Accessing TGI or Premier TGI

While media-owners featured in the 34 TGI volumes or 9 Premier TGI volumes buy the entire sets of 34 or 9 volumes, it is possible for advertisers and advertising agencies to buy individual volumes or even separate product fields. These volumes are based upon the 12 month period April to March.

TGI as a 'single source' measurement and computer analysis allows any part of the survey to be analysed against another. For instance, media exposure can be related to product usage. Schedule analyses can thus be based on product and brand users, analysed by their extent of use and other demographics. TGI is frequently used to produce data identifying the media consumption of these target markets so that, for instance, press schedules can be based upon the cost rankings of media featured in TGI. There are two ways to access the TGI database:

1. Desktop PC based analysis packages. By subscribing to a computer bureau subscribers can use their own desk top computers to analyse the database.
2. Special analysis by Bureaux. A TGI subscriber who has a relatively low use of this analysis can use one of five bureaux able to interrogate the database.

The bureaux concerned are:

BMRM
(Hadley House, 79–81 Uxbridge Road, Ealing, London W5 5SU)
IMS (Interactive Media Systems Ltd)
(Grosvenor Gardens House, Grosvenor Gardens, London SW1W 0BS)
HRS (Holborn Research Services)
(Grosvenor Gardens House, Grosvenor Gardens, London SW1W 0BS)
Telmar Communications Ltd
(21 Ivor Place, London NW1 6EU)
Media Plan
(Enigma House, 30 Alan Turing House, Research Park, Guildford, Surre, GU2 5AA)

TRAC (TUBE RESEARCH AUDIENCE CLASSIFICATION)
(see **TDI TRAC** *above)*

VFD (VERIFIED FREE DISTRIBUTION LTD)
(Black Prince Yard, 207–209 High Street, Berkhamsted, Herts HP4 1AD)

Verified Free Distribution (VFD) is a wholly owned subsidiary of the Audit Bureau of Circulations (see separate entry) and is the independent certifying authority for all publications whose distribution is not through regular newstrade channels or by single addressed copies mailed through the Post Office.

The VFD operation

1 On application each publication's records and distribution system are subjected to a close inspection by a VFD Inspector to determine eligibility to join the system. This check confirms good record-keeping and distribution control, including agreed standards of backchecking on delivered copies on a regular and systematic basis. Further VFD inspections are carried out as a regular routine. (If the publication cannot meet VFD standards, the application is suspended until the publisher's system has been revised and checked again.)

2 Issue-by-issue records for standard six-month periods are kept by the publisher on VFD forms, and these are then audited by an approved independent firm of chartered accountants.

3 If the results are approved, VFD Certificates of Average Net Distribution are issued for each standard period, January to June and July to December. Also stated are the average number of pages achieved, and the percentage of advertising content. This information, in addition to a description of the distribution area, form the basis of the VFD Certificate for each registered title or group of publications.

4 All publishers are required to maintain lists of households checked for regular delivery, and these records are subject to random tests by a research company arranged by VFD.

The Scope of VFD

Verified Free Distribution operates in three divisions:

1 Free local newspaper-format publications and free magazines (delivered as single copies).

2 Free directories (delivered).

3 Courtesy magazines (not delivered as single copies but available for pick-up at hotels, airlines, clubs, etc). This service is known as Bulk Verification service and has a different certificate from 1 and 2 above.

Optional services

1 Three Star. VFD operates an optional additional certification service based on a national standard of interviews with recipients of free delivered publications in designated areas, either by telephone or face-to-face interviews, which confirms the level of regular receipt of the particular free publication. Publications taking out this service successfully are granted three stars within the VFD logo as a mark of confirmation.

116

2 *Leaflet Distribution*. VFD operates an optional additional service to provide certification of systems employed by publishers in membership of VFD to control the distribution of leaflets either within their publications or solus.

VIDEOTRAK
(Media Vision Research Ltd, 102 Dean Street, London W1V 5RA)

VideoTrak provides estimates of viewing figures for commercials in pre-recorded videos. It is based on information collected by BARB and utilises the time-shift viewing technology in BARB.

Media Vision Research's (MVR) system encodes pre-recorded videos with a signal throughout the length of the tape, which is recognised by the BARB equipment. Detailed information on who is viewing commercials on these coded videos can be provided in the same way as for broadcast commercials. As a result, agencies can plan, buy and evaluate this type of advertising with a 'currency' equivalent to broadcast commercials. MVR have a range of services which include:

- *TitleTrak* – analysis of individual title performance, including demographic and regional profiles and daypart viewing.
- *Market Trak* – overview of the rental market covering weekly trends nationally and by region, market share, consumer profiles and comparison with in-home media consumption.
- *Campaign Trak* – assessment of video advertising performance across demographic and regional groups over the campaign period.
- *Cover View* – a study of the impact video advertising has on the overall media schedule, including reach and frequency and unique cover analysis across video, TV and satellite/cable.
- *MediaScope* – tracking consumer behaviour to measure the effectiveness and impact of TV advertising and trailering on video performance. It determines the number of viewers who watched trailers or TV advertisements then actually watched the title itself. It also identifies how effective advertising was, analyses which TV programmes those viewers watched, helping to plan future schedules and assesses the optimum number of impacts required.

OTHER SOURCES

There are other useful sources of media information, in addition to those already mentioned. Some are covered later in Chapter 6, which is devoted to the specialist services available, and necessarily overlaps with this chapter since various organisations just described make available services additional to the basic ones mentioned. Other data sources belong more rightly to this chapter.

Media-owners' research information

As a means of making valuable information available to potential advertisers and also to assist current advertisers in producing more effective media schedules, many media-owners subscribe to various research and other services.

Some media-owners also commission their own research. It is rare for a media-owner to undertake research to disprove the information provided centrally, although such action might be taken if he considered the findings presented an unfair picture of his medium. More usually, media-owners seek to provide additional information which might persuade advertisers and agencies to view their medium favourably.

Media-owners' own surveys can provide much useful information and often venture into fields untouched by central research. As examples, media-owners have undertaken research into the effect of advertisement size in relation to page size, into the effect of advertising on retailers, and into page traffic and the 'life' of advertisements in publications which are kept for reference rather than read and thrown away.

Media-owners who are not, for some reason or other, included in the central reports may commission research to provide comparable information to permit their medium being assessed on the same basis. Where no central research exists, media-owners may have no choice but to provide details of their medium's coverage and to undertake research to obtain this information.

Media-owners' information activities are many and varied, and this aspect of the media-owner's work is discussed again in the later chapter devoted to 'The Media-Owner'.

An interesting development in recent years has been the increasing provision of co-operative research and activities. Rather than compete with each other for larger slices of the same size advertising cake, rival media-owners have joined forces to promote the advantages of their combined media group over others to increase their share of total advertising expenditure. Most such co-operative campaigns have been reviewed within this chapter and, viewed as a whole, these combined activities have made valuable contributions to the provision of media research data.

A major difference between central research and media-owner's own information is that whereas the former is provided on a regular basis, media-owners undertake research activities often on a more *ad hoc* basis, from time to time whenever they wish to prove a point about their medium. Another difference is that, somewhat understandably, advertisers and agencies are likely to suspect it of being biased in favour of the medium sponsoring it. In this respect it is worth noting that the Media Research Quality Committee of the Institute of Practitioners in Advertising provides a service for member agencies in appraising such published surveys and sends out its report in the form of an appraisals bulletin. The IPA has published a booklet 'Producing useful Media Research' by Guy Consterdine, and also welcomes advance consultation in regard to any surveys proposed by media-owners.

Some media-owners undertake a great deal and do so frequently, whereas others provide very little information. This makes it difficult to include within this book any formal list of the additional research information available from this source. Nevertheless, any executive concerned with the effective use of media should be aware that some extremely valuable research has been undertaken and should certainly check out this source of information.

Agency- and client-sponsored research

This field of reseach is comparable in many ways with media-sponsored research, in that it is aimed at providing additional information. One example is a study by a media agency, sponsored by Unilever, of radio effectiveness. An article in *Campaign* mentioned that it was designed to 'measure whether the effect of radio ads could be observed across a number of unnamed researched brands'. This article highlighted some of the additional drawbacks of this type of research: failure to cover all the media in the group, or being carried out at irregular intervals. A further disadvantage (other than to those directly concerned) is that the information may not be freely available, which is understandable since the advertiser or agency incurred considerable research expense to gain a competitive advantage. Such research is, in fact, a business investment and is rightly regarded as confidential information.

OTHER INFORMATION SOURCES

In addition to the wealth of useful information contained in reference publications, it would be wrong to leave this section without mentioning that some media-owners and trade and professional bodies have their own publications which they use to communicate items of interest and that, in addition to these special interest publications, articles of specific interest appear from time to time in a host of other publications, both newspapers and magazines.

In conclusion, it is worth mentioning that some of the organisations mentioned are not just sources of media information, but powerful influences on the way media will develop in the future.

Chapter 6

Further Information and Additional Information Sources

FURTHER INFORMATION

The published reports just discussed are mainly available in hard copy form, with printed tables showing numerous data. There is increasing pressure, however, for 'raw' data to be made available, so that analyses can be individualised to the particular needs of each brand. Research sources such as BARB are so detailed that the main method of analysis is now electronic and, as electronic facilities are increasingly available, other sources such as NRS, JICREG and TGI have also become available in this form.

The majority of the vast range of data sources are, however, still available only in paper form. There has, however, been rapid growth in the provision of electronic facilities to obtain further information from paper-format research sources (at a fee appropriate to the cost of providing the analyses required).

These can be provided by the organisations which commissioned the original research, by obtaining on-line access, by purchasing your own copies of the tapes, or by specialist data-processing firms having authorised access to the research data. Some of these bureaux were listed in Chapter 5.

ADDITIONAL INFORMATION SOURCES

A number of readership surveys were not included in the previous chapter because they relate to specialist areas. Some extend their coverage beyond media research figures, to include what are called 'U&A' studies covering *Usage* (read regularly, read half or more etc) and *Attitudes* (best source of new ideas, usefulness of advertising etc) as well as other media (direct mail, exhibitions, seminars, television etc). Specialist surveys include the following:

- Agridata (Agricultural Readership Survey)
- Archbuild (Building Industry Readership Survey)
- Airline Readership Survey
- Builders Merchants Readership Survey
- Commercial Catering Industries Readership Survey
- Commercial Property Publications Survey
- Commercial Vehicles Operators Survey
- Computer Market Readership Survey (Banner)
- Construction Industries Readership Survey
- Defining the *Vogue* Reader
- Electronics Industry Readership Survey
- Engineering Industries Readership Survey
- Farm Advisors Readership Survey
- Gardening Market Study
- Hospital Media Readership Survey
- Hotel and Catering Industry Readership Survey
- Independent Grocery Market Readership Survey
- JICMARS (GP Readership Survey)
- Motor Show Survey
- National Architects Survey
- Packaging Industry Readership Survey
- Parenting Magazines: The Essential Medium
- Personnel Market Readership Survey
- Readership Survey of Social Workers
- Road Transport Survey
- Travel Agents Readership Survey
- Vanity Fair: Influences

Many of these specialist surveys were discussed in Martyn Davis' other publication *Business-to-Business Marketing and Promotion* (Century Business).

A problem which arises with some specialist surveys is that, unlike the general surveys mentioned in the previous chapter, the research is not always undertaken on a regular basis. Some are in fact 'one off' exercises, mounted and published, but never repeated.

There is, of course, no sharp dividing line between general and specialist surveys – some of the general databases discussed in the previous chapter also provide 'specialist' information, while advertisers seeking to reach general markets such as 'business executives' would find a wealth of information in the specialist surveys listed above.

Furthermore, the list is not exhaustive, in that there is a steady flow of new media information as new research material becomes available.

Chapter 7

Media Evaluation – Criteria for Comparison

To use media to full advantage, it is clearly essential to evaluate them to select those most suitable, and many criteria exist by which you can compare one medium with another. There are various factors you must take into account when making decisions. Part 3 will review criteria for evaluating complete advertising schedules, but this chapter looks first at how you can compare individual media.

A first step in establishing criteria for media comparison is to differentiate between *quantitative* and *qualitative* aspects. Quantitative data refer to the *numbers* of copies sold or read, or viewers or listeners reached, while when reviewing qualitative criteria media planners must express *opinions* as to the value of, for example, sound or movement or high quality colour reproduction. The difference between quantitative and qualitative criteria is essentially a simple one: particularly interesting, however, are the recent attempts to quantify qualitative aspects through the 'U&A' studies already mentioned, which measure Usage (number of pick-ups, proportion read, etc) and Attitudes (most/least useful source of new information, helpfulness of advertisements, etc). These quantitative and qualitative factors can vary in priority according to each advertiser's marketing objective and so, in reviewing them below, they are not necessarily in your order of importance.

QUANTITATIVE CRITERIA

These include:

Who will your advertising message reach?

One major consideration is the market covered by the medium in question. Market investigations have a high priority in the work of advertiser and agency alike, both of whom will make a straight cross-check between the market covered by the medium and the market they wish to reach. Clearly the closer the approximation, the more effective the medium.

The term used here is *demographics*, commonly defined as a means of analysing information by sex, age and social status or other classifications. Information about age is usually given in fairly broad groupings, eg 15–24, 25–34 and so on. The social grades commonly used are those pioneered in the National Readership Surveys and are normally based on the occupation of the chief income earner of his or her household. There are six such grades:

Social grade	Social status	Chief Income Earner's Occupation
A	Upper middle class	Higher managerial, administrative or professional
B	Middle class	Intermediate managerial, administrative or professional
C1	Lower middle class	Supervisory or clerical and junior managerial, administrative or professional
C2	Skilled working class	Skilled manual workers
D	Working class	Semi and unskilled manual workers
E	Those at lowest levels of subsistence	State pensioners or widows (no other earner), casual or lowest grade workers

Many of the data sources described in Chapter 5 include a wide range of other demographic classifications (such as terminal education age, or ownership of consumer durables) but in some cases, eg with industrial or technical products, your interest may be in the job description of the people your advertising message will reach, the industry in which they are employed, or their special interests, rather than their personal attributes. In other instances, your interest may be in product-related data. Are they heavy or light users of your product? Or in their attitudes. Are they conservative in their buying habits, or are they likely to respond favourably to new products? Are they in need of your product and *ready* to buy? Whatever the categories, the fundamental question is a basic one. Who do you wish to reach, and to whom will the medium in question deliver your advertising message?

Where?

This cross-checking procedure applies equally to geographical location, since this aspect of the media audience is just as important as its composition. This information may be available in terms of the Registrar-General's Standard Regions, or perhaps by television area. Marketing areas vary, and there must be strong correlation between your own marketing area and the area to which the medium would deliver your advertising message. For local advertisers the two areas should coincide as closely as possible. Even so-called 'national' media vary in intensity of coverage across the country and you should clearly take account of these variations.

Another way of asking the 'Where?' question overlaps with 'Who?' when we look at the residential areas in which individuals live and, to use more precise terminology, segment your markets *geo-demographically*. ACORN (CACI's A Classification of Residential Neighbourhoods) is a consumer classification system which can be used in conjunction with media research surveys such as NRS and TGI (discussed in Chapter 5), to give a more in-depth view of individuals and their purchasing and lifestyle habits. ACORN identifies 54 distinct types across the population of Great Britain eg: Home Owning Family Areas, Estates with High Unemployment and Agricultural Villages, Home Based Workers, etc taking marketing analysis and planning an essential step further than traditional socio-economic classifications. To the marketing and advertising executive its importance lies in its ability to show clear lifestyle differences between neighbourhoods leading to many differences in consumer behaviour. Being area-based, ACORN leads to a more scientific answer to the marketing question '*Where* should I . . .?'

Other ways of classifying media coverage geodemograpically are described in Chapter 13

How many?

In evaluating media you need to know not only the composition and location of the media audience covered but also its size, together with the number of individuals in each of the various categories. How many of each type and in each area? Breakdowns may be required for several categories simultaneously, to show how many people of a given sex, age and socio-economic group receive your advertising message within a defined area.

There may be different stages of answer to this 'how many?' question. With press media, for example, you may have at your disposal circulation figures and also readership – but much depends on definitions and research methods. To illustrate this point, contrast the differences in the data available about television audiences and press readership.

For television advertising, measurements can be made at the time of viewing, and numbers may be quoted to you in terms of TVRs or Television Rating Points. A television rating is the number of individuals viewing, expressed as a percentage of all such individuals viewing, provision being made for guests, but excluding children under the age of four. The term can apply to any time period, such as one minute, a quarter-hour, a rate card segment, an individual commercial or a programme.

The term can apply to a range of categories of individuals such as adults, men, women, children. Indeed, a wide range of demographic sub-groups can be utilised as well as a number of specific viewer categories such as business spenders, pub-goers, motorists, shoppers with dogs, dependent on the target audience sought by the advertiser.

One TVR represents 1 per cent of the potential TV audience and a viewer is defined as someone who is present in the room with the set switched on. Viewing starts from the moment the person records their presence, provided the viewing persists for a minimum of 15 seconds. Viewing figures are processed and reported on a minute-by-minute basis. You should note that the term 'in the room' covers anything from attentive watching to a casual glance while undertaking some other activity. The Newspaper Publishers Association, in promoting the merits of national newspapers, cited research which showed that 'viewers' might in fact be engaged in a range of other activities – or not even in the same room as the switched-on TV!

With press media, by way of contrast, advertising contact can be made over a considerable period, and the definition of a 'reader' is equally important. With the National Readership Surveys, a key concept is the *issue period*. Average Issue Readership (AIR) is the number of people who claim to have read or looked at one or more copies of a given publication for at least two minutes during a period dating back from the date of interviewing equal to the interval at which the publication appears – a daily newspaper is thus held to have an issue period of one day, a weekly publication has an issue period of seven days, a monthly publication has four weeks and so on.

You should note that the term 'reading or looking' covers anything from thorough reading to a casual flip through, and that it does not matter *which* issue – any issue will do. Readership may also be affected by other problems of definition:

(a) Parallel readership This refers to people who read more than one issue within the issue period prior to interview. No matter how many back issues had been read, it would still be counted as reading one issue, and average issue readership would thus tend to be deflated.

125

(b) Replication This refers to cases where the respondent reads the same issue of a publication (perhaps a 'special' which may have been kept for reference) across two or more publication periods. This would inflate average issue readership, since it does not truly represent additional readers.

(c) Page exposure The counter-argument to replication is that some publications will be 'read or looked at' more frequently than others, thus increasing the numbers likely to receive your advertising message. Hence the increasing importance of the 'U&A' studies.

You should also bear in mind that any figures are necessarily dated in themselves: readership surveys, for example, are sometimes 6–12 months old before new data is published. Research on other media suffers from a similar weakness, with some reporting quarterly and others on an annual or even less frequent basis. This, ironically, benefits media in decline (unless you arbitrarily reduce readership pro-rata according to the latest available circulation figures which, for national newspapers, are published with greater frequency). When considering the number of people your advertising message will reach, you should therefore always remember that whilst numbers are important, the research methods which produce them are by no means perfect. This statement is not made with a fault-finding attitude, but simply to set matters in context. Furthermore, it is always comforting to reflect that in many countries of the world even authentic circulation figures are not available, let alone readership (or viewing or listening) figures. Under such circumstances, we must be grateful for the wealth of data at our disposal, and not cavil at any minor imperfections. Furthermore, we should remember that with television and press the research needed to provide such information is well established but, as earlier chapters made clear, with a number of other media you will not have all the data you need.

Penetration versus profile

In discussing the number of people your advertising message reaches, you need to know the degree of penetration or coverage represented by the number reached. In simplest terms, penetration means the *proportion* of the total market covered. If you seek to reach housewives, for example, it will interest you to know that by using a certain medium you can reach 20 per cent, 50 per cent, or some other proportion of *all* housewives.

Later, when considering advertising planning, we will consider the cumulative coverage or 'reach' achieved by a full media schedule, but within this chapter, the term 'penetration' is restricted to the proportion of the total market to which any given medium will deliver your advertising message.

A medium's 'profile' typifies the categories of people reached. Profiles differ from penetration in always adding up to 100 per cent. A simple example which illustrates the difference between the two terms is that of women's magazines. A women's magazine read by half the women in the country has a 50 per cent penetration. If you look at the magazine's profile, however, this will be 100 per cent women. (In point of fact, the profile might well be 95 per cent women and five per cent men, since even women's magazines have some male readers). This is of course an over-simplification since profile information may be broken down in numerous different age-group, socio-economic, area or product usage categories but, whichever sub-groups are detailed, the total profile always adds up to 100 per cent.

A 'trick' question which illustrates the difference between penetration and profile is 'Which newspaper will give you the highest coverage of AB business executives – *The Sun*, or *The Financial Times*?'

The answer is not in fact *The Financial Times*. While *The Sun*'s profile includes only a relatively small percentage of AB business-people, a small proportion of a very large readership gives a larger number than a high percentage of a relatively small readership. Those wishing to reach AB business-people might not consider *The Sun* the ideal medium, however, for various reasons. One might be wastage, discussed next, while others concern qualitative considerations discussed later.

Wastage

It is unlikely that any advertising medium will give you perfect coverage of your market. Some potential purchasers will not be covered and so you will not achieve 100 per cent penetration. Equally, some of the people you *do* reach will not be in the market for your product. Since you nevertheless have to pay a charge based on the medium's total circulation, readership, viewership or listenership, you will clearly want to assess what proportion of its audience is likely to constitute less valuable coverage. Such considerations will clearly influence your choice of media, but should not lead you to undervalue that part of the total coverage which *is* of your target group. If coverage of the people you want to reach is properly evaluated, then coverage of others can be considered as a bonus rather than 'wastage'.

There is one further quantitative criterion: Cost. This will be discussed later, since media planners must consider whether or not the qualitative criteria which follow are worth the money.

QUALITATIVE CRITERIA

These include:

The medium

A factor of prime importance in media selection is the means by which your advertising message is delivered. What form does it take – do people read it, watch it or listen to it? Television gives you the benefit of movement to demonstrate your product in use, together with sound in the form of music, and the human voice to speak the advertising message. Cinema advertisements, too, have movement and sound. Both can have the advantage of colour. Posters have colour and size but not movement. Many newspaper advertisements are printed in black and white. In magazines, colour is more frequently available, to attract attention and show your products in their natural colours as they appear on retailers' shelves. Colour availability is not enough in itself, however, for quality can vary considerably, and this will influence selection within the range of colour media.

When selecting media, you should therefore make more than a superficial study of the actual means by which your advertising message will be delivered to your target audience. Changes in technology are not restricted to press, and have equally important implications for other media.

Mood/Environment

Your prospective customer's state of mind when receiving your advertising message can directly enhance or weaken your campaign effectiveness, so this consideration should be well to the fore when you contrast the media available to you. In this respect you should distinguish between media where advertising is an intrusive element and others where it is acceptable or, better still, has positive interest value. By advertising in women's publications, for example, your advertising message will reach women – the 'Who?' question tells you this – but you will know that it will reach women when they are in a receptive state of mind. They will be relaxed and seeking information about homes, beauty, fashion or food, and thus receptive to advertising messages about merchandise in these product fields. Special interest publications similarly offer you the double benefit of reaching a selected group of likely purchasers and of delivering your message when they are in a receptive mood, and the same is true of many exhibitions. This principle can be extended to specific positions within a medium: an advertisement on the gardening page of a newspaper selects gardeners out of the total readership and delivers the advertising message when they are mentally 'tuned in' to the subject of gardening.

In that editorial reflects readers' interests, any advertiser is advised to check previous issues to see how frequently there has been editorial relating to his particular product area, since this should give a further indication of whether readers are likely to be in the market for his product.

A medium's editorial content may influence mood in another way by lending an atmosphere of authority or expert knowledge of a subject, with consequent benefit to the advertiser and his product.

In preparing advertising campaigns, many people make the mistake of concentrating on their own activities, rather than thinking in the terms of their potential buyers. An extension of the mood question can place the emphasis where it should be – on the consumer. Rather than asking 'What will my advertisement do to people?' you should ask 'What will people do to my advertisement?' The answer to this question depends not only on the creativity of your advertising campaign (which is of course beyond the immediate scope of this book) but, equally, on the state of mind they are in when they receive your advertising message. This question thus links back with the 'Who?' question – if a medium reaches people ready to buy your product, and delivers your advertising message when they are likely to respond favourably to it, the medium is likely to be highly effective. Usage and Attitude studies, when available, clearly provide highly relevant information about your target market's mood when receiving your advertising message.

The extreme example of mood/environment is advertising in certain directories or works of reference, the very nature of which indicates that those people consulting them are not only potential customers but are in the market *now* and thus reach and eager to buy – why else should they be consulting the directory?

When?

Timing your advertising message is a vital consideration. For some advertisers this is a question of seasons: promoting summer goods in the summer and winter goods in the winter. Others may need to be more precise, and deliver their advertising messages on a given day of the week. Some media, such as point-of-sale displays, deliver your message seconds before the purchase is made. An important timing question is that of either maximising the opportunity of peak sales, or limiting the troughs of low season sales and so spreading the sales load more evenly. Perhaps your advertising should appear at the beginning of a traditional climb in the graph towards a peak, so that sales start to climb earlier and grow faster. These are complex questions, the answers varying according to the needs of each advertiser who must consider when is the most effective time for the advertising message to be received, and when will the various media deliver it.

Frequency

A second aspect of timing concerns repetition: the regularity with which your advertising message can be delivered. Some low cost media allow many advertisers to afford heavy repetition. Media such as posters are structured to achieve high frequency, whilst others permit daily, weekly or only monthly contact with your targets. Consumer buying habits – day and frequency of repeat purchases – thus directly influence your use of media.

Speed

A third aspect of timing relates to speed of operation rather than when and how often your advertising message is delivered, since some media must receive advertising material far in advance of publication date. Should you need to deliver an urgent sales message such as a price reduction, you would choose the medium with the shortest copy date in order to make your announcement as speedily as possible. Conversely, if your future plans are subject to constant change, you might be averse to using media with long copy dates (perhaps months in advance of actual delivery of your advertising message) since this means you have to decide your message on a long-term basis, whereas immediate short-term considerations are of major importance. You might equally be wary of using media that demand notice of cancellation long in advance of publication date, and thus do not permit flexibility in planning.

This is another area where, yet again, changes in technology are of vital importance: copy dates are being reduced, thereby making media attractive to new potential advertisers, and more flexible for those already appearing.

Flexibility

Speed is not the only factor affecting flexibility in media usage. Direct mail is perhaps the ultimate example – not only do you control timing and frequency but also *quantitative* aspects – you can turn the tap on or off as you wish to increase, decrease (or stop) stimulating your target group as market conditions dictate.

Span of attention

The attention that prospective purchasers pay to your advertising must be considered from two aspects: the duration of your message and the amount of time for which it will receive attention.

Some advertising messages have a very brief existence: a ten-second television or radio commercial, for example, clearly cannot receive attention for more than ten seconds and, once transmitted, the prospective purchaser cannot refer back to it (unless it is recorded and until it is broadcast again). Newspaper and magazine advertisements exist for a longer period, and so can be studied at leisure.

Equally important is the amount of time prospective purchasers will devote to your advertisement. Posters exist 24 hours a day, seven days a week (even if they are not at work all that time) and thus have a longer life than most media. Nevertheless, your advertising message must usually be kept short, since most posters are only glanced at by people hurrying past. Posters on stations or in buses and trains, where there is a 'captive audience', may be studied for longer periods.

These two aspects of attention must be considered from the communications standpoint, for brief duration is neither good nor bad until related to a specific advertising task. Hence, you must consider how much information you need to convey. Is your message brief enough for a ten-second commercial or poster, or do you need to convey details about prices and sizes and so on?

A balance must be struck between the amount of time needed to convey your message and the duration of interest the message will receive. The decision you reach has direct media implications.

Life

Some media repay their use within a very few days, while others give you full value for money only over a much longer period. From the advertisers' point of view this means you may receive results in one short burst or spread over weeks, months, or even years. Since this affects the period for which the market for your product is stimulated, the life of any medium is an important consideration. A television or radio commercial, for example, delivers its full impact at the time of transmission, whereas a magazine printed on high quality paper may go on bringing results until it literally falls to pieces. Here you should distinguish between publications that are read once and thrown away, those that are passed to others (thus providing 'pass-on' or secondary readership), and those that are kept for reference.

This consideration affects not only evaluation of media, but also of campaign results – it would clearly be unwise to evaluate the results of any advertisement before the medium has had full time to deliver its message.

Indirect influence

Some media bring results through their effect on important groups other than the main media audience. Such influence frequently bears on retailers, who stock and display merchandise in the belief that advertisements in a given medium will stimulate consumer demand from which they can profit. Manufacturers place tremendous importance on obtaining good distribution and display, and any medium that helps in achieving this has a marked advantage over others. The example most frequently quoted is television, which exerts a strong influence on retailers as well as the main media audience. Co-operative campaigns, where your stockists' names and addresses are featured in advertisements, can be equally effective in influencing retailers. Where this is the case, you should clearly take account of it in reaching media decisions.

Availability

This heading in fact covers three criteria for media selection. One is fundamental and governed by the rules and regulations relating to certain media, which might categorise certain types of advertising as unacceptable. Products or services that are not acceptable for advertising on television, for example, include tobacco; and also gun clubs, soothsayers, private detectives, and breathalysers! Television as a medium is thus not available to such advertisers. Bear in mind, however, that such restrictions may vary over time, as circumstances change. The ITC changes its rules from time to time, as does the ASA whose codes apply to all non-broadcast media.

A second availability criterion, that links with the question of *how* the medium will deliver your advertising message, relates to creative scope and thus could be asked under either heading – what colours are available (specials or publisher's choice only)? More directly under this heading of availability, however, what precise sizes and positions does the media-owner accept? Is it possible to have your printed material included, either as a bound-in insert or as a loose insert? It is beyond the scope of this book to list all the standard transport sizes and positions, for example, or to detail the various sizes and position available in newspapers and magazines, and you would of course want to study these when making a more detailed review of those media of interest to you. In making this review, the fundamental question is a simple one. What advertisement 'units' – or choice of units – must you think in terms of when preparing your creative proposals? To give an extreme example, there would be little point in preparing a campaign based on diagonal half-pages, only to find this size totally unacceptable when you attempt to make your bookings.

Clearly your creative proposals must be put in hand in a practical manner, in a form acceptable to media-owners. The range of units is considerable and most media-owners are keen to co-operate, so this need be no creative straightjacket. And it is always worth asking the media-owner if odd shapes will be accepted.

Thirdly, under this general criterion of availability, you will most certainly need to know what advertising spaces or positions are actually available. Should all the best positions be already booked, or only a limited number of spaces available, you have little choice but to consider spending the balance in other media.

Constraints

Some media-owners impose house-rules about the types of advertising they will accept, and reject any offending advertisements. It is therefore clearly advisable to know if there are any limits on type size, for instance, or restrictions on white-on-black advertisements, since this would perhaps constrain creative content.

Reliability

How certain can you be that your advertising message will in fact be delivered? Any advertiser who has based his selling efforts on the belief that his market will be stimulated at a particular time will naturally be wary of any medium that omits his advertisement for some reasons or other. Equally important, how reliable will the delivery *quality* be – in terms of, for example, colour? And, if your advertising message is not delivered to your satisfaction, what compensation can you expect?

Competitive activity

This overall heading covers various criteria for media selection. First, before booking with any medium it is advisable to check if rival manufacturers appear regularly, and in what sizes and positions and with what frequency.

Secondly, you should also consider the general weight of advertising, and in a publication carrying a vast amount of advertising you may think it necessary to book a larger advertisement or a special position, to ensure that your advertising message receives attention.

Thirdly, there is the matter of the company you will be keeping: the fact that a medium carries (or does *not* carry) well prepared advertisements for leading firms can, in itself, influence the mood of the media audience.

Facilities

The range of facilities offered by media is wide. However, they can all be grouped together under the general theme of what the media-owner will do in addition to delivering your advertising message.

Many media help encourage readers to obtain further information about advertised products as well as helping to handle that response. Response services offered by some magazines include a telephone number to call for brochures as well as reply cards for readers to obtain information about more than one advertised product. Similarly, television contractors encourage Direct Response advertisers by providing telemarketing response services such as 0800 numbers and call handling support.

Other facilities offered by magazines include run-ons (additional copies of the advertisement), direct mail to the trade about the campaign, and point-of-sale material reminding shoppers where they saw the product advertised.

Television rate cards also feature added-value services such as commando sales forces and direct mail to sell the product to retailers, help with production costs, studio visits/presentation facilities and subsidised research.

The provision of valuable research data by media has already been mentioned. This can include special computer runs to help with media scheduling. One example of the sophistication such research can reach is the panel of 750 Superpanel homes in the Meridian TV region. Advertisers can access single-source effectiveness data, because the research records not only TV viewing patterns but also product purchasing from the exact same households. Less ambitious, but nonetheless vitally important, is the assistance given to inexperienced advertisers by media representatives in preparing and producing effective press or radio advertisements.

Some of these facilities may be provided free as part of the media-owner's normal service, whilst there may be an 'at cost' charge for others. It is also sometimes possible to persuade media-owners to share costs as part of the buying negotiations. Such facilities can be most useful and you should most certainly check them out and use them as necessary. You should, however, beware of 'letting the tail wag the dog'.

Media-owners, quite understandably, want repeat orders: hence the range of additional facilities to help you achieve a successful campaign. The prime reason for using any advertising medium is, however, to deliver your message and, in evaluating media, the answers to the questions listed above are of greater importance than any secondary facilities that the media-owner might offer. Of even greater importance is the answer to the next question: cost.

QUALITATIVE AND QUANTITATIVE:

Cost

The factor deliberately left until last, though it is of course a prime consideration in media selection, is cost. Much depends on the size of your appropriation, for some media call for large expenditures and may thus be out of the question for advertisers with small budgets. Cost is basically a straightforward question but nevertheless presents considerable problems in terms of booking unit, size, position, amount of advertising booked and other considerations discussed below.

Booking unit

The complication here is that advertising is sold in different units, making straight comparisons impossible. Newspapers, for example, are usually sold by the 'single column centimetre': one centimetre in one column costs £X and space is sold in multiples of this. A 20 cm × 2 cols advertisement simply means 20 centimetres taken in two adjacent columns, or 40 cm, and the cost of this advertisement is thus 40 times the basic unit cost. Similarly, a 25 × 4 cols advertisement is charged at 100 times the unit cost. Media planners often make cost comparisons of charges for the same-size advertisement in two publications, but a straight comparison is not possible. Even when advertisements in two media are the same size, they may appear in publications of different page sizes. It is argued, for example, that a given-size advertisement in a tabloid newspaper is more effective than in a broadsheet, because it is more dominant in the smaller page than the larger and will thus attract higher readership.

Research can overcome this problem, but comparison of media on a straight cost basis is still difficult to achieve, especially when the basic unit differs. Magazines, for example, are usually sold not by the single column centimetre, but by the page or fractions of a page: half-page, quarter-page, eighth-page, etc, and posters sold by number of sheets, cinema, television and radio advertising are sold by time – 10, 20, 30, 40, 50 or 60 seconds and so on.

The problem of contrasting media that sell advertising in different units is further complicated by the fact that cost varies with three factors: size, position and amount of advertising booked.

Size

There are three obvious advantages to large advertisements – more people see them, there is scope to include more information and better creative work, and the advertisements themselves usually have greater impact. The bigger your advertisement the higher the cost, but the complication arises that cost does not always vary 'pro rata' in *direct* proportion to size, when calculated on the unit rate. Some media offer large advertisements at a 'bargain' rate to encourage you to take such sizes: other media, where larger sizes are in heavy demand, may charge higher premium rates so that, for example, a 25 cm × 5 cols advertisement costs more than 125 times the single-column centimetre rate.

On television, rates are usually quoted pro-rata to the 30 second rate, but not always. For instance, one contractor charges 10 second spots at 50 per cent of the 30 second rate instead of the expected 33 per cent.

This is a straightforward matter of supply and demand for the media-owner, but for the advertiser and his agency it makes more complex the already difficult problem of comparing competitive media.

Position

The cost of an advertisement also depends on its position. An advertisement on the front page is seen by more people than one inside the publication: similarly, a 'solus' advertisement may receive more attention than one that has to compete with other advertisements. A poster on a main road is seen by more people than one in a side street, and the same is true of a television commercial transmitted at peak viewing time rather than in the afternoon. Some advertisers pay extra to be the first spot in a break and it is possible to benefit from being the only spot in a break. Good position results in high coverage of the total potential audience and there is accordingly a higher charge, which advertisers try to evaluate in relation to what they are getting for their money.

If you do not book a special position, your order will be at a less expensive 'run of paper' (ROP) rate which permits the media-owner to place your advertisement anywhere within the issue.

Your advertisement's position affects not only the number but also

136

the type of people who see it. An advertisement on the motoring page is more likely to be seen by motorists, and a similar argument applies to advertisements on sports pages, fashion pages, home hints pages and so on, which select likely customers for betting shops or football pools, fashion houses and food products. The editorial content of such pages also influences the mood of the media audience, who will be more receptive to the advertising message. With other media, position can equally well influence the type and mood of the media audience.

Size and position

Size and position may be fixed jointly by some media-owners, so that no choice is offered. The position on the front page of a newspaper, for example, may be guaranteed to be solus, but the publisher restricts it to a certain size and may, in effect, be offering a 20 cm × 2 cols front-page solus. Similarly, the publisher might offer a 25 cm × 2 cols, facing TV programme page. Both these advertisements would be charged at special rates, since they are important sizes and positions. With other media, the same reasoning may apply.

The effect of size and position

Size and composition of the media audience directly affect media selection, yet surprisingly there is, for some media, very little information available about the different audiences that will be reached by varying sizes and positions. The National Readership Surveys, for example, give only overall readership figures for publications. Common sense tells you that more people see large advertisements or a front-page solus, and that an advertisement on the women's page selects women out of the total readership, but this is by no means precise enough: you need to know exactly the size and composition of the audience you will achieve with a given advertisement on a certain page, rather than a general picture of the medium's average issue readership.

Similarly, with television, you do not know what difference it will make to your audience if you have a 20 or 30 second or some other length of commercial, but the television audience surveys do indicate, on the other hand, both the size and composition of the media audience you are likely to achieve if your commercial is transmitted in a particular time segment. Similar information could be made generally available for press media, but some practitioners have questioned the research techniques used to measure page traffic and the effect of advertisement size and, in addition, there are the usual problems of agreeing, organising, supervising and – above all – financing such research.

Amount of advertising booked

Cost varies not only with size and position but also with a third factor – the total amount of advertising booked. This is because most media-owners, in order to encourage repeat bookings, offer some form of discount to advertisers who support them regularly.

Series orders bring direct advantage to the media-owner, since it is most helpful to know what bookings are in hand for future issues. Furthermore, there is a considerable economy in time, salary and selling expenses if, say, 12 orders are achieved through a single call instead of the representative having to make 12 separate calls to achieve the same results.

Newspapers and magazines frequently offer a 'series' discount if the booking is for a minimum number of insertions. There is a similar 'volume' discount for television, and other media usually decrease their rates as the size of the total booking increases.

Special discounts

Cost varies with size, position and total booking, and most variations appear on published rate cards, but other types of discount may also be featured. A television rate card selected at random included test market incentives (providing up to 50 per cent discount to new advertisers), business incentive discounts (providing between 5 per cent and 25 per cent discount depending on volume and proportion of spend committed to that sales house) and advance booking discounts. These and many other variations may be featured on standard rate cards, which clearly merit detailed study.

From time to time, however, media-owners often find it expedient to extend other special offers to boost sales in otherwise slack periods. These offers are many and varied but divide into two basic groups – a discount offer to sell the same amount of advertising at a reduced charge, or alternatively a bonus offer of more advertising at no additional cost. These offers may be made known by special mailings and sometimes, when the offer applies for an extended period, special rate cards may be issued.

Another type of discount relates to 'packages' of advertising: if you help media-owners overcome possible selling problems, they in turn help you by giving lower rates. Most media-owners, seeking to balance supply and demand, offer financial incentives to advertisers who are flexible in their requirements regarding both timing and/or geographic location. If, however, you want precise control of when your commercials are to appear, which precise sites feature your posters, or which specified cinemas show your commercial and in which weeks, you must book at the full price in the normal way.

Some or all of these offers may be linked with the other question raised above – how many? – in that the advertising offer is linked with a guaranteed minimum audience, as revealed by research. With television advertising, for example, the rate card mentioned above features a range of 'Guaranteed TVR packages', that allow advertisers to achieve an agreed level of rating points. The television channel guarantees that your commercial will achieve at least the minimum, say 30 TVRs during daytime viewing, for a relatively low investment. As these packages are under the contractor's control they are likely to comprise more than one spot and your targets will receive the commercial message more than once. In consequence, the *net* coverage of your target is likely to be less than the TVR target. Similar guaranteed audience 'packages' are frequently available for other media, such as radio and cinema.

Many advertisers employ both methods – their media plan includes a carefully-targeted component to ensure a minimum number of advertising messages are delivered to the right people in the right place at the right time. This planned component is then backed up by the purchase of 'bargain packages' which offer good value for money when delivering additional messages.

Finally, media-owners may find themselves called upon to negotiate special 'contract' arrangements at top level, particularly where big advertising expenditures are involved. Basically, this amounts to hard bargaining between the media-owner and the advertiser or his agency, both sides seeking to agree a contract, often for a year across a number of brands to their own best advantage. The advertiser and agency seek lower rates or, what amounts to the same thing, premium positions without paying a higher rate. The media-owner, naturally enough, seeks the maximum amount of revenue he can secure. Before undertaking any bargaining, you should of course consider the media-owner's relative strength in the marketplace, since this will influence the flexibility of his attitude. Some media-owners see discounting as anathema: a signal that a publication is in trouble.

Cost and value for money

1 *Cost per thousand* Cost is frequently considered together with quantity, and one medium compared with another, by what is termed CPT or 'cost per thousand' – the cost of reaching each thousand of the target universe (homes, housewives, adults, etc). It is usually expressed in pence, and is used as a general yardstick of media cost and efficiency. Cost per thousand is calculated by dividing, for example, the single-column centimetre rate of a publication by its circulation. To illustrate

this with simple hypothetical figures, a newspaper charging £1 per s.c.c. and with a circulation of 20,000 thus has a cost of £1.00/20 = 5p per thousand circulation. Another newspaper might charge £10 per s.c.c. and have 500,000 circulation and here the cost per thousand circulation is only 2p. The second paper costs more in outlay – £10 instead of £1 per s.c.c. – but the circulation is larger, and so in this respect you get more for your money.

The cost per thousand concept is frequently used in evaluating different media and is, therefore, one with which you must be thoroughly familiar. It is also perhaps the most misused: it can be treated as a precise measuring instrument but in many cases it is used much too loosely. To quote 'cost per thousand' is meaningless unless it is made clear just what is being measured. Before accepting any cost per thousand figure for one medium in comparison with its rivals, you should ask a very basic question – 'Cost of *what* per thousand *what*?' Costs per thousand are most frequently quoted per s.c.c. for newspapers (or per page for magazines) per thousand circulation, but very few advertisers are interested in total circulation, and few (if any) plan in terms of single-column centimetres. Their interest lies in the advertisement size required, and only that part of the total media audience likely to buy their product. For this reason, cost per thousand calculations are frequently extended to compare actual advertisement costs – the cost per thousand of a 20 cm × 2 cols insertion or of a solus position in one publication rather than another. Equally, it may be calculated not for circulation but for readership, or for readership of a particular category – cost per thousand housewife readers in the 16–24 age group and in a stated socio-economic category. Similarly, television cost per thousand is sometimes based on numbers of homes and the cost of a 30-second commercial: many advertisers, however, use commercials of a different length and calculate costs per thousand for specified target audience groups, rather than the number of sets switched on.

2 Weighted values Cost per thousand calculations are useful in comparing one medium with another as regards value for money in terms of the audience numbers you are likely to reach, but the approach is sometimes extended to allow for qualitative as well as statistical values, through including 'media weights' in your calculations. A media weight is necessarily subjective and reflects the importance you place on intangible factors. If you think colour or high-quality printing of particular importance to your advertising, or feel that the mood of the potential customer receiving your message through a magazine is of greater or lesser value in comparison with the same message received through a newspaper, you may wish to allow for this in your calculations since this would provide a more relevant measure of cost effectiveness than cost per thousand alone.

The concept to be used under such circumstances is called Valued Impressions per Pound, or VIPs:

VIP = (Media audience × Media weight)/Cost

The media weight is the value you place on intangible factors such as colour, expressed in numerical terms.

Quite apart from allowing for subjective views as well as statistical information, there is another important difference between VIPs and cost per thousand. One calculation is the inverse of the other, ie the *higher* the VIP index then the *more efficient* the medium, whereas with cost per thousand calculations you seek the lowest possible figure. The two different methods, nevertheless, have the same underlying aim – they are simply alternative methods you can use in assessing value for money.

Production costs

Another factor that indirectly affects media planning is production costs, as distinct from the charges levied by media-owners. With some media, production costs constitute only a small proportion of total costs, while in others they are important enough to demand major consideration. In some cases, such as direct mail or display material, production charges are of course inseparable from media costs. The importance of keeping up-to-date with changes in technology is again apparent.

OVERALL MEDIA COMPARISON

Bearing in mind the wide range of comparison criteria, it is clear that there can be no such thing as the *best* medium. All media have their respective advantages (and drawbacks) and your task is to assess the contribution they can make to achieving your advertising objective. This task, together with the problem of balancing conflicting demands for impact versus frequency versus coverage, is considered in Part 3.

Part 2
THE ORGANISATION OF MEDIA

Having considered the range of media, this Part turns attention to those organisations and individuals responsible for their use. You cannot separate media planning principles from the people applying them or the firms in which they work: the first chapter in this Part therefore covers the media-owners and subsequent chapters concentrate on the advertisers and their agencies. The fourth chapter in this Part describes the role of the media independents, and a fifth outlines some of the specialist services available.

Any media representative must fully understand how advertisers and their agencies operate if he hopes to gain an order, and it is equally essential for advertisers and agencies respectively to appreciate the working of the other two parties to the advertising contract, if they hope to use media to best advantage.

Any reader who wishes to skip the chapter describing that part of the industry in which he is employed – on the premise that he knows its contents from everyday working experience – is welcome to do so. However, as a refresher, this section is of course recommended for at least a cursory read.

Chapter 8

Role of the Media-Owner

THE MEDIA-OWNER'S STRUCTURE

All media-owners differ in their precise organisational pattern, but it is nevertheless possible to describe a basic structure around which individual media-owners make those variations best suited to their particular operation. This chapter discusses the media-owner's various departments, the inter-relationship of their activities and how they can best work with advertiser and agency respectively for more effective advertising.

The financial circle

Before examining the component activities of any media-owner's various departments, it is important to realise their inter-relationship. If a medium is of a quality which attracts a large audience, it not only gets considerable cover revenue but can also sell space to advertisers wishing to reach that audience. High cover and advertisement revenue enable the media-owner to maintain, or even improve, the already high quality and to promote the medium's sales effectively. This will increase the audience even further, and so the financial circle is complete: in this case in a beneficial upward spiral.

Conversely a medium of poor quality will not attract many purchasers. Without a worthwhile audience, the media-owner will find it difficult to sell advertising space. Poor sales of space means poor advertisement revenue as well as poor cover revenue. The media-owner thus has insufficient funds to produce a medium which consumers wish to buy, and no funds to promote it to them. In this case, the financial link is a vicious circle, with a downward spiral.

There are of course other factors – such as the state of advertisers' markets and the relative efficiency of other media – but the financial circle should be borne firmly in mind when reading the following review of the media-owner's various departments and their relationship. The review is mainly in terms of press, since this is still the largest medium in terms of advertisement revenue. The principles apply to other media, however, where the financial circle is equally applicable.

The degree of application will of course vary between different media, and a primary factor is the extent they are reliant on advertising revenue. Posters are totally reliant; radio and terrestrial television are all but totally reliant (there may, of course, be income from programme sales, but our concern here is with advertising). On the other hand, satellite television and cable gain more revenue from subscriptions than advertising and cinemas gain more from admission revenue than advertising.

The editorial department

With most media, advertising is not their reason for existence but only a means of helping them exist. Newspapers and magazines are read for their editorial content and television watched and radio listened to largely for news and entertainment, and it is editorial skill in interpreting and satisfying target audience taste that determines the size and type of media audience. This in turn influences the possibilities for using these media as effective means of advertising.

The editorial size is frequently sub-divided, with special sections appealing to particular groups within the overall media audience. Newspapers, for example, have special gardening or motoring features, or pages written expressly for women readers. On television and radio, there are similar specialist programmes. Some features appear regularly (whether daily, weekly or monthly) while others appear only on particular occasions. The latter category could include features giving special coverage to, for example, the Boat Show or the Royal Academy Summer Exhibition.

Editorial is not always the reason for the existence of an advertising medium, however. Outdoor advertising, for example, has no editorial content and justifies itself solely as a publicity medium. With some media, advertising also serves as 'editorial': the 'editorial' of an exhibition for example, is of course the advertisers' stands. It is worth bearing in mind that advertising serves the media audience just as much as the advertisers and media-owners. Exhibitions provide a clear example of this but the same point applies equally to press media.

The production department

The writings of the editorial staff together with relevant illustrations must be put into print, and readership depends not only on the editorial being of interest but also on it being well printed. Printing quality also affects advertising effectiveness and is one of the factors that advertisers and agencies should consider when selecting media. Those using media should therefore keep themselves up-to-date with changes in printing technology, since these directly influence the efficiency with which your advertising message will be delivered to your target market.

Similarly, television and radio programmes must be produced and transmitted. Poster sites must be constructed and the posters themselves pasted up. For some media, such as point-of-sale display material, production is of major importance and constitutes the main part of the advertising: the same applies to direct mail and to exhibitions. Technological changes are equally relevant to these media.

The circulation department

There is more to successful publishing than writing and printing alone, for printed copies are of little use until they are delivered to actual readers. This is the task of the circulation department and the sheer physical work is often under-estimated. The flow of printed copies coming from the press must be bundled and addressed, and special transport is frequently necessary: fleets of delivery vans, trains, or even aircraft. A few minutes' delay in the delivery chain may lead to missing a vital connection, and thus to loss of sale of thousands of copies. A whole network of wholesalers and newsagents is involved and the media-owner must ensure that his publication is available in sufficient quantities and well displayed. In this respect, the work of the circulation representative is similar to that of most consumer goods salesmen. In addition to the routine circulation operation, complex enough as it is, the circulation department may often arrange special distribution facilities for extra sales at important events or exhibitions. Some media-owners, rather than undertake this complex work in-house, prefer to sub-contract the task to an external service organisation.

Changes in printing technology are having their effect here also. No longer is it necessary to print in one location, and for the circulation department to then physically transport heavy bulk supplies to other parts of the country, or to other countries. As already mentioned, *The Financial Times* is printed simultaneously in eight different locations and circulates in 140 countries. New printing technology means that material can be written and typeset in one location but actual printing takes place at another (perhaps where there is spare printing capacity) thus speeding up the circulation process at the same time as cutting distribution costs.

With a number of publications, magazines particularly, a considerable proportion of copies are not distributed through newsagents, but posted direct to readers on a subscription basis. Free newspapers, on the other hand, omit the wholesaler/newsagent/subscription link, and the media-owner achieves circulation by direct delivery to the home. By contrast, with some media there is no 'circulation' in the sense of a separate physical activity. With direct mail, for example, circulation is really only an extension of production work and, with television and radio, building of audiences depends not only on production and transmission of the programmes but equally on their promotion. To this end, many media-owners develop promotion departments. Circulation, subscriptions and promotion departments may operate as separate units, or may be joined to form an overall publishing department.

The subscription department

Many publications rely to a great extent on subscriptions for their distribution. Subscription circulation is important not only as a source of revenue, but also because it implies regular readership, which is of prime importance to potential advertisers. Indeed, analysis of subscriptions, as a form of research, can provide valuable information about the type and location of readers. With magazines on controlled circulation, where copies are sent (free of charge) addressed by name to individuals in certain defined categories, this research aspect is dominant, and the subscription revenue foregone. Publishers of controlled-circulation journals count on the assurance they can give potential advertisers about circulation and thus readership to bring them an advertising revenue which more than compensates for the loss of subscription income, so that in this respect the readership aspect is all important. The same applies to specialist journals received by members of various professional bodies, as part of the service they receive in return for their membership subscription. The research is becoming increasingly sophisticated as the relevant databases become computerised.

The promotion department

With subscription copies of publications, or those sold through newsagents or booksellers, the promotion department plays a key role. Other media, which do not have the equivalent of circulation or subscription departments, rely equally on the promotion department.

The size of audience that views a television programme, for example, or attends an exhibition, turns on the skill of the promotion department. This department may also sponsor special events such as sporting and arts events or exhibitions, as part of the medium's overall promotional programme. In recent years, some promotions have become increasingly lavish, with rival media-owners competing for readers by offering scratch cards or other forms of promotion with 'Free Houses', 'Free Holidays' or 'Pay Off Your Mortgage' prizes.

In considering the promotion department's activities, any media-owner should be considered a manufacturer in his own right, with merchandise to sell, who must plan his advertising with as much care as other producers. It is not unknown for a media-owner to have an advertising manager (responsible for promoting the medium) as well as an advertisement manager (responsible for advertising revenue).

The advertising manager may plan a number of distinct campaigns. There may be a promotional campaign aimed at the public, persuading them to buy a publication, to watch a television series or attend an exhibition. Just as manufacturers usually have a second campaign aimed at retailers or wholesalers, so the media-owner will mount promotional campaigns aimed at wholesale and retail newsagents, with the object of persuading them to stock up and display his publication. Media-owners differ from other producers in needing a third campaign to potential advertisers and their agencies, to bring in advertisement revenue. Most media-owner undertake a great amount of promotional activity, to back up the efforts of their media representatives. These campaigns include a whole range of material: direct mail shots, trade press advertisements and sales aids for media representatives to use in their presentations. The promotion department will also devote considerable attention to making known the work of ancillary services such as the research department.

The research department

Much research is undertaken centrally: the readership or listenership surveys and television audience reports described in Part 1, for example, provide information about reading, listening and viewing habits which is readily available to all advertisers and agencies, and serves as an important tool in media evaluation. Given the existence of this central research information, you may wonder why a media-owner should run his own research department. Quite simply, the main purpose is to provide additional information not contained in the central research, which might persuade advertisers and agencies to view the medium more favourably.

In describing the data available, Part 1 pointed out that much valuable information was available from media-owners' own surveys, and such work is the province of the research department which may also subscribe to the various research services available: all this activity has the common aim of providing information that might be useful to you in your planning. This information might well be provided by the media-owner undertaking special computer runs of the central surveys, to present additional tabulations not available in the surveys' standard formats. Much of this information will equally be of assistance to the media representatives in their selling tasks, but there is however a major problem underlying such research activities by media-owners.

The surveys commissioned centrally and those sponsored by media-owners complement rather than duplicate each other. There may be areas of overlap and differences may arise through use of varying research methods, but these problems are of minor importance in comparison with the underlying question of whose responsibility it is to undertake and finance the research.

Advertisers and agencies can justifiably claim that the media-owner has a responsibility to provide information about the coverage of his medium. No difficulties arise when a medium is included in the central research, but where the media-owner starts to provide additional information a fundamental problem does occur.

An overall review of media-owners' research shows that much of it is at one of two levels. The first level of research provides information about the medium's coverage, to enable media planners to judge the medium's power to reach that market. But should the market not be worthwhile, no amount of research will persuade manufacturers to use the medium. Hence some media-owners tend to provide 'second stage' research information to show the value of a market – and thus persuade advertisers to mount a campaign in that market, in which case the media-owner should get his share of the advertising expenditure, and can use his first-level research to ensure inclusion in the schedule. Some media-owners go even further, into what can be termed 'stage three' research, by checking the sales in their market of particular groups of products, to show manufacturers of these products the desirability of mounting a campaign in the area. In short, the media-owner researches the market he serves, rather than the medium itself.

Such research is really aimed at providing marketing information and this is where the controversy arises. Why should it fall to media-owners to provide costly marketing information which advertisers or their agencies should have collected themselves, if they are to mount successful marketing campaigns? And, again, to *whom* should the media-owner make the information available? The marketing information was collected to influence marketing policy, and it is only *after* this is decided that media planners make their contribution – selecting media to reach the market that is the target of the campaign. Yet many marketing surveys are sent to media planners, to whom they are not of immediate *media* interest. The same problem arises when media-owners promote their areas as ideal for test marketing. The decision to mount a test campaign is a marketing decision and not a media one, yet media planners are frequently bombarded with such information, just as they are mailed about merchandising services. Media-owners thus have the problem of distinguishing between the tasks of selling the market and that of selling the medium, since these call for selling activity directed to different individuals. This problem, however, is relatively easily resolved in comparison with the more controversial one of who is to finance the research, and the answer to this has yet to be agreed.

Returning to less controversial but perhaps more interesting matters, it is worth noting that some media-owners are moving into 'stage four' research – providing 'Usage and Attitude' or 'Advertisement Recall' information about the ability of their media to *communicate* and whether the same message received through Medium A is more effective than if received through Medium B.

'Stage five' research occurs when rival media-owners, rather than fight each other for an increased share of a static market, work alongside their immediate competitors to mount co-operative research about their media group and its advantages over other media. Part 1 described the many interesting developments in this type of research, undertaken for cinema and video, direct mail, business press, national newspapers and general magazines, posters, radio and the regional press.

The need for marketing information has resulted in some media-owners' research departments operating to an entirely different end, acting as an internal service organisation for the advertisement department. The research role here is to assemble facts and figures that advertisement representatives will find helpful in their contacts with advertisers and agencies. In addition, research staff may analyse current advertising to predict future trends. Where research is entirely devoted to securing additional business, the department may be known by another name, such as 'Sales Research', 'Marketing Services' or 'Business Development', and operate independently of the research department, which devotes itself to field research.

Marketing and merchandising departments

In many cases, a research department marketing survey is linked with an outline of the various merchandising services provided by the media-owner to assist advertisers in ensuring the success of their campaigns. The one 'Marketing and Merchandising' document thus includes details of activities such as trade mailings, conference facilities, reprints, display material and many other aids which, when criteria for media comparison were discussed in Part 1, were grouped under the general heading of 'Facilities'.

The advertisement department

The advertisement department has the vital task of obtaining maximum advertisement revenue. For some media such as terrestrial television, radio or posters, where there is no income from sales or subscriptions, advertising is the sole source of revenue on which the medium depends for its existence. Even where a medium does not wholly rely on advertisement revenue, such as a publication sent to association members in return for their subscriptions, advertisement revenue is still of importance in that it permits publication of larger issues with better quality printing. Never forget, also, that the advertisements communicate information and are thus a service to readers.

The individual who controls sales of advertising within a medium is usually known as the advertisement manager or director (a very different individual from the advertising manager, whose responsibility is to buy advertising). In other media he is known as a Sales Manager, but for consistency, we shall refer to the post as advertisement manager. Before starting to sell, the advertisement manager – and his representatives – must know exactly what is available to sell. For press media, the advertisement manager must negotiate with editorial and production staff, and agree precisely what advertising space he can sell. He must then decide the units into which the total advertising space can best be broken down, and obtain agreement on precise size and positions. The advertising rates at which these spaces and positions will be charged must also be decided.

The exercise, which must be performed for every issue of the medium, is not a one-way process with the advertisement manager asking what is available. The degree of advertising support achieved by the advertisement side directly influences the size of the issue and the number of pages of editorial that can be included. With other media, a similar process will apply. Television and radio representatives must know how many minutes of advertising time are available, in what units, and the precise positioning of the commercial breaks. Exhibition organisers must know what stand space can be accommodated within the exhibition area, and the location and size of individual stands. Once advertising availability is known, the advertisement manager can set about achieving sales.

The advertisement manager as head of a department The advertisement manager is head of a department in just the same way as the editor, the production manager, the circulation manager, or a manufacturer's advertising manager. He must evaluate the amount of selling to be done, the number of calls to be made, their geographical location, and the level at which contact must be made, since some selling jobs calls for representatives with special experience and skill.

Assessing the market and division of work A list of potential advertisers must be built up, and a careful analysis made of each. Once the list of potential advertisers and – if appropriate – their agencies is built up, the advertisement manager's next task is to divide it among his various representatives and provide each with a call list. There are various ways in which this can be done and the advertisement manager must decide the most suitable division for his medium. It may be a straightforward sharing of work, each representative having a list of advertisers and agencies on whom to call. Alternatively the division may be by type of advertising, some representatives being responsible for classified advertising, for example, and others for display. There may be further specialisation within each division, with one representative having special responsibility for, say, car or fashion advertising. Again, calls may be split by area, each representative being responsible for all advertising within his defined territory.

Where division is by area, this reflects the advertisement manager's responsibility for predicting levels of activity, for such division assumes that there is adequate potential within each area and sufficient work to support, say, a Northern representative. Should there not be sufficient work to justify full-time employment, the advertisement manager may arrange for his representatives to make field trips from time to time to various areas. A final point is that some media-owners find it preferable to contract out of advertisement selling altogether, and to appoint space-selling agencies to undertake the work. For certain mainly local media, representation by national sales houses accounts for a significant proportion of advertising revenue. Naturally, these methods of dividing the work are not mutually exclusive, but frequently overlap. In various media, this has led to London-based sales houses responsible for sales to National advertisers, whilst local offices relate to regional or local advertisers. This structure applies to regional press, ITV and commercial local radio.

The advertisement manager must also bear in mind possible future expansion and increase his staff in good time to meet it. For even when the new man arrives he cannot be put to work immediately and, however experienced, will still need training to acquaint him fully with the new medium he is selling. The advertisement manager thus has a major responsibility in the selection and training of representatives, as well as their control. Some media-owners now pay more than lip-service to this matter and have appointed training officers, but the advertisement manager still remains directly concerned, as the type of training given will depend upon his view of future requirements.

Staff training This activity is an important and also a controversial one, since there has been considerable criticism of the calibre of representatives employed by certain media (some media-owners have been equally critical of client and agency staff!). It might be helpful to review briefly the knowledge required if a representative is to make a positive contribution to effective use of the medium. This knowledge reflects the tasks of the advertiser and agency described in Part 3 of this book, on the effective use of media:

1 *The product* The representative must be fully acquainted with the physical means by which the medium delivers your advertising message, advertisement sizes and positions and rates, copy dates, and all the mechanical production data regarding the advertisement material required.
2 *Editorial policy* Though the physical format remains the same, editorial content changes with each issue and may open up prospects of attracting advertisers previously not interested. Hence the representatives must be fully conversant with overall editorial policy, and with all future details: in this respect, training is a never-ending task.
3 *Media audience* Potential advertisers are directly concerned as to the audience they can reach through the medium. One of the first tasks of advertiser and agency is to define their market and, in evaluating media, they make a straight cross-check – with what certainty will the medium reach the defined target market? Accordingly, the representatives must have at their command readership or viewership figures, or other research information. Indeed, the majority of sales representatives (for instance in consumer magazine groups) have desk top access to research data.
4 *Potential advertisers* Representatives must understand thoroughly the marketing and advertising problems of the advertisers and agencies on whom they are to call. What type of advertising do they undertake, in what sizes, with what frequency, and on what dates? What are their marketing objectives? When does their season start? Which groups constitute their market, and what coverage of these groups does the medium offer? Which agencies are employed, and how is the work shared with the advertising department? Who plans the media schedule, and when? Part 3 discusses these investigations in more detail but here it is sufficient to point out that if media representatives are to be of service to potential advertisers and their agencies – and thus obtain the orders they seek – they must have this knowledge at their fingertips.

5 *Competition* Since the media-representative is selling against rival media, a knowledge of the competition is important under each of the headings listed above. This applies to indirect as well as direct competition: specialist publications, for example, compete not only with rival journals but also with alternative media such as direct mail or exhibitions.

6 *Media selection and planning* Understanding the potential advertiser's objective, and the principles by which media are evaluated and schedules planned, the advertisement representatives can then help ensure that their particular medium makes its maximum possible contribution to the success of the overall campaign.

7 *Creative skills and constraints* With some media, it is not sufficient for the representative merely to sell space. Where advertisers are inexperienced, it may be necessary to create and produce advertisements for them, for without this help it would be impossible for them to use the medium. This aspect of the advertisement department's work is discussed in more detail below, as are the legal and voluntary constraints affecting creative content.

8 *Selling techniques* Even when representatives have full knowledge of the physical format of their medium, its editorial policy, the market covered, the potential advertisers and the contribution which the medium could make to achieving their advertising objectives, there still remains the basic task of selling. While 'salesmanship' is important, it must be based on sound knowledge and reasoning, for all the sales talk in the world cannot compensate for lack of basic reasons for advertising in the medium. This is stressed because there are still a few media representatives who believe that stringpulling will bring orders.

A well-stocked wardrobe and superficial charm will not alone induce a media planner to include a medium in an advertising schedule. The same applies to lavish entertainment. Advertisers and media planners are busy people, with better use for their time than wasting it on unwanted hospitality, and are unlikely to accept invitations from media which do not merit serious consideration.

Supervision and control While the representatives are making calls, the advertisement manager must keep himself informed of their progress. Some media representatives, like their colleagues on the manufacturing side, are required to submit regular call reports, so that the advertisement manager knows what orders have been received or are pending, and can maintain up-to-date records.

The direction of selling The advertisement manager and his representatives must decide the best direction for selling. Should their sales effort be directed to the advertiser or advertising agency or both, and which individuals in these organisations should they contact? Here the detailed structure of the advertiser and agency, described in the following chapters, becomes significant.

The direction of selling is affected by client/agency relationships. Deciding which individual should be the target for sales effort may be a problem as sometimes more than one individual, or even a committee, is concerned. Advertisers employ agencies for their expert advice and experience, but this generalisation masks numerous possible variations. Division of the budget into 'above the line' expenditure handled by the agency and a 'below the line' budget handled by the client can vary from case to case, depending on each client's expertise and inclination, and the expertise of his agency. Even with 'above the line' expenditure by agency planners on the more conventional advertising media, client/agency relationships can vary, thus influencing the media-owner's selling activity.

Much depends on the relative dominance of the advertising department and agency. In some relationships the agency is the dominant partner, planning and executing the campaign, the client paying the more passive role of briefing the agency on the problem, and checking and approving the proposals. With a number of companies, however, particularly those with strong marketing orientation, the tendency is for the advertiser to adopt the more dominant role. Where a company's marketing manager is responsible for the full range of marketing activities (including advertising, selling, merchandising and sales promotion, research and even product policy and pricing) it follows that the client/agency relationship must differ from cases where the advertising manager is responsible for advertising alone.

Marketing-orientated companies are not necessarily dominant in every aspect of advertising and marketing: all depends on the relative strength and expertise of the individuals in both advertising department and agency. Furthermore, a change in staffing on either side could result in a shift in this pattern of dominance: another reason why it is so vital for media-owners to keep up-to-date with staff changes.

The background and experience of the individuals concerned influences the approach as well as the direction of media selling. When calling on an advertising manager, for example, much depends on his specialist expertise (or any weaknesses in his knowledge). By definition, an advertising manager should have an all-round knowledge of advertising matters, but clearly any individual must be more expert on some topics than others, and will therefore be more searching in his questions on his special advertising interest. An advertising manager who trained originally as a copywriter or visualiser is bound to have a different outlook from one whose background is research or media. One will be influenced by the creative possibilities of the medium, while the other will make a far more statistical assessment. Clearly the approach made by the media representative must vary accordingly, and for this reason a thorough personal knowledge of prospects is essential. The same is true when calling on an agency account executive.

On contacting a client's advertising manager, the media representative will frequently be referred to the agency. The key figure through whom the client makes contact with all the agency specialists is the account executive and so, naturally enough, his is the name mentioned when referring representatives to the agency. Many representatives make the understandable mistake of insisting on speaking only to the named executive, and virtually refusing to accede to his request to contact the agency's media department. This practice is likely to upset both parties: the executive wants the expert advice of his media department and not constant phonecalls from the media representative, however well-meaning he may be; and equally the media planners are unlikely to view favourably any media representative unwilling to speak to them initially, and then doing so only with an attitude of 'second best'. By all means media representatives should maintain contact with the account executive, but they should remember that he relies on the advice of his media department and directs their selling efforts accordingly.

When contacting the agency's media department, many representatives find themselves unable to decide *who* to speak to – group heads, media planners, media buyers, media assessors, media researchers or any of the other titles that abound in agencies. With the growth of global agency networks handling world-wide accounts strategic planning may be undertaken centrally, with local offices having varying degrees of autonomy within the overall plan. These arrangements vary from advertiser to advertiser and from agency to agency and the representative must be aware of the nuances of control. The various media department structures and the wide variety of organisation patterns described in Chapter 10 make it difficult to give general advice, but many media-owners have found it helpful to extend their central records to include information about advertisers and agencies. Thorough and continuous investigation into which people are influential in media decisions can build up a 'structure chart' for advertiser and/or agency. In this way, the record can show the names of the advertising manager, the account executive, media planners or buyers and so on. More important, 'weights' can be allocated to each (just as media planners often assess media) according to the relative influence each has on media decisions. Where different representatives from the same medium call on the same agency, media-owners often build up a structure chart for each agency in the same way, based on the combined view of all the representatives concerned. The structure chart can then be up-dated as necessary, to take account of staff changes.

Media/agency/client contacts

There are occasions when the representative may feel that his medium has not received the attention it merits in the client's media schedule, and he therefore seriously considers that his case could not have been adequately presented to the client, or was insufficiently considered by the agency. It is usually advisable for the representative to be open with his views, rather than go to the client 'behind the agency's back' or to try to play off client against agency (or account executive against media department). A clear statement of his case to the agency, with adequate reasoning as to why the schedule should be revised to include his medium, will have more effect than complaining to the client, quite apart from any ill-will that may be caused. Agencies do not often make mistakes, but they do occur from time to time, and an agency would naturally prefer to correct its own error, rather than have it pointed out by their client at a media-owner's prompting. If, after requesting the agency to review the position, the media-owner feels that his case has not received due consideration, the representative should most certainly go direct to the client, but should pay the agency media staff the courtesy of notifying them of his intention to do so. And the media representative should make sure he *has* got a case to present – many representatives are, understandably, over-enthusiastic and biased towards their own medium, perhaps in excess of its merits. Advertising managers do not like to have their time taken up reviewing situations that have already been considered by their agency. The media representative may see the advertising manager the first time but, unless he feels the visit was justified, the chances are that the media representative will not be so lucky on the next occasion. All being well, however, this selling activity will result in an order being placed, and attention should now be focused on the media-owner's next task.

Confirming the orders

Most media-owners keep some form of 'space register', or 'flat plan', showing the amount of advertising space available for sale in future issues. This shows the total amount and sub-divides it into run-of-paper and special positions (or their equivalent for other media). The register must be kept up-to-date so that the advertisement manager and his representative can see at any moment what space has already been sold and what is still available. Leaving space unsold, through oversight rather than through lack of effort, means loss of potential advertising revenue.

Immediately an order is received it must be checked carefully for accuracy of vital facts such as size, position, cost, discounts, etc, and to ensure that the order has been duly signed and is correct in every way. This done, the order must be checked against the register to see if the space requested is in fact available. For run-of-paper insertions this is a straightforward operation, a simple check that total bookings do not exceed the amount of space available. For special positions, however, the operation is more complex since it means placing a named advertiser in a particular position in the medium. Such positions can be sold only once, and considerable ill-will would result if the same space were promised to two advertisers. It might even lead to future business from one advertiser going to another medium, perhaps less suitable, but where it was certain to appear as promised. Reliability was one of the criteria for comparison discussed in Part 1.

The space register is of vital importance even before an order is received, for its accuracy may determine whether or not the order is placed. With many media the space register is used by representatives who telephone in during discussions with advertiser and agency, and make immediate bookings based on the information given. Under such circumstances, information must be literally up-to-the-minute.

Space registers are maintained by publishers, and owners of other media have similar systems. Television and radio contractors, for example, have 'time registers' showing the booking position for commercial breaks between programmes. Poster contractors must know their site bookings, and be able to say which will become available and when. Even where the medium has a high production and service content, such as direct mail, and there is no top limit to the amount of advertising that can be sold, the direct mail houses must know when their various machines are fully occupied, and when they have capacity to accept further work.

Immediately the order has been checked against the register, an appropriate entry must be made and the order duly acknowledged, either by returning the tear-off slip which may be incorporated in the order, or by sending the media-owner's own acknowledgement form. Most media-owners use computers for the detailed record-keeping and some communicate directly with major agencies using a dedicated computer system to complete the administration involved in buying advertising time or space. Two actions then follow: the production staff must obtain the necessary material, and the advertisement department must consider where best to place each advertisement, and decide upon the most suitable 'make-up'.

Production and creative services

Advertising material must be obtained from the advertiser or his agency. Even when this is received well in advance of copy date, the prudent media-owner checks all material immediately it arrives: is it of the right size and type, and does the advertisement conform to the various voluntary codes and legal restrictions, and to any rules that the media-owner himself imposes? Advertisers and agencies have thorough administrative systems but the possibility of errors still exists, so material must be checked without delay. Should the material be at fault, prompt notification enables the client or his agency to rectify the mistake and supply correct material. It will be too late to check at the last minute, as there would then not be time for errors to be corrected. For other media, similar action is involved, according to the production process.

To minimise the likelihood of mistakes occurring in production, an advertiser or agency may provide advertising material in the form of complete artwork, films or, increasingly, in electronic form on disk or by ISDN (Integrated Systems Digital Network) telephone lines direct to the publication or the printer. Even where the advertiser or his agency supplies a complete advertisement, its appearance in the medium still involves some production work. With press media, for example, the advertisement must be inserted in the appropriate place in the medium and correctly printed. For other media, similarly straightforward production work is involved.

Frequently, however, additional services are called for, particularly by smaller advertisers. Where a complete advertisement is not supplied, but only typed or even hand-written copy, the media-owner must undertake typesetting and is thus involved in more production work. Indeed, without this production work it would be impossible to accept the advertisement.

The service may extend to creative work and some media employ special staff to prepare creative suggestions for prospective advertisers, so that their representatives can submit copy and design proposals. Alternatively the representatives themselves may prepare these creative suggestions.

Creative and production services may equally be provided by other media. Many television and radio contractors offer facilities for special 'budget' commercials, quoting special low all-inclusive rates covering scripting, actors, studio and production. The same applies to the cinema, where stock films may be available which local advertisers can purchase at much less expense than they would incur in producing a film for themselves, and which they can personalise by including their own name and address. Direct mail houses similarly extend their services beyond production alone, and offer creative advice to those using their medium.

It is not only for inexperienced advertisers, who for lack of expert staff might be precluded from advertising, that media-owners provide these creative and production services. In other cases, media-owners have virtually been forced into such activity to safeguard their own interest. Some media-owners, for example, have encountered advertisers who do not take full advantage of the creative possibilities of the medium and, in extreme cases, produce advertisements that are actually *negative* in effect. Clearly the advertiser would receive little or no benefit from his campaign in such circumstances and would decide, wrongly, that there was no point in using the medium, since it had 'proved' itself ineffective. Incredible though it may seem, this was the case in the early days of television, when many advertisers withdrew from the medium for this very reason. Direct mail houses still find the same thing today. Some media-owners therefore extend their facilities, taking the more positive attitude of ensuring that their advertisers produce effective advertisements, and no longer take the more passive role of providing help only when asked. Action such as this is, of course, self-defence for the media-owner since if the advertisements do not bring results he will not get repeat orders.

Preparing the make-up

Where advertisers have booked special positions the problem of make-up does not arise, since the location of such advertisements is determined by the booking. Many advertisements, on the other hand, are booked on a 'run of paper' basis and it is left to the advertisement department to place these in the most suitable position. And to do so is in the advertisement department's own interest as well as being a service the advertiser expects, for a well-placed advertisement results in better response, and thus greater likelihood of a repeat order. Clearly an advertisement for a garden product is better placed on the gardening page and a car on the motoring page, than *vice versa*. Such obvious cases speak for themselves but, in practice, positioning is usually more difficult and the advertisement department finds it a problem to satisfy all the conflicting calls for right-hand page, top of column, outside edge, front half of publication, and similar requests. Once the detailed make-up is decided, however, the media-owner can then proceed to the next stage.

Final proofs

The production staff proceed simultaneously with two separate tasks - editorial and advertising. The advertisement department's make-up, placing advertisements next to the most favourable editorial, serves as production's guide in placing the advertisements in position. Further proofs are produced by computer but not circulated to advertisers, since they are for internal use only. Their purpose is to ensure that all is in order and that no mistake had slipped through the previous careful checks. The advertisement department may, for example, have sold space in the belief that a 25 cm × 2 cols advertisement is to appear on a given page, while the editorial staff have designed on the assumption that space was needed only for a 20 cm × 2 cols advertisement. Or perhaps, through a production slip by advertiser and agency, an advertisement of the wrong column width was sent in error and, through an equally unfortunate error, this was not noticed on receipt. Again, page proofs may reveal that two advertisements containing coupons have been placed back to back: under such circumstances neither advertiser could get maximum results and the advertisement department would lose revenue by having to give both advertisers a rebate.

Page proofs may also bring to light unfortunate positioning which may have to be corrected: the advertisement department's make-up may have placed an advertisement for holidays abroad on a general news page, but if the news of the day happens to describe riots or some other unfortunate event in the country concerned, the tour operator would not be at all happy to see his advertisement next to news that must inevitably reduce response to his offer. Events or mistakes such as these are rare, but the possibility that they may occur nevertheless exists; hence the rule for the media-owner – just as much as for the advertiser and agency – is meticulous checking and double-checking to remove all possibility of error. If all goes well, no last-minute changes will be necessary and publication can proceed.

Publication

Copies must be printed and physically distributed to newsagents or subscribers. Television and radio programmes and commercials must be transmitted, and cinema films screened. Although the advertisement department is not directly concerned with this side of affairs, its activities still depend on the successful completion of this vital stage: the actual communication of advertisements to the media audience. Immediately the advertisements appear, the accounts department must be given all the information they need to invoice advertisers correctly.

Invoicing and voucher copies

The advertisers or their agencies must be invoiced before they will pay, and the invoicing task is to ensure that every advertiser is charged at the correct rate for each appearance of his advertisement. A smoothly operating accounts department avoids any loss of advertisement revenue through failure to invoice, and directly affects the speed of payment. Invoice queries by advertisers or agencies often cause ill-will or frayed tempers, and hold up payment. Delayed settlement can cost money in bank charges, and if settlement of many invoices is held up the consequent shortage of funds could place the media-owner in a difficult financial position.

Equally important is an efficient voucher service, for before the advertiser or agency will settle the invoice they will want to check that their advertising appeared as booked. The voucher may sometimes take the form of a 'tear sheet' rather than a full copy of the publications. With some media it may not be possible to provide a voucher copy or physical proof of appearance, in which case the media-owner may send a 'certificate of transmission (or of posting)' or some other assurance that the advertising has appeared. Failure to send the necessary voucher copy or certificate means that payment of the invoice is delayed until this omission is rectified. The smooth functioning of the voucher section is just as important as an efficient accounts department: the purpose of all this activity is receipt of advertisement revenue.

Follow-up

Once the advertisements have been invoiced, do not imagine that the operation is complete and the way now clear for further selling. Adequate follow-up of the issue just published is essential. The representatives who obtained each advertisement should check them with as much attention as the advertisers and their agencies will devote to them. Did the advertisements print well? What ratings did the television commercials receive? Did the exhibitor have an attractive stand? Evaluation of results, with a view to improving future performance, is of major importance to both advertiser and agency, and advertisement representatives, in selling future issues, must be equally concerned with the advertisement which has just appeared. This also provides them with the ideal opportunity to seek repeat orders.

The new issue

The financial circle mentioned at the start of this chapter has now been completed. All being well, this should be a beneficial upward spiral. Every issue of their own medium, and competitive media, present opportunities to follow-up previous advertising and affords scope for new sales, which means we are now considering the operation of the advertisement department from the same point at which we started.

Chapter 9

Role of the Advertiser

The actual tasks of the advertising manager which, overall, make for good advertising, are:

1 *Situation analysis* Gathering the company, product and market data essential for effective planning.
2 *Advertising strategy* Deciding your campaign objective, which directly effects both media selection and the creative approach to be featured.
3 *Budgeting* Fixing the advertising appropriation, so that you spend the right amount in achieving your chosen objective.
4 *Preparation of advertising proposals* Planning an advertising campaign, creating advertisements and selecting media, to achieve your determined objective.
5 *Approval of proposals* Checking, prior to executing the campaign, that your proposals are likely to be successful.
6 *Execution of these proposals* Putting your plan into effect.
7 *Follow through* Ensuring that the company is geared up to cope with the response generated by your advertising.
8 *Evaluation of results* Checking that you received value for money, and seeing what lessons can be learned for the future.

This process is a closed loop, and evaluation of the results of this year's campaign should provide additional information on which to base next year's planning. All these tasks will be examined in detail in Part 3. This chapter, however, reviews the role of the advertising manager and how he can best tackle them.

ADVERTISING IN PERSPECTIVE

Before examining how the advertising manager sets about his tasks, consider for a moment the goods or services to be sold. Advertising will *not* sell poor merchandise: if it does, buyers will soon realise that the goods are of poor quality, there will be no repeat purchases and the harm done goes beyond your initial sales. Advertising should therefore never be used to sell 'mistakes'. If customers will not buy goods when they see them on the shelves, why on earth should they buy them just because they are advertised? This point is stressed because manufacturers or retailers do sometimes try to clear dead stock through advertising, and then blame advertising when no sales result. Clearance items can be featured with profit from time to time, at attractive bargain prices, but these are special cases. For advertising to be effective, it must offer customers a benefit, such as a new or improved product, lower prices, or newly arrived stocks. Thus a first essential for effective advertising is a good product.

The second essential is that your products must be made known to the right people. This is, perhaps, obvious, but there is no point in telling people about goods which are of no use to them, however much of a bargain is offered. So careful consideration of your 'market' is another essential. If potential purchasers do not know of your merchandise they will not buy it, hence effective advertising means telling the right people about the right goods.

With the right merchandise and the right people to inform, a third consideration is the right means of conveying information to these people. There are many ways to reach prospective customers with your advertising message (and this book concentrates on how to use them effectively). There is no *one* medium that is best – they all reach different markets by different methods. So it is vital for you to select the advertising medium that reaches the people you want, and which will deliver your advertising message most effectively. Correct media selection is therefore vital to effective advertising.

A fourth essential in planning advertising is to get the right message. If you have the right goods, know who your prospective purchasers are and have the means of contacting them, then for successful advertising your message must attract their attention and convey your product's benefits. Hence great care must be paid to the wording of your advertisement, the choice of illustration and the overall layout.

Fifthly, but of equal importance, is timing. Advertisements that appear too early or too late, before your customer is in a position to think about buying or after the purchase has been made, are wasteful.

Finally, your goods must be readily available in the shops when the customers go to buy. Any weakness in distribution will result in your advertising merely increasing your *competitor's* sales, for the retailer – rather than lose his profit – will recommend an alternative brand.

In short, for your advertising to be effective, careful planning must ensure that several factors are right:

Right products – which people would buy if they knew about them.
Right people – to whom your product is of interest.
Right media – which reach these people effectively.
Right message – which conveys your product's benefits.
Right time – when your potential customers are likely to buy.
Right distribution – when your goods are available in the shops.

A Jewish colleague once illustrated this by remarking that there was no point in trying to sell bacon to Jews by advertising in the Catholic Herald on a Friday! Amusing though this anecdote is, it does not cover *all* the essential 'rights' – it stresses wrong product to wrong market in wrong medium at wrong time, but ignores the vital matter of message. This omission nevertheless only reinforces the importance of right product and right market, for *no* advertising message, however brilliantly created, could ever persuade people to buy a product that is forbidden them. Another omission is right budget, so you do not spend too much or too little on achieving your objective.

This planning of 'rights' is an over-simplification, but it does make clear the need for planning. It is vital that your advertising is carefully planned. Advertising is not a separate operation unconnected with your company's other marketing activities: advertising, sales and display effort must all be co-ordinated. With careful planning, advertising expenditure is controlled and spent to best advantage, and ensures results that bring profits which more than pay for the advertising. Part 3 describes how this planned advertising can best be achieved.

THE CHANGING STRUCTURE OF THE ADVERTISING DEPARTMENT

The structure of the advertising department will vary with the firm and with circumstances, and the background to such changes must now be considered. Advertising is no longer treated in isolation: advertising and marketing activities now play an important role in influencing overall policy rather than merely reflecting it. Advertising and marketing executives are found on Boards of Directors and the status of their departments has changed accordingly.

Another aspect of change relates to the range of work carried out by the advertising department, whose manager may find himself with responsibilities such as public relations, merchandising, marketing, sales promotion and market research. Again the structure varies: in some firms, one individual controls all these activities and his title (and that of his department) changes accordingly, while in others they are

166

divided among two or more executives, each the head of his own department.

Whatever the structure, it is essential that all these activities interlock: unless advertising ties in with merchandising, sales promotion and public relations in aiming to achieve the identical marketing objective, it is impossible for advertising media to be used to maximum effect. For this reason, we should examine these allied activities.

Public Relations

The chapter on Other Media stressed the importance of giving attention to both editorial and advertising columns. Press relations is an important part of PR. The Institute of Public Relations defines PR as 'the deliberate, planned and sustained effort to establish and maintain goodwill and mutual understanding between an organisation and its publics'. Advertising is one of the tools used to achieve mutual understanding, but public relations is another far broader one which covers every contact made by the organisation in every field.

To illustrate its wide scope, take the launch of a new product by your company. Certainly you would need to inform the public and forewarn retailers, and public and trade press advertising would play a key role in ensuring public and retailer acceptance of your new product. Public relations activities, however, operate on a much wider front, for the new product is also 'news' and the editors of consumer and trade publications need information to keep their readers up-to-date. The same applies to other media such as television and radio.

It would be a great mistake, however, to regard editorial mentions as 'free advertising' and to set about public relations work with the intention of 'getting something for nothing'. Instead, you must consider the special requirements of each editor and what will interest his readers. The art of good press relations is knowing just what is of news value to different media, and so presenting the editors with the information *they* want, in the form they want it, and in good time for them to use it. Sending out extra copies of a News Release to all and sundry publications in the belief that 'they may use it, and it only costs a stamp' will, in fact, do your firm a disservice. Editors who repeatedly receive useless News Releases from the same source will, before long, no longer bother to read them. Then, when something occurs which is of genuine interest, your Release will not get the attention it would otherwise have received. Editors are busy people, working under pressure against the clock, and cannot be expected to waste their time reading releases in the hope that one in a hundred will be of interest.

Public relations activity does not end with the issue of News Releases but covers any contact, on any topics of interest, with the different sections of your public. Many people will be personally affected by the new development, and should be told directly of its implications rather than being left to read about it by chance. Those on the factory floor will want to know about the new product and the sales staff will be equally interested. Many other staff divisions – such as warehouse, despatch and accounts – will want to know how the new product affects their work and, even outside the firm itself, there will be many sections of the community affected by or interested in your new product. Retailers and wholesalers, for example, will be directly interested, as will be the suppliers of raw materials or machinery, while your company's shareholders will most certainly want to know how their money is being spent. In each of these cases there is need for public relations activity to ensure a flow of clear information – a flow which, in the Institute's definition, is deliberate, planned and sustained. Failing this there could be lack of mutual understanding and, in extreme cases, even ill-will, all of which could have been avoided had you taken the trouble to inform people of what was going on, rather than leaving them to find out for themselves.

Public Relations practice in depth is not the subject of this book, although it does cover *every* contact, and not only those made as a result of paid-for advertising. Playing a vital part in your firm's operations, it demands top-level attention and in some organisations public relations work is linked with that of the advertising manager. In others, it is developed to such a scale that a full-time public relations officer is necessary, often with his own department. Alternatively public relations consultants may be employed, or the advertising agency's PR service used. Clearly then there is a variety of ways in which your company's public relations can be safeguarded and promoted: the important thing is that this must never be neglected and must integrate with other activities, if advertising media are to make their full contribution to achieving your business objective.

Merchandising and Sales Promotion

The advertising manager's responsibilities may also extend to merchandising and sales promotion, since an advertising campaign's success depends as much on your goods being in the shops at the right time, or on potential purchasers actually *trying* the product, as on the effectiveness of the creative work and media schedule. Many companies ensure that their advertising is backed up by extensive merchandising and sales promotion campaigns. These tasks may be undertaken by the advertising manager as an additional responsibility, separate merchandising and sales promotion managers may be appointed, or the work may be shared with the appropriate section of the company's advertising agency or with outside services.

Sales Promotion is defined by the *Institute of Sales Promotion* as 'comprising a range of tactical marketing techniques designed within a strategic marketing framework to add value to a product or service in order to achieve specific sales and marketing objectives'.

For planning purposes, however, it is better to separate what has been grouped together under the single heading of 'sales promotion' since this does not distinguish between two very different objectives. In consequence, I offer an alternative definition: 'Activities which pull people towards products, or which push products towards people.'

Sales Promotion

To stimulate trial by potential new purchasers, to encourage brand loyalty among existing customers, or to persuade purchasers of rival products to switch brands, manufacturers often mount sales promotions such as product and price offers (including banded packs and free samples), coupons, free and paid-for gifts, prizes (including competitions, free draws and instant win offers), editorial offers and charity linked promotions as well as in-store demonstrations, offers of informative booklets or any of a host of other incentives which can serve as useful devices for pulling potential customers towards your products.

Having stimulated the market through advertising (supplemented by appropriate public relations and sales promotion campaigns) what a waste of time if potential customers then find that retailers know nothing about your new product or free trial offer, or are not prepared to redeem your coupons! So, in addition to your public campaign, there should be a second campaign aimed at your distributors.

Merchandising

Before retailers will stock or display new merchandise they must be convinced that the line will sell. This means stimulating their enthusiasm by telling them of your forthcoming advertising and the demand it will create, and persuading them to stock and display the new product.

To secure maximum distributor co-operation in pushing your products, your 'dealer campaign' might include trade press advertisements, sales letters telling of future consumer advertising, and the provision of display material. There may also be arrangements for 'co-operative advertising' in which retailers join your firm in local media advertising, perhaps on a shared-cost basis, to announce that they stock the advertised brand. For retailers unskilled in display, you may provide a special window-dressing service. In addition, there might be competitions for best performance, dealer conferences, and 'stocking-up bonuses' or other financial incentives. All these activities can be grouped under the heading of merchandising, in that they aim to make sure your products have wide distribution and are well displayed in the shops when your advertising campaign breaks on the public.

Merchandising can also help your company's salesforce in persuading retailers to stock and display the goods. Accordingly, for effective marketing, your salesforce must be kept fully informed.

Sales force activity

The vital links with distributors, or indeed with customers direct, are your sales representatives, so merchandising activities should extend to them: they then push products towards distributors, who in turn push them towards ultimate purchasers. Many of the same merchandising techniques apply, but this time aimed at sales staff rather than wholesalers or retailers.

Promotion plans may include a sales conference at which your production manager explains the new product range, the sales manager talks about sales targets, and the advertising manager – aided perhaps by the agency – outlines the advertising campaign. The advertisements and media schedule are shown to the sales staff and the thinking behind your advertising explained. The purpose is to make sure that all representatives know of and understand the advertising support that will back up their sales efforts. And it is of vital importance that representatives *do* understand the campaign, for even when a product is widely advertised it cannot be bought until it is in the shops, and shopkeepers will not stock it unless the sales staff have convinced them it will sell.

The trend towards re-engineering company structures highlighted the high cost of running a sales force and led many manufacturers to review the number of salesmen employed. The result is increased use of less costly methods of communicating with lower priority customers, particularly through advertising supported direct marketing.

The consumer advertising campaign can thus serve as an additional means of persuading retailers to stock and display your lines, and a portfolio containing specimen advertisements and details of your media schedule can be used as a sales aid when making presentations to potential stockists or mailed direct to them.

Although separated for ease of analysis, advertising, merchandising, public relations and sales promotion are not watertight compartments, and there is no hard and fast line between one activity and another. Advertising might be the means of announcing a sales promotion incentive (which also achieves editorial mention through effective press relations). Response to the offer may in turn serve a merchandising function, by providing leads for sales representatives. These many activities also clearly influence mutual understanding, and thus have public relations implications. The important thing is for your company to consider all aspects of marketing communications: this in turn has direct implications for the role of the advertising manager.

Marketing

The Chartered Institute of Marketing has adopted the following definition:

'Marketing is the management process responsible for identifying, anticipating and satisfying customer requirements profitably.'

Marketing thus directly influences the work of the advertising manager. Sometimes his work is linked with that of the marketing manager, or both functions might be united in a single post – perhaps with the added responsibilities of public relations, merchandising and sales promotion, and market research.

The modern concept of marketing has in fact revolutionised production and selling. In the early days of large-scale production, a firm manufactured a product, the sales manager sold it and the advertising manager devised a suitable campaign. Their joint effort was aimed at achieving sales of a product already in production. Salesmen perhaps passed back any comments they received from retailers regarding public reaction to the product or, more recently, there may have been some research to define the market and to learn consumer attitudes to the product. Then, on the basis of this somewhat meagre information, the company or its agency designed the pack and planned the advertising campaign. In essence, however, all this activity was aimed at selling a product already produced: in other words, the product came first and was followed by the selling and advertising decisions.

This brief description over-simplifies the process, but serves to illustrate how the modern concept of marketing has meant a complete reversal of this attitude. Instead of manufacturing a product and then selling it, marketing now attempts to locate and define a need and to ascertain in advance in what size, shape, colour, packaging and at what price consumers would most want the product. Only then does marketing assess how best to produce, distribute and promote the product itself. Thus, long before any production facilities exist, and when the idea is still at concept stage, marketing plans the complete production and selling operation. Research ascertains the form and

171

quantity that will best suit the market: an obvious prerequisite to production, for how else can management decide what facilities are necessary to manufacture the product in the right quantities, and in the packaging and at the price required? Marketing also considers distribution of the product, the type of retail outlets, trade discount and sales force structure, and the degree of emphasis to be placed on advertising and personal selling.

Today, most marketing plans go even further: they look to the future by attempting to predict your product's life cycle (introduction, growth, maturity and decline), and also include research and development activity to improve existing products as well as providing new products for your company to market in the future.

Marketing unites advertising, selling, market research and many other activities. None of these is new: the only new concept is linking these various activities under the common heading of marketing. The marketing man must have a full appreciation of the parts played by market research, production, packaging, price, advertising, personal selling, merchandising, sales promotion, and distribution in successfully producing and selling his company's lines and in planning future products. Sales and advertising departments have always been complementary, but the new concept of marketing is leading to these 'separate' activities being united under a single marketing director, who controls a number of executives responsible for various aspects of the marketing mix, or brand managers responsible for individual products within the range. Even in companies where sales and advertising remain separate, the concept of marketing implies that the staff in both departments must work in close co-operation, fully 'market-orientated' and conscious that the all-important factor is not what they wish to sell but what the customer wants to buy. The two are not necessarily the same and, where there is a difference, it is increasingly rare for the manufacturer to regard his view as the dominant one. The consumer is sovereign and has freedom of choice: maximum profitability for the company must be balanced by a corresponding satisfaction for its customers.

Direct and Database Marketing

Marketing itself is changing: direct marketing has increased partly through increased use of direct mail. Direct mail, a formerly static medium, has undergone major changes in the light of new technology, particularly the computerisation of mailing lists. This situation is very much chicken-and-egg – has use of direct mail grown because of increased direct marketing, or has direct marketing increased because of improved direct mail technology?

Direct marketing has been described as *'any activity which creates and profitably exploits a direct relationship between seller and prospect.'* Its two essential requirements are recording names and addresses, and measurement of results – both of which directly affect advertising planning, and in particular the use of direct mail.

The new concept of database marketing is rooted in an old philosophy – that of getting closer to your customers. An organisation which identifies its customers, understands and meets their needs, and treats these customers well, will do well even in the most competitive environment – and database marketing is basically a sophisticated new means of serving this old philosophy. Its principles apply particularly to direct mail advertising but are equally relevant to other aspects of marketing: the same approach can increase salesforce or telemarketing effectiveness, with results fed back into the same database.

A mailing list should be more than a collection of names and addresses; it should be a complete database of your target markets. Information is usually stored on computer, and arranged so that:

- Your records contain purchasing history as well as names and addresses and other customer details.
- Different sections of your list are readily identifiable, by purchasing patterns or other criteria.
- The database includes promotional history – which customers were targeted, type of company, number of employees, what messages were delivered through which media, who responded, when and how?
- It is regularly up-dated – lapsed customers identified and removed, and new enquiries/purchases or address changes etc entered as soon as possible.
- Addresses are postcoded, for efficiency of mailing – as the earlier reference to *Mailsort* made clear, there are valuable discounts for those who carry out sortation work that would otherwise be undertaken by the Royal Mail. Database marketing can thus help stretch your advertising budget even further, quite apart from improving campaign effectiveness.

The final stage of advertising planning, evaluation of results, applies particularly to database marketing. Your advertising campaign can result in off-the-page sales or enquiries which serve as sales leads, which in turn permit a tracking system far more sophisticated than simply recording cash sales or enquiries, and enquiries converted into orders. The database should not only specify goods sold but should also analyse purchases in 'Recency, Frequency and Value' terms, as well as including conventional data such as age, sex, socio-economic group, and geodemographic classification or location. These details, fed back into your database, then serve as an integrated information system.

An effective database enables you to maximise customer potential, and to:

- select individual customers whose records indicate they are ripe for possible repeat purchases
- select those whose purchase patterns suggest that they are prospects for other products/services in your range
- apply regional or timing controls to your direct mail activities
- send these selected customers a personalised message, related to their individual needs
- select specific market segments for further advertising attention.

With conventional marketing, market segmentation is often achieved by 'desegregating' large market groups into smaller target categories, whereas database marketing achieves accurate segmentation in the opposite way – by aggregating individual customer records.

This information can help target 'cold' mailings to potential customers with whom you have had no previous contact. Such new lists should of course be merged and purged against those names already on your records, the response to mailings evaluated, and your database adjusted accordingly.

Database marketing can help you move these potential new customers up a five-rung 'ladder of loyalty', leading them through five market stages:

1. *Suspects* – potential customers who have not yet indicated an interest in your product or service, but who merit a 'cold' mailing
2. *Prospects* – those recipients who have indicated interest, but not yet purchased
3. *Customers* – those who have purchased
4. *Loyal customers* – those who buy regularly
5. *Advocates* – those beyond passive brand loyalty, who actively recommend your product or service to others.

Apart from these advertising applications, database marketing also improves salesforce effectiveness, as it can:

- assist with call and journey planning
- facilitate effective telemarketing
- produce pre-call briefing documents for sales representatives
- standardise post-call reporting.

Database marketing is thus not just a means of communicating with customers, but rather a new way of defining supplier/customer/

advertising relationships. It is also a new way of doing business that provides marketing and management information: database marketing could eventually replace conventional market research through advertising campaigns planned to provide all necessary information by seeking and measuring customer response. By mapping market trends, database marketing helps ensure opportunities and threats are swiftly identified, and speeds up the process of capturing these market opportunities and neutralising any threats. The system can also provide management ratios, such as advertising expenditure to enquiries, enquiries converted to actual sales, and average order value. It can further help evaluate both media and messages.

The database approach thus serves as a functional basis for management and marketing planning, salesforce control and telemarketing, just as much as for direct mail and other advertising. It can also help you to co-ordinate these separate activities so that they all interlock to maximum effect.

A final but extremely important point relates to external constraints on your direct marketing activities. A later chapter discusses the *British Code of Advertising and Sales Promotion* in general terms, but it should be noted here that it includes specific rules on list and database practice, and also refers to the Data Protection Act and the Mailing Preference Service. The European Union has, for some time, been drafting a Direct Selling Directive which could have a dramatic effect on your ability to use direct marketing. This potential for change proves a point repeatedly made throughout this book: the vital need to keep up-to-date with new developments.

Marketing Research

When database marketing is not applicable, the purpose of market research is to provide information which will help advertisers anticipate consumer needs so that they can decide how to satisfy these needs in a profitable way, and the need to adopt a marketing approach has already made clear the vital role of research in locating and defining consumer needs. The many different applications of marketing research, and the various ways in which information can be obtained, call for major attention and cannot be covered within the scope of this book. All that need be said here is that research may be an additional task for the advertising manager, or it may be the responsibility of the marketing manager, perhaps through a specialist market research manager, through the research department of the advertising agency or through an independent market research company.

ADMINISTRATION OF THE ADVERTISING DEPARTMENT

The advertising manager as head of a department

The advertising manager is head of a department just as much as the head of production, sales, transport or any other section: he thus has responsibility for staffing his department, and its size depends to a great extent on whether or not any advertising agency is employed.

Where the firm does not use an advertising agency, the advertising manager must have in his department creative staff to prepare the advertisements, or be in touch with freelance workers on whom he can call. Similarly he must be able to deal with the work of media selection, planning and booking, and the physical production of advertisements.

Even where this work is undertaken by an advertising agency (or by the creative and media independents described in later chapters), it does not follow that there is no staffing problem for the advertising department. Careful control must still be kept of schedules, accurate records maintained of the company's advertising, and voucher copies and invoices checked. Perhaps the advertisements call for readers to fill in a coupon. This simple request involves a vast amount of work in sending out booklets, sorting out the coupons and perhaps passing them on to the firm's representatives as sales leads, and analysing the response to the campaign. Responsibility for advertising involves a great deal of executive, creative and purely routine administrative work, even when an agency is employed. Division of work between advertiser and agency varies but, whatever the circumstances, the advertising manager must ensure he has staff to cope with whatever work he accepts as his responsibility.

Agency selection and liaison

The advantages and disadvantages of using an agency will be covered in the next chapter, but clearly the decision whether or not to employ an agency rests largely with the advertising manager and he will be called upon to advise his Board of Directors accordingly. If it is decided to do so he will be responsible for selecting a suitable agency, negotiating arrangements for handling his advertising, and for briefing the agency on his company's requirements. After this briefing he will throughout the campaign work closely with the agency team in the preparation and execution of proposals, and the evaluation of their results.

The importance of agency liaison must never be under-estimated and, in fact, it largely depends on the client's advertising manager whether or not the agency produces a good scheme. There is no question of the advertising manager sitting back and leaving everything to the agency, for even the finest agency, staffed by experts in every specialist branch of advertising, can give of its best only if it receives full backing and co-operation from the client.

Division of work

Some advertisers rely on their agency for the full range of advertising media, while others undertake part of the work themselves. More usually, 'above the line' media such as press, television, radio, cinema and outdoor advertising come within the agency's orbit, while control of other media may rest with either party. 'Below the line' media such as exhibitions, direct mail and display material are frequently retained under the advertising department's direct control, even when an agency is employed. Some advertisers adopt a policy of dividing their appropriation into two parts: an 'above the line' budget to be spent by the agency and a 'below the line' budget which is retained by the advertising department. There is no uniformity about where the client's work ends and the agency's starts, and much depends on the staffing arrangements the advertising manager considers most effective under the circumstances in which his firm operates.

The size and structure of the advertising department

There is no limit to the variety of structures within different companies' advertising departments. A firm may or may not employ an advertising agency and, either way, the advertising manager may rely on only a few staff or alternatively he may have a large department containing numbers of expert staff, equivalent to a fully-equipped agency. The advertising manager may in fact have in his department a number of specialists who are the counterparts of the agency experts. Many large advertisers, who have centralised their media planning/buying into a single agency, employ a media manager to co-ordinate these activities. Similarly, agency creative proposals are checked by creative staff, production budgets by production experts, research proposals by research staff and so on, with the advertising manager in overall control and taking an overall view. Alternatively, these experts may undertake the full advertising task without outside assistance.

Where a company has several different divisions or products, there may well be separate advertising departments, each under its own advertising manager and co-ordinated by an advertising director. Each of these departments may produce its part of the company's advertising without agency assistance, but in other cases the advertising departments may employ one or more advertising agencies.

177

In some cases, this structure may be extended to include the media independents (described below). One company used four separate advertising agencies for its four separate divisions. Since all four advertised heavily on television, the company then employed a media independent to co-ordinate their activities and to prevent any possibility of the divisions wasting valuable resources in pre-empting each other's television spots.

There is thus a wide variety of organisational patterns, but there is certainly no question of one business structure being 'better' than others: each firm adopts the organisational pattern most suited to its circumstances and adapts itself as the business world, and the firm itself, changes. The advertising manager must consider future expansion, perhaps caused by additional products to be marketed and, reverting to his role as head of a department, must recruit and train new staff and/or review his agency arrangements accordingly.

In-house or agency?

There are, as always, advantages and drawbacks to both in-house and agency operations. What is not always immediately apparent is that one is the converse of the other: the advantages of agency service, reviewed in the next chapter, are the drawbacks of undertaking the work yourself. Conversely, the advantages of in-house work are the drawbacks of agency service.

There is, however, one further factor: added flexibility. Should you take on additional staff in anticipation of additional work, there may be redundancy costs involved if the anticipated work does not materialise. Using an agency means that they, rather than you, have the work-load problem. Much the same applies to quality of work: it is relatively easier to change agencies than the staff of a department, should the advertising they produce not match up to the standard required.

Who represents advertisers generally?

Most major advertisers belong to the ISBA (Incorporated Society of British Advertisers). The benefits of ISBA membership include:

- **expert communication advice and consultancy**

The ISBA consultancy service provides confidential information and expert guidance on matters such as:
  - recommendations for and formulation of agency/supplier agreements

- agency payments: negotiating a fair deal
- production cost effectiveness: advice on television and press production costs
- agency evaluation systems
- codes and statutory requirements for high standards in advertising

- **benchmarking information to help advertisers achieve more value-effective marketing communications**

One of ISBA's main aims is to raise standards of practice among advertisers. 'Best Practice' initiatives have been developed in a number of communication areas.

- **representation of the specialist views of advertisers**

The ISBA represents UK advertisers' views on advertising to media owners and agencies. It also promotes and protects the role of advertising and the standards of self regulation.

Specialist 'Action Groups' meet regularly to discuss and take action on matters affecting all areas of media including television, radio, cinema, press, outdoor, direct marketing, research, sponsorship and new media

- **publications**

The ISBA publishes a newsletter: *Nutshell*, as well as other publications. Recent titles include: *Advertising Briefing Procedure, Media Buying – the Alternatives for Advertisers, Guide to Outdoor Advertising, Guide to Sponsorship*.

Chapter 10

Role of the Advertising Agency

Whether undertaken by advertiser or agency or shared between them, the various component tasks which overall make for good advertising remain the same. These tasks were listed at the start of the last chapter. The aim of this chapter is not to consider these tasks as such but to review how the agency sets about them in partnership with its client.

It is interesting to recall that agencies were originally media-owners' service departments, not independent organisation. In the early days of advertising, agencies acted as representatives for newspapers and sold space in them to advertisers. At first, the agencies bought space in quantity, and made their profit by selling it in smaller units for as much as they could get. Later still, agencies started to sell space on a commission basis, and a commission system is still the basis for agency remuneration, many agencies taking their profit from commissions granted by media-owners rather than fees from advertisers.

Finding it easier to sell space if they suggested how it should be used, the agencies started a copywriting service, and soon afterwards design and art services were added. By this time, agencies were really working more for the advertisers than for the newspaper proprietors, and before long they became fully-fledged service organisations giving their clients a complete range of advertising services. They also became independent, and bought space in whichever newspapers or other advertising media they thought best served their clients' interests. Today, the term 'agency' no longer applies in the legal sense, since the agency makes contracts in its own right – with its clients on the one hand and with media-owners on the other – and remains a party to the advertisement contract, which it would not were it an 'agency' in the legal sense of the word. Agencies are thus liable in law for debts to media, even though they made the bookings on their client's behalf. To minimise the risk factor, many agencies take out indemnity insurance, to ensure they can settle their accounts with media-owners, should any client unfortunately fail to meet financial commitments.

Media-owners, in their turn, also take action to protect themselves, to prevent a situation in which an agency might be unable to meet its financial obligations. Often this defensive action is taken on a collective basis through the appropriate trade organisation, which may operate an agency-monitoring system. For instance, the Periodical Publishers Association (PPA – described earlier) Credit Management Committee assesses the credit worthiness of applicant agencies, which must satisfy the following minimum requirements:

- trading record of at least two years
- annual billings of a stated minimum in press media
- net assets of at least a stated minimum
- current assets in excess of liabilities
- a profit before tax in the most recent financial year
- client base of at least four companies.

The Committee continuously monitors payment performance and reviews each recognised agency's annual audited accounts. Should this monitoring process give cause for concern, the agency's directors may be asked for management accounts, personal indemnities, bank guarantees or an insurance bond.

If a delay occurs in forwarding management or audited accounts, or the accounts themselves suggest that the agency no longer fulfils PPA requirements, the agency will be invited for interview. In extreme cases, the agency's recognition could be withdrawn. This would seriously affect the agency's cash flow as it could now be required to pay in advance for advertising, but its client would still be invoiced in arrears.

THE ADVANTAGES OF USING AN ADVERTISING AGENCY

There are a number of reasons why a manufacturer employs the services of an advertising agency instead of relying on his own advertising department.

1 A team of experts Primarily, agencies exist to provide a team of experts to work in closest co-operation with the client's own advertising staff. The team includes specialists in all the many aspects of advertising practice including, of course, media. There are, however, many other advantages to agency service.

2 The work load problem The advertiser could no doubt recruit experts on his own staff, but there might be insufficient work to keep an expert on, say, media, fully occupied. The agency, on the other hand, can afford to employ the specialist, since he will be working full-time for a number of clients, according to their varying needs for his expert advice. Alternatively, the client might himself employ a number of independent consultants but they would not be accustomed to working together, whereas the agency has the experts immediately available and already working as a team.

Points 1 and 2 viewed together mean that perhaps an advertiser who cannot offer adequate scope and challenge (quite apart from remuneration) may fail to attract staff of the right calibre.

3 A new approach A further advantage of employing an agency is that it brings a fresh approach to a problem, since its staff are detached from the company's day-to-day operations, whereas an advertiser's own staff often become so involved in detailed work that they no longer see the wood for the trees.

4 Experience in allied fields Again, since they are handling different products for a number of clients, agencies have wider experience and their personnel, not being restricted to any one company's problems, are unlikely to take a narrow view. Besides, the knowledge and experience gained from one marketing problem can frequently be adapted to meet another, and in this way each client derives benefit from the agency's experience in other fields – an advantage of particular importance today when markets and trading patterns are changing so rapidly. An agency keeps abreast of new developments through direct contact with the marketing problems of a number of advertisers, and can advise its clients in the light of its wider knowledge and experience. Advertisers, of course, also keep themselves up-to-date but, because they operate in only one product field, their experience is inevitably limited.

5 Buying power The advertising agency's total expenditure must necessarily be larger than any one client's individual budget. Accordingly, when buying on its clients' behalf, it can bring considerable pressure to bear on suppliers and media-owners – far more pressure than most advertisers can exert on their own. This buying 'muscle' can be exerted by the agency not only on media purchases but on all other items, such as print or artwork, that the agency buys on its clients' behalf. Added to expert knowledge of the market climate and of which suppliers to approach, this can result in considerable savings for the agency's clients.

6 Reduced cost A further advantage of agency service arises directly from the commission granted by the media-owners, which helps reduce the costs of using the agency's team of experts. Media-owners grant commission, usually ranging from 10 to 15 per cent, to recognised advertising agencies, and agencies get commission on almost everything they buy on a client's behalf. If an advertisement costs £1,000, that is the amount the client spends whether he makes the booking direct or through his advertising agency. But by booking it through his advertising agency, though it still costs him £1,000, the agency receives 15 per cent commission, or £150. Where the commission granted by media-owners is less than 15 per cent, the agency may 'round up' the charge made to clients, at +17.65 per cent of the net cost, to recoup the difference in income from that advertisement.

For some clients, where the commission is enough to cover costs and provide a sufficient profit, the agency will work on commission alone, and the advertiser then reaps the benefit of agency service without charge. Should the client consider that the commission received from his account is more than sufficient to cover the agency's work on his behalf, he may – when negotiating arrangements – call for the commission level to be reduced. On the other hand, if an agency finds its expenses in handling the client's advertising exceed the commission received, or leave an insufficient margin of profit, it will charge a 'service fee' to obtain the additional income necessary. Even where the advertiser pays a service fee, however, this is usually still less expensive than taking all the experts into his own staff.

For many years there has been talk of the commission system breaking down but, despite much controversy and discussion of alternatives, it still survives – even if in changing form.

Commission is granted only to 'recognised' advertising agencies, and the financial vetting of applicant agencies is undertaken by the appropriate media-owners' trade organisation, as a central service for its members. Following the extension of restrictive practices legislation to services, however, the recognition system came under review.

After discussion with the Office of Fair Trading, it was agreed that financial vetting of applicant agencies was an essential area for continuation of collective action, and thus acceptable within the terms of the legislation.

All matters relating to payment of commission are now for the individual decision of each media-owner. Accordingly, under these arrangements, recognition does not carry with it any entitlement or conditions regarding the payment of commission. Recognised agencies do, however, benefit from the central trade body's recommendation to its members that such agencies should receive credit terms.

Further legislation or new rulings by the Office of Fair Trading may lead to other modifications. Alternatively, internal business pressures within the advertising industry may still lead to the commission system breaking down, or perhaps being amended to allow for two or more commission levels, on a decreasing scale as advertising expenditure increases. A further possibility is payment on a straight-fee basis. There are three main types of fee arrangement:

Hourly rates where the time spent by each executive on the account is charged to the client at varying rates. Thus a Media Director will be charged out at a higher rate than a media planner. Overall control ensures that the charge to the client does not exceed an agreed amount.

Retainer Fee where clients pay a standard monthly fee, irrespective of the time spent that month. Some months the agency will undertake more work, and less in others. The intention is to achieve a satisfactory balance over the contract period, usually a year. The agency benefits from consistency of cash flow, and clients need to ensure they get value for money over a year.

Payment by results an agreed minimum fee is paid to cover agency costs, and profit is dependent on reaching agreed targets. The problem here is to assess the value of the agency's contribution. For instance, if media is bought at substantially less than rate card cost, how does the client ensure the quality of the time/space bought?

7 Other savings Other benefits of agency service, though of less importance, can nevertheless result in considerable administrative savings. Any company placing its advertising direct receives individual invoices from all media on the schedule, as well as accounts for artwork, production of press advertisements, and for making television, cinema or radio commercials. When an agency is employed, however, the advertiser receives comprehensive accounts covering all these many and varied items, which he can then settle with a single payment. In addition, there are clerical savings in that spread sheets of media schedules and other documents are provided as a normal part of the agency's service.

A final note

As pointed out in the previous chapter, the advantages of agency service are the drawbacks of the client undertaking the work within his own organisation. Conversely, the disadvantages of agency service listed below are the advantages of in-house work.

THE DRAWBACKS OF AGENCY SERVICE

Employing an advertising agency is not without its drawbacks, though in most cases these are outweighed by the advantages.

1 Divided attention One disadvantage is that agency personnel work on several different accounts at the same time (thus helping to overcome the workload problem) and clearly cannot give their undivided attention to all of them simultaneously. If something urgent crops up with one client, agency personnel may be prevented by other commitments from devoting all their time to dealing with it, whereas a manufacturer employing his own advertising staff knows that his problems receive undivided attention all the time.

2 The time lag Again, agency service is not always as speedy as direct working, and a manufacturer whose advertising is constantly subject to unexpected changes might prefer to do the job himself. If the content of the advertising campaign is under continual review, this could well apply: a mail order firm, for example, might wish to drop one item from an advertisement immediately stocks were exhausted and replace it with another line. Similarly, a tour operator might wish to stop advertising his Italian holidays just as soon as all places were booked, and to substitute another country where he still has vacancies.

3 Cost A further drawback arises from the commissions received by the agency, the service fee charged, and the amount of work involved. For some types of advertising, the commission may be so small and the service fee so high that it becomes more economical for the advertiser to engage his own experts and to set up an advertising department which amounts to a small agency. Much depends on the nature of the advertising, for where media costs are low the agency receives little income from commission. On the other hand, it takes just as much effort to prepare an advertisement for a business magazine as for a national newspaper, yet the former task will bring the agency far less revenue than the second, simply because it receives commission on a smaller sum.

4 Built-in 'inertia' The income *versus* workload problem can be extended, since the agency receives roughly the same commission on £50,000, whether it is spent on a single advertisement or on hundreds, but its costs will vary considerably. A bargain flight company, for example, might get far better results from classified insertions than from display advertisements and would consequently want to advertise in this way. From the agency standpoint, however, this could be extremely uneconomic – imagine how many classified or semi-display advertisements you could buy for £50,000 – each one would necessitate typing an order, preparing copy and type mark-up, checking proofs and vouchers, and paying an invoice. The administrative costs would leave little or no profit from the commission. The commission system thus has a 'built-in' temptation for agencies to achieve maximum income with minimum effort.

The same argument can be applied to changes in advertisement content. The agency incurs lower staff costs by preparing one advertisement and letting it run week after week for a year than if it changes the content each month. The income from commission remains the same, yet monthly changes of copy mean 12 times as much work, with consequent higher staff costs and lower profits.

Agencies need to make a profit, and to some extent this can be achieved by charging a higher service fee to recoup the additional staff costs involved. The higher the service fee, however, the more attractive it becomes for the advertiser to run his own advertising department, or to transfer to an agency charging a lower fee.

Agency directors are of course more than aware of all these drawbacks, and take the necessary steps to overcome them. Agency management is thus of great importance in ensuring that advertising skills are used to maximum effect, on behalf of the agency's clients. Equally, responsibility for the disadvantages rests to some degree with the advertiser: drawbacks should ideally have been ironed out at agency selection stage, and client/agency relationships be compatible.

AGENCIES AND MEDIA-OWNERS

Employment of an advertising agency should bring benefits to media-owners as well as to advertisers. Ideally, it means that a media representative presents his sales argument to an advertising expert who will appreciate his medium's various selling points, evaluate them in terms of the client's marketing strategy and prepare a schedule in which all the media dovetail in a carefully planned campaign.

With companies which have little experience of advertising – particularly small firms – media representatives often find selling a difficult task, because before they can present the case for their medium, they must devote considerable time to selling the need to advertise. With some inexperienced advertisers the media representative has to go even further, even to the extent of writing copy and suggesting layouts. This point brings to light another benefit that media-owners receive from agency service: when an agency is employed, there are expert staff to create advertisements and the media-owner's production staff can expect to receive the necessary material in good time. In many cases, media-owners receive from agencies complete advertisements, and are not involved in any typesetting expenses. Furthermore, when proofs are submitted, they are returned promptly with alterations indicated with the accepted proof correction marks instead of the crossings-out and arrows used by the inexperienced layman.

As every media-owner knows, there are times when the agency does

186

not deliver as promptly as it should (perhaps because of pressure caused by rush campaigns for a number of clients simultaneously) and the media representatives find themselves chasing the agency for material or the return of corrected proofs. For the most part, however, the media-owner's life is made easier by the smooth function of agency procedure.

There can also be financial benefits, since the media-owner is dealing with an advertising agency he recognises (either directly or through his trade association) rather than a number of perhaps little-known clients into whose creditworthiness he would otherwise have to make individual and time-consuming investigations. The agency is liable in law for space or time booked on its clients' behalf, and the media-owner can thus look to the agency direct for payment, hence the importance of the central media trade organisation's recommendation that the agency be recognised as creditworthy.

AGENCY PROCEDURE

When a company appoints an agency, the first task of the agency personnel is to find out all about their client's activities and problems. The agency's investigations, discussed in detail in Part 3, necessarily duplicate those undertaken by the advertising manager when he was first appointed, since the agency staff need an equally clear understanding of the client's company background and marketing objectives. The agency will spend considerable time making a thorough investigation, for not until the advertiser's requirements have been accurately defined can the agency attempt to meet them. The size of the appropriation and the period to be covered are also important to the agency, as are precise instructions on what the appropriation covers. Are production charges included or only media costs? Is the client undertaking part of the campaign himself and keeping back a 'below the line' budget for this purpose? Practice varies with the firm, as we have seen, and there are no hard and fast rules. Obviously, however, the agency must know what money is available and what it has to cover.

Ideally, the client will give the agency *all* the information it needs when he gives his advertising 'brief': the quality of work produced by the agency to a considerable extent depends on the client's skill in giving his agency all the information it needs in order to prepare advertising proposals on his behalf.

Once the agency is confident that it has a correct understanding of the situation, it can start the vital work of preparing an advertising campaign to help its client achieve his marketing objectives. In many cases, to ensure that its understanding of the problem is correct, the agency will prepare a 'facts book' detailing the marketing situation, which the client will double-check for accuracy.

Planning the campaign

An important person in defining and solving the advertising and marketing problem is the agency's account executive. This title is rather misleading, since the executive has little to do with accounting as such, although he certainly bears responsibility for expenditure of the appropriation. The account executive is, in fact, responsible for *all* aspects of handling the client or 'account'. He is usually selected soon after the agency is appointed and attends the meeting at which the agency is briefed on the problem. It is true to say that no client, however well-intentioned, ever gives a 100 per cent perfect briefing and it is up to the executive to ensure, by asking the right questions, that his agency has all the facts it needs to solve the problem. In some cases, inexperience may prevent a new advertiser from giving a proper briefing. In such circumstances it is up to the account executive, through relevant questioning, to get one.

The account executive has a two-way role, in that he represents the agency to the client and the client to the agency. He is the individual to whom the agency staff in all departments turn for information: equally, it is through him that the client's problems are channelled to the appropriate agency specialists, and their work co-ordinated. Frequently you may encounter different levels of account executive. Some larger agencies have account executives backed by assistant executives who handle the day-to-day work on each account. At a higher level, there may be account supervisors, each responsible for a number of account executives handling a similar number of accounts. Again, there may be account directors at a still higher level, with overall responsibility for the campaigns handled by their account supervisors. Another variation is that an individual on the executive side may be responsible for a number of accounts rather than just one. For greater cross-fertilisation of ideas, and to prevent them getting into a rut, many agencies deliberately give their executives varied responsibilities. This practice also helps the agency overcome the workload problem discussed earlier. You may also meet agencies where the term 'account executive' is not used, executive staff being referred to as 'representatives' or 'managers'. For the sake of simplicity, however, the term 'account executive' is used from this point on, to identify the executive function.

Once the problem is clearly defined, the agency staff can start to solve it, and here the account executive plays a key role. He may start by calling a meeting of a 'Plans Board' (formal or informal) on which will be representatives of all the important agency departments. Creative staff are present to consider the theme to be featured in the advertising, and the media department to advise on whether the prospective customers could best be reached by press, posters, television or some other medium. Both media and creative departments *must* be represented on the plans board, since the decision of one department directly affects the other.

Use of any medium also involves *production* considerations, for there is obviously no point in booking space if the advertisement cannot be prepared in time to meet the media-owner's copy date or if the medium's ability to *deliver* your advertising message is not utilised to full advantage. Production costs, too, are important and can influence media selection. The agency production staff are thus directly concerned in media decisions, and will give their views at plans board meetings. Others beside creative, media and production staff may also be represented on the plans board, including any experts in the agency's team who can contribute to solving the particular problem. The plans board may also include other account executives, in addition to the one handling the particular client, for the benefit of their experience and advice. Similarly, other senior members of the various departments may sit on the plans board, even though they are not involved in the day-to-day running of the account. Thus the client gains maximum benefit from the combined talents of the agency.

The plans board discusses the client's overall marketing problem from every angle and finally agrees on a basic solution. Since any advertising campaign represents a combination of interlocking decisions regarding marketing, media, creative, production and other aspects of advertising, clearly broad agreement must be reached by the board as a whole.

Account planning

Some agencies set about solving their clients' advertising and marketing problems in a different way by separating out the account-planning function. Drafting advertising strategy is considered too important and too time-consuming to be undertaken by busy account executives on a 'part-time' basis. This task is therefore made the primary full-time responsibility of an account planner, whose aim is to bring a stronger discipline to the essential first stage in creating effective advertising campaigns – developing the advertising strategy on which creative and media proposals are based, and by which they are evaluated and justified.

The planner's initial role is to collate and analyse relevant available data, and to propose any new research required to supplement this information. The planner must understand the target market's needs and motivations so that media strategy can be set in a real world environment. In the light of these findings, the planner then drafts the advertising strategy document for discussion and agreement by the account team or plans board, before it is presented to the client. In due course, the account planner will interpret any research feedback about consumer reactions, to see whether the advertising objectives are being achieved, and recommend any necessary modifications to strategy in the light of this new information. Account planners also think beyond the current campaign, assessing long-term market trends in order to develop long-term strategies. Their multi-skill function is one of increasing importance, and formally recognised as such in the departmental structure of more and more agencies.

The research department

When agency staff attempt to define their client's marketing problems they may decide that they lack sufficient information to reach a sound and reasoned judgement and will call in the research department. This department may already have a representative on the plans board, for the benefit of his general advice, but when more detailed information is required the research department starts to function in its own right.

A tremendous amount of information is readily available in published form, so before any 'field' research is undertaken there is always 'desk' research, which involves checking through existing sources of information. In some agencies desk research staff form a separate department and may be known by another title such as 'Information' or 'Library', while a second department ' usually with the formal title of 'Research Department' – looks after field research.

Desk research is carried out before field research, as a matter of form, but if some vital questions remain unanswered, or if some of the information available was published some time ago and is thus out-of-date, then field research becomes essential and the agency research department takes action. Its task lies in planning the operation rather than undertaking the actual 'fieldwork', which is usually carried out by a specialist market research organisation. The agency selects and works with the most suitable market research company in planning the research and supervising the fieldwork. Equally, it gives much thought to interpreting the results and making recommendations for action.

Some 'research departments' have converted into account planning sections, as described above. Many research staff found that restricting their activities to gathering data did not give them job satisfaction: they wanted to be directly involved in the practical application of the valuable information they had gathered. This feeling coincided with the management view that drafting advertising strategy could not be undertaken by busy account executives on a spare-time basis.

As soon as the information collected has been carefully checked and interpreted, there are further meetings of the plans board to consider the advertising and marketing campaign. Once the overall campaign strategy has been agreed, the individual departments set to work to crystallise their ideas and to produce detailed proposals in accordance with the agreed broad plan.

The media department

The media department is represented when the overall campaign is discussed at plans board level. Once the general strategy is agreed, it is then up to the media department to get down to detailed planning with the aim of spending the client's appropriation in such a way that his advertising message reaches prospective buyers as effectively and economically as possible. The media planners are experts on the full range of media and have at their command all the relevant statistics about press, posters, cinema, television, radio and other media.

There is often considerable specialisation within the media department. At its head there may be a media director who represents the media viewpoint on the plans board and agrees the overall strategy. Immediately responsible to him may be media planners whose task is to take the broad strategy and go into the detail of specific media, size, position, number of insertions, dates and so on. Once this stage is agreed, specialist media buyers may take over to put the plan into operation. For example, specialist television time-buyers may negotiate with the programme contractors for the best possible implementation of the media planners' proposal and decide in exactly which breaks, at what times and on which days the client's television commercials will appear. The time-buyers keep this schedule under constant review, adjusting it in the light of changes in rival BBC or commercial programmes, statistics on audience size and composition, or any additional information likely to influence the schedule's effectiveness.

The time-buyers may also be responsible for radio and cinema advertising, or these two media may be the province of separate specialists. Even in the field of press media, specialisation may occur, one space-buyer concentrating on national newspapers, a second on the regional press, and another on, say, women's magazines. In some agencies, exhibitions may be the responsibility of specialist staff. For outdoor media, separate poster specialist agencies may be consulted to give advice to the main media department on poster planning and buying. These different experts have, however, a common aim: to communicate the client's advertising message as effectively as possible through the media which are their own particular responsibility. Other agencies find it more effective to avoid over-specialisation and require their staff, at all levels, to handle the full range of media, and to be responsible for both planning and buying.

Some agencies have specialist media research staff, sometimes called 'media assessors'. Media-owners issue a great deal of useful research material and the flow of information is such that some agencies appoint staff whose main task is to evaluate these documents, thus leaving others free for their main function of planning and buying.

In larger agencies there may be many experts and the media department may operate on a 'group' system, each group containing both planners and buyers, with the media director exercising general control over all groups.

Whatever the agency structure, the experts' skill lies not so much in their detailed knowledge of media (although this may call for years of experience) but in applying this knowledge to their client's advertising problems. If the media specialists are to match the advantages (or drawbacks) of the wide range of advertising media with the requirements of each client's individual marketing problem, they must fully understand that problem. A full briefing of the media department is, therefore, essential if it is to come up with the right answers.

Given this efficient briefing, the media department can then evaluate the range of media, select those most suitable in the light of the client's requirements and prepare detailed proposals. This work is complex and merits more attention than can be given in one chapter dealing with an advertising agency's overall operation. Media evaluation, selection and planning are, therefore, the subjects of later discussion in Part 3.

The creative department

While the media department interprets in detail the broad approach agreed at plans board level, the creative staff take their work to a more advanced level. They may produce alternative concepts, which are then researched as a formal stage in developing the advertising. Once the ideal creative concept is agreed, the actual advertisements – or executions – are prepared. For this, copy is written for press advertisements or printed material, and layouts prepared. For posters or display material, roughs or dummies are made, and storyboards drawn up for television or cinema commercials. Detailed discussion of these activities is outside the scope of any book on media, although clearly the creative content of advertisements is vital: there is little point in spending hours on devising a complex media plan only to have it deliver the wrong message. The reverse is just as true – even a superb advertisement cannot work to best advantage if delivered to the wrong audience. Creative and media aspects of campaign planning are of equal importance if you are to use advertising media effectively. In larger agencies there may be several creative as well as media groups.

Review of proposals

As soon as detailed media and creative proposals are ready, the plans board meets again to review the work. Possibly there may now be a formal change of title, and the committee becomes known as the 'Review Board'. In some agencies, the review board comprises precisely the same individuals as the plans board and would therefore probably continue under the same name. In others, the individuals as well as the name are changed. Whatever the practice, the purpose is to check meticulously, point by point, the proposals to be submitted to the client to ensure that there are no discrepancies in the work of the individual departments, that all the various aspects of the campaign interlock, that the proposals conform to the basic strategy agreed by the earlier plans board, and that the quality of the work matches up to the agency's standards.

This, then, is the pattern of agency work – investigation, analysis of the problem, agreement on a basic solution, working out a detailed plan, and careful checking to ensure that the proposals are faultless. The various stages involved are an indication of the care which agencies take in their work, even though the procedure may not always be on a formal basis. Indeed, a plans board meeting may sometimes be completely informal, with the account executive talking over the problem with individual members of the various departments, after normal office hours and away from the usual distractions. Some practitioners argue strongly against formal plans or review boards on the grounds that they stifle individuals and impose an agency style on all clients regardless of their requirements. For this reason, meetings may sometimes be completely informal.

Presentation of proposals

Once the detailed proposals have been approved by the review board, they are made ready for presentation to the client. The media schedule is prepared in its final form, as is the advertisement copy, and finished versions of designs are prepared by the creative staff. These are then presented to the client, and the inter-relationship between copy, design and media explained. It is essential that these three are presented together, for the client would be unable to approve a media schedule without knowing the advertisements to be featured, nor could he approve creative work without knowing the media in which it was to appear. Creative and media proposals are accordingly presented together, with other parts of the plan.

The presentation of campaign proposals is of major importance and should not be viewed as 'selling' the proposals to the client but rather as careful explanation of the individual parts of a complex plan and how they are related. Presentation of proposals is, in fact, the very reverse of the agency's first task. When the problem was first discussed, it was broken down into individual components for detailed work by the various departments, whereas in the formal presentation the specialist proposals are joined together and presented as a co-ordinated plan.

At the presentation, the account executive usually outlines the market situation and the agency's approach to the client's problem. He then introduces individual members of the agency team who, in turn, present their own sections of the campaign and explain the reasoning behind them. The research staff outline how prospective customers were defined; the media planner in his turn presents the schedule designed to reach the market defined by research; and the creative staff show and discuss the proposed advertisements. Experts from other departments may also be called on to clarify their particular part of the plan. Finally, the account executive concludes the presentation by summarising the major points made and the reasoning behind them. After the verbal presentation, a detailed document is given to the client confirming the points made.

An effective presentation is of major importance, because the client's acceptance of an agency's proposals depends on a clear understanding of the many complex and interlocking sections of the campaign plan. Cases are not unknown where a campaign has been rejected, not because the plan was a bad one but because the agency failed to explain adequately the thinking behind it. For this reason, agencies often go to considerable lengths to ensure that the client has a clear understanding of the proposals. On the media side, spreadsheets are used to prepare the schedule in visual form, accompanied by a written report clarifying the reasons why this particular media pattern has been selected.

Where the presentation is on a major campaign, the agency may call on all those concerned to make a 'dry run' beforehand, amounting almost to a rehearsal, and may go to the extent of preparing scripts for the entire proceedings, showing the order of speaking, the words to be spoken by each individual, and the charts, slides or other visual aids to be used. Some agencies even put the entire presentation on video and screen this to the client, rather than risk the possibility of error that is always present in a 'live' presentation. Presentation techniques have become increasingly sophisticated, with agencies using computer generated and controlled presentations, rather than the standard visual aids. This sounds an elaborate procedure, as indeed it is, but it could be well worth while in ensuring that the campaign is faultlessly presented. It is all too easy when speaking to overlook some point or fail to express it clearly, or to take points out of order and so destroy the logic of an argument. The more complex the scheme, the greater the need for the details and the reasoning behind them to be made completely clear. As marketing problems and advertising planning become more complex, so the need for lucid presentation becomes even more vital.

Execution of proposals

Before giving the agency formal approval to proceed, the client checks the proposals to ensure that they are sound and that they dovetail with his company's marketing activities. Once the agency has the client's agreement, the advertising proposals can be put into effect: the media schedule must be converted into actual orders to media-owners and parallel action must be taken by creative staff and other departments to bring their proposals to finished form. The detail of this work is described in Part 3.

The control department

The control department is often described, and with justification, as the nerve centre of an agency. Its function is evident from the various titles by which it may be described – 'progress', 'traffic', 'control', or 'copy detail'. It controls the progress or traffic of detailed work, and the smooth functioning of the agency turns to a great extent on the efficiency of this department.

Copies of media orders come to the traffic department and set in motion the complex procedure of producing an advertisement. Take, for example, the task of handling a straightforward insertion in a Christmas issue. The booking may be made many months in advance, but it would be foolish to wait until the last minute and then do a rush job, since this rarely results in effective advertising. The control department, therefore, undertakes the complicated arithmetic of routing the advertisement through the agency. The copy detail staff must prepare a detailed time schedule, working back from the media-owner's copy date, which may be weeks or even months in advance of publication date. Time must be allowed for typesetting and production and for correction of proofs by both client and agency. Account must also be taken of the time needed to produce artwork, and to mark up copy for typesetting. Before this work can be done, the copy must be written and a visual prepared, and adequate time must be allowed for these to be submitted to the client and approved. Even before the creative team can start work, the account executive must contact the advertising manager, to see if there are any special requirements for this Christmas advertisement, and this, too, must be allowed for in the time schedule.

The control department must anticipate the time needed for each of these stages and build in a safety margin to allow for unexpected delays and, if necessary, the revision of copy, visuals, or proofs. A time-schedule must be prepared, allowing so many days for each stage, and careful watch must be kept to ensure that no delays occur anywhere along the line. If there is delay on the part of someone early in the chain, some other unfortunate individual will, later on, have to race against time. Too much haste seldom produces good work, as well as greatly increasing the possibility of error – and mistakes in advertising tend to be *very* expensive. A good control department thus makes for efficiency and prevents costly errors, as well as directly affecting the quality of the agency's work.

In addition to press advertisements, the control department is frequently responsible for the progress of television and radio commercials, printed material, exhibition stands – in fact all agency work, whatever the medium. With a major campaign, where media and creative proposals are submitted together for approval, the work of the department even extends to ensuring that the proposals are ready in good time for submission (and prior checking by the review board). Once the proposals are approved, the control department also supervises their execution.

Vouchers and accounts

Just as the advertising manager checks to see that his company receives value for money spent on advertising, so does the agency. The voucher section checks that the correct advertisement appeared on the appointed day, in the position booked and that the printing quality was up to the required standard. Not until the voucher copy has been checked is the media-owner's invoice passed through for payment. The location of the voucher section varies: in some agencies it is part of the media department, in others it is attached to the production or control departments or is an extension of the accounts department.

Other departments

The general pattern of agency operations remains the same whatever the variations in size and agency structure: problem analysis, preparation of media and creative proposals to solve that problem, and execution of the approved proposals. The proposals are based on the three functions of advertisement creation, media selection and production work, and these three form the essence of agency service.

In the course of time, however, and reflecting the increasing complexity of marketing problems, many agencies have extended the scope of their services by developing other departments, staffed with experts capable of solving specialist sections of their client's marketing problem. Some agencies, for example, have a special research department, and other activities such as television, marketing, merchandising, sales promotion, below-the-line media, direct marketing, public relations and international operations may also merit the status of separate departments, each under its own director. Some agencies develop these activities in another way, by establishing subsidiary or associated companies which operate on a commercial basis, and offer their services to all rather than restricting them to the agency's immediate clients. As well as being profitable in their own right, such companies can also play an important part in attracting new clients to an agency.

Television The specialist nature of television advertising once led some agencies to group the various specialists together in a working unit, rather than leave them in the various departments that would normally house them. Production of television commercials calls for different expertise than for printed media; the agencies therefore include specialist television producers on their staff. Similarly, on the creative side, the agency's staff may include specialist storyboard artists and scriptwriters, who think in terms of moving rather than still pictures, and the spoken rather than the printed word. On the media side, as we have seen, specialist time-buyers may be employed.

Whatever the agency structure, the aim is to create effective television commercials and to screen them to best advantage. It is now rare to concentrate all television staff in a single department and, where separate television departments do still exist, they tend to concentrate on the production side, and to leave time-buying to the media department.

Merchandising In reviewing the advertising manager's work the point was made that, as well as stimulating public demand for his company's products, he must also ensure that they are on display in the shops and readily available for customers to buy. In consequence, a considerable amount of merchandising activity is aimed at retail outlets and the company's sales force to ensure that the public campaign is well backed-up at point of sale. Some larger agencies have specialist staff to advise clients on this vital work or, where the advertiser does not have experts in this field, to mount complete merchandising campaigns for him.

Sales Promotion Just as larger agencies have specialist staff to advise clients on merchandising, many have special Sales Promotion sections.

Public relations As we have already seen, PR may be added to the responsibilities of the advertising manager or may be delegated to a specialist section of the agency. A number of agencies have specialist PR subsidiaries or associated companies, fully staffed with experts who work in co-operation with their clients. Either way, the aim is still a 'deliberate, planned and sustained effort to establish and maintain goodwill and mutual understanding between the organisation and its publics'.

Marketing Like merchandising, marketing may be the province of the agency as well as the advertiser. Some agencies have special marketing staff who co-operate with clients in analysing and assessing consumer wants and needs and devising marketing programmes to satisfy them.

Some agencies have even gone to the extent of establishing their own retail outlets which operate independently on a profit-making basis. Such shops provide the agency with invaluable first-hand information about the market, and can be used for testing products, packaging, or other elements of the marketing mix.

Direct Marketing The increase in direct marketing has been accompanied by a growth in the number and size of agency Direct Marketing services, either specialist departments of traditional agencies or independent services.

As with other activities, such as Sales Promotion, some agencies have 'integrated' direct marketing into their main agency service.

Some Sales Promotion specialists have merged with Direct Marketing specialists to become 'Direct Promotion' agencies. In the main, however, Direct Marketing agencies have remained separate, in view of the wide range of specialisms involved. Apart from the strategic and creative areas, these specialisms include list renting/building, computerisation, printing, insertion and response handling.

International With the increasing number of clients operating internationally, agency selection and management takes on an added importance.

As an example, a UK-based advertiser or their advertising agency could buy overseas media from their domestic base by using specialist offices which represent overseas media in the UK.

Some advertisers, however, prefer to use agencies who have extended their service overseas. There are various ways that agencies satisfy this demand.

Some agencies have loose associations with 'affiliate' independent agencies in each country, with similar philosophy, structure or size, who do not have a share in each other's business. They use each other's services, tailor-made to suit individual client needs.

Other agencies forge permanent arrangements with overseas organisations. They build networks of branch offices, often by buying part or full ownership of existing agencies. They exchange personnel so that expertise in different countries is developed throughout the network.

Essentially there are two types of network. Firstly there are multinational networks, where each branch consistently provides the same full service and is a mirror image of the head office. These networks have many branches, in some cases over 100 throughout the world. Their size provides substantial buying power which in turn attracts large multinational clients and quality personnel. Some agencies, very experienced in the international field, have developed extensive support networks, including inter-office computer communication facilities.

The second type of network, also used by multinational agencies, is where each branch is more of a satellite than a full branch office. This structure is often called 'hub and spoke' with the branches used mainly to support centrally-driven activities. This cost-effective method provides a multinational network without the high cost of duplicating full services in each branch. The hub originates and co-ordinates, whilst the spokes focus on servicing local client needs.

The trend for major advertisers to 'centralise' domestic media planning and buying is spreading to international operations. For instance a major German car manufacturer recently appointed a single media agency to co-ordinate its multi-million pound Pan-European account.

Advertisers are increasingly appreciating the benefits that can accrue from appointing a Pan-European or even global network to co-ordinate strategy, enhance understanding of the diversity in media and research, whilst taking advantage of possible cost savings.

AGENCY SYSTEMS

Quite apart from departmental variations, agencies also differ in their system of operation. Some use the 'pyramid' system, under which directors are responsible for a group of accounts (rather than for staff members) and the executive, media, creative or other staff may all work on several accounts, each of which may be under the control of a different director. Others operate on the 'group' system whereby the agency is divided into two or more separate units, each of which amounts to a self-contained agency.

The group system adopted by many larger agencies has various advantages: each account group becomes a profit centre, it enables the agency to handle competing accounts (provided clients agree), and staff can be switched between groups from time to time to bring fresh input to the accounts handled.

The media department may work on either the pyramid or group system.

Specialist agencies

Some agencies, rather than expand by diversifying their departments, prefer to concentrate their abilities, as in the case of an agency specialising in technical advertising. Copywriting for industrial products demands a degree of technical knowledge that the average consumer-product copywriter does not possess. Similarly, technical illustrations such as cross-sections of machinery may prove outside the average agency creative expertise. Specialist agencies, whose staff have the necessary technical knowledge and skills, thus take their place on the agency scene. Similarly, the particular needs of recruitment advertising have led some agencies to concentrate on this specialist area. Others have specialised in below-the-line media, sales promotion direct marketing, or business-to-business.

Other 'agencies' concentrate their abilities in a different way. Rather than provide the full service of advertisement creation, media planning and buying, and production work, they restrict their expertise to one of these three functions, and it is thus possible to call on specialist services for creative work only. On the media side, the media independents (described in the following chapter) – the companies that undertake responsibility for buying media on behalf of advertisers (independently of the agency providing the creative work) – are now an important feature of the current advertising scene.

Agency Groups

The advertising agency world has always been a fast-changing one, but has become increasingly so in recent years. Some agencies have taken over others, or set up specialist subsidiaries, to broaden the portfolio of services offered to clients.

Some larger agency groups have become what amounts to a conglomerate of autonomous companies so that they can handle competitive clients in 'watertight' agencies. As well as operating the full service concept, these groups offer an 'a la carte', 'cafeteria' or 'boutique' service from which clients select whatever service they wish.

Agency standards

The range of services provided – and the standard of these services –

must necessarily vary from agency to agency, and so we should not leave this chapter without a brief discussion of the Institute of Practitioners in Advertising – the agencies' professional body. Whilst there is nothing to prevent someone without any real knowledge of the subject from hiring an office and putting up a sign proclaiming himself an 'advertising agency', it is a very different state of affairs if a firm wishes to announce that it is an advertising agency in membership of the IPA, because, before agencies are permitted to style themselves 'Incorporated Practitioners in Advertising', they will have to conform to the rigorous standards laid down by the Institute regarding – amongst other criteria – professional competence, independence, ability to mount a national campaign, financial stability and income level. The applicant agency must also agree to uphold legal and ethical standards, including the IPA bye-laws and the codes of practice issued by the ITC, the Radio Authority and the Committee of Advertising Practice.

The applicant agency is required to demonstrate its professional competence as an organisation concerned primarily with providing strategic advice on marketing communications, creating and/or placing advertising. Such services can include, or represent, specialisation in consumer or business-to-business advertising, media placement, direct marketing, creative consultancy or recruitment advertising.

The applicant agency must show that it maintains an independent judgement in professional matters, and is not directly or indirectly controlled by an advertiser or group of advertisers whose advertising it handles, or by concerns wholly or mainly interested in the sale of advertising media or services. There is an overriding proviso that the agency should not have entered into any engagement which would cause it to devote its main energies to the service of any particular advertiser or limited group of advertisers.

There are of course other requirements. The IPA looks at the financial resources and credit standing of the agency, its recognition by the various media trade bodies, the agency's experience, and the range and variety of accounts handled.

The top 30 agencies are all members of the IPA, and it is estimated that member agencies handle well over 80 per cent of all the advertising placed through agencies in the United Kingdom.

Chapter 11

Role of the Media Independents

BACKGROUND

As pointed out in the previous chapter some agencies, rather than expand by diversifying their departments, prefer to concentrate their abilities. Rather than provide the full service of advertisement creation, media planning and buying, and production work, they restrict their expertise to one of these areas. These independent companies now form such an important part of the current advertising scene that they merit separate attention in this chapter.

What was originally thought to be a temporary phenomenon has turned out to be a substantial and permanent feature of the advertising industry. These organisations are no longer described, as they were originally, as media-brokers or buying shops. The term 'Media Independent' is not fully adequate but does describe these companies which specialise in all aspects of the media side of advertising, yet are independent of the traditional agency structure, and of any specialist creative or production company.

In order to understand why these specialist media planning and buying companies have prospered, we must examine both the service they provide and the clients who use it.

SERVICES PROVIDED

Media independents are specialised and have grown because they are cost-effective streamlined organisations which employ skilled media talent. Because they have no other distractions, and no other pressures are brought to bear, they are able to devote this talent with undivided attention to the task of media.

Why should any organisation call on the services of a media independent? There is no single answer. A number of advertisers found that conventional full-service agencies did not meet their particular needs or budgets. The economic climate forced some companies to look for alternative systems and, as media costs continued to rise, many advertisers turned with new interest to ways of stretching their budgets. The media independents offered them a system that side-stepped the fixed 15 per cent commission rate and employed some of the best media-buyers in the business. Clients with expert marketing departments could formulate their own products, select a skilled team of creative people to prepare the advertisements and appoint a separate team of experts to plan and book the schedule.

As marketing departments grow more skilful, so they are better able – and are often more inclined – to commission specific tasks, and they now have a far wider range of specialist teams from which to choose, to perform these selected tasks. Some companies adopt the system of using a roster of several creative companies to develop different campaigns for different brands, and one 'centralised' media independent to place the advertisements. As clients became more sophisticated, and the media independent (and complementary creative independent) prospered, some full service agencies hived off their media departments, rebranded and ran them like media independents or, more precisely, like media dependents.

The difference between a media independent and a media dependent is that the former is not owned by an agency whereas the latter is. More over, it is dependent on the parental agency for at least initial clients. However, like a media independent, they compete in the open market place for media-only accounts. Some dependents have been particularly successful in attracting additional business into the parent agency. Some agencies have still kept the 'traditional' structure of a media department integrated into a full service agency, but also compete for media-only accounts.

AGENCIES VERSUS INDEPENDENTS

One extreme view – held by some independents – is that a trend has started which will mean the end of many traditional agencies, particularly those of a medium size which cannot afford to match the talents available within independents. It is argued that clients get a better service because independents employ the best talent to do nothing but media, and this in turn means that they must be extremely competitive. With a full-service agency, the client might find some services extremely good but others, particularly media, weak. The media independents point out that a small team of experts in media planning is usually better than a large team which includes some middling talent, and that a client using an independent can be sure the company is surviving by being competitively successful at one particular thing. Of particular relevance here is the high cost of technology – linking every media executive to computer networks that give access to the numerous research databases featured in Chapter 5 and providing the sophisticated software necessary to analyse them in a creative manner. The independents are not cheap, but claim to give better value for money: they make better use of the funds allocated to them and give their clients a better financial deal. There is an appreciable cost-saving and the money saved can be used to buy more media, which is the main purpose of the exercise in the first place. This school of thought argues that there is no reason for advertisers to use a full-service agency to plan and buy their media requirements, unless the agency is prepared to waive the 15 per cent commission rate in favour of a payment system better than that offered by the independents – and, even if this were granted, the independents would still do a *better* job.

The opposing school of thought – found, of course, in the agencies – is that there will always be a need for the superior resources and fertile inter-connections of the full-service agency. Companies without internal resources of experienced advertising and marketing staff need help in straightening out their advertising strategies and marketing planning. While a media independent will perform its allotted task very efficiently, all depends on what it is asked to do, and the independent may not have the agency's wide knowledge of marketing and of the client's marketing in particular. It is not only unsophisticated companies which need full-service agencies, however. Advertisers with a wide variety of communication needs, and different levels of campaign running simultaneously for a range of different products, need a full-service agency to co-ordinate for them. But, whether the client has few internal resources or is extremely sophisticated, the underlying point is the vital one: that by using a media independent advertisers lose the benefits resulting directly from the integral structure of the full-service agency, where creative, media and account people work together as one team under the same direction. The criticism made of the independents is that everything is brought down to the lowest common denominator: cost. Furthermore, as media independents run the risk of being divorced from the creative strategy, they are less efficient than their agency counterparts in making media choices which acknowledge creative demands, and the penalty of not using a full-service agency must be measured by the loss in effectiveness of the total advertising investment.

The casting vote between these extreme viewpoints must be with the clients who appoint the media independents in the first place and decide what services they need, so it is important to recognise that it is not only advertisers who employ the independents' services. The client profile for the media independents now covers the whole gamut of opportunities – advertisers, agencies, creative consultancies and design groups, and even media-owners and management consultancies.

Many small agencies now place some or all of their media planning or buying in the hands of the media specialists, but it is not only the small firms who do this. In a few instances, medium-size agencies have co-operated with a media independent to launch a jointly-owned media specialist, dedicated to the clients of the medium-size agency whilst benefiting from the resources of the media independent. Media independents are getting business from new agencies without media departments, set up by people who are building agencies they would like to be different from the large ones they have left. They have decided not to offer clients a full service in-house but to use media independents to do their buying (and often their planning) for them, and some new agencies without media departments are viable only because of the independents. These companies are providing the top creative and account-handling experience that complement the media independents' own services to clients. Added to this, the rise of separate media planning and buying companies has also opened up the field for the creative consultants, whose work has multiplied over the years.

The media independents are now in a period of evolution rather than revolution, and the 'either/or' syndrome no longer applies so rigidly –advertisers and agencies recognise that the independents have a lot to offer, can save time and money and cut down administration costs.

EVOLUTION OF MEDIA SPECIALISTS

It is interesting to note the wide variety of services now offered. Some independents work in an advisory capacity but do not plan or buy campaigns – while others specialise in international business. Furthermore, the ways in which the media independents are integrating have become increasingly flexible – they co-operate not only with creative consultancies and the new-type agencies but also work freely with advertiser/agency partnerships direct – some advertisers now use media independents working alongside their existing agencies, rather than seeing them as competitors as was the case in the past. Media planning and buying have always been difficult tasks, and the growth of new media opportunities (including the proliferation of terrestrial, satellite and cable TV channels and the expansion of press and radio media) has meant increased demand on the independents' talents.

The gradual convergence of computers and telephony added another dimension to the gradual fragmentation of media. Furthermore, government de-regulation of media ownership has been followed by a greater freedom in the commercial use of media leading to such developments as sponsorship and advertiser-supported programming.

Many media independents (as well as dependants and media departments) are now involved in the planning, buying and measurement of this broader based use of media. And specialist companies now exist to handle areas such as sponsorship, product placement, econometric measurement, research and media consultancy.

To give all these types of company a voice in the industry, a new trade association was launched in 1995: the Association of Media and Communication Specialists (AMCO). Members include media independents together with a wide variety of companies in the new media areas. AMCO's stated aim is: 'to encourage media development in a wide and diverse market place and to enhance the means of measurement and accountability.'

Chapter 12

Specialist Services

This chapter is brief and necessarily overlaps with earlier material: the chapter on media research and services pointed out the possibility of special computer runs based on available data, and the media-owner chapter touched on the many additional services provided in addition to delivery of your advertising message.

The purpose of this chapter is to draw attention to the fact that it is not only advertisers, agencies and media-owners who can contribute to your effective use of media: there are other specialist services which can assist in improving your advertising effectiveness.

Media independents merited a special chapter, which also mentioned the corresponding growth in creative consultancies. On the media side, national and specialist sales houses play an increasingly important part, enabling media-owners to sub-contract or supplement their media sales operation, thereby providing a better service to advertisers and agencies.

Computer bureaux or in-house facilities also make an increasingly important contribution, in respect of data handling. This broad heading covers not only the provision of further tabulations of existing data, but also a wide spectrum of additional data-processing activities. One end of the scale covers the relatively straightforward (but nevertheless vital) 'housekeeping' functions such as orders, schedules, vouchering, invoices, payment advice, and budget versus expenditure analysis, etc. At the other end of the scale are sophisticated media-planning operations which could include cross-tabulations and market area breakdowns, cost per thousand and cover rankings, duplication tables and cumulative coverage, schedule construction and analysis, evaluation of schedule performance over time, and the many media-planning activities discussed in detail in Part 3.

There are many firms active in the 'housekeeping' and/or media-planning aspects of data processing. There are specialist voucher checking companies and, in addition to the Computer Bureaux mentioned in Chapter 5, Donovan Data Systems (DDS), for example, provide a full range of services specifically designed for advertising agencies, embracing the entire spectrum from 'housekeeping' through to media planning. Twenty-nine of the top 30 agencies/media independents are among its 170 clients.

Needless to say, not all these companies offer the full range of data-handling activities listed, and others specialise in particular aspects of media service.

Other 'house-keeping' aspects of advertising can also be contracted out. It may well be vital to do so because any firm which invests advertising money in stimulating the market should gear itself up to respond swiftly to the interest generated. It would be very unwise, for example, to underestimate the task of handling the deluge of simultaneous calls which might result from featuring your phone number in a TV commercial. Specialist services not only have the technology to respond with minimal delay, but can also undertake prompt despatch of literature. Even when no 'instant' response is required, 'fulfillment houses' can relieve you of the 'mechanical' chores of storing and despatch. Such sub-contracting serves a double purpose: it reduces the risk of losing prospective purchasers by speeding up response and, at the same time, frees your own staff to concentrate on their proper functions.

While many special needs have existed for years and are covered by the services of long-established companies, the swiftly-changing nature of the business world means that new needs are constantly arising. More often than not, new organisations are set up to cater for these new needs.

Part 3
THE EFFECTIVE USE OF ADVERTISING MEDIA

Having considered the range of advertising media available to communicate your advertising message, and the organisations and individuals concerned, we can now examine the *effective* use of media under the following chapter headings:

a *Situation analysis* Gathering the company, product and market data essential for effective planning.
b *Advertising strategy* Deciding your campaign objective, which directly affects both media selection and the creative approach to be featured.
c *Budgeting* Fixing the advertising appropriation so that you spend the right amount on achieving your chosen objective.
d *Preparation of advertising proposals* Planning an advertising campaign, creating advertisements and selecting media, to achieve your chosen objective.
e *Approval of proposals* Checking, prior to executing the campaign, that your proposals are likely to achieve success.
f *Execution of these proposals* Putting your plan into effect.
g *Follow through* Ensuring that your company is geared up to cope with the response generated by advertising.
h *Evaluation of results* Checking that you received value for money, and identifying what lessons can be learned for the future.

These are the component tasks that overall – whether undertaken by advertiser or agency, and in which the media-owner is directly involved – make for good advertising. These tasks should be a closed loop, and evaluation of the results of this year's campaign should provide additional information on which to base next year's planning.

Chapter 13

Situation Analysis

Before you start planning to use advertising media, it is essential to analyse the current situation. You must have a full background knowledge of many business aspects before considering any advertising, for unless your campaign reflects these facets of your business, it cannot work to full advantage.

YOUR FIRM

A full knowledge of all aspects of your firm is essential. Is it old-established so that emphasis could be placed on tradition, or is it alternatively a newly-formed pioneer? Where is it based? Are you, in fact, considering a single organisation, or perhaps a range of companies? Do they operate nationally, on a Pan-European basis, internationally or multinationally? Do these companies operate individually with separate advertising identities, or does some corporate theme link them together? If the latter, this should surely be reflected in your own advertising. If the former, how are these autonomous profit-centres co-ordinated? It would clearly be a waste of advertising money to pre-empt your own companies on television rather than your competitors! Does your firm have access to the management services and skills of a parent company? Is sufficient finance available to mount an extensive advertising campaign? Clearly all these considerations affect not only the size and type of your advertising campaign but also its contents, so a thorough knowledge of these different aspects is essential.

YOUR PRODUCTS

Equally important is complete knowledge of the products or services to be advertised (both individually and over the complete range), since this can affect media policy just as much as creative content. Are they marketed individually or under a 'family' brand? Prices, sizes, colours, flavours, packaging – all are important. What are the limits to the amount your factory can produce: there is no point in over-selling and thus boosting sales of competitors' lines. What does your product actually do? Does it have a single use, or are you considering a multiple-use product? Sales might be increased, for example, by including recipes in the advertisements, thus pointing out additional uses for your product. Is there any special guarantee, or after-sales service? Is the service element more important than the product itself, as far as users are concerned? Perhaps you are considering a service as such, and your firm is a service organisation rather than a manufacturing company.

Clearly all these different aspects have direct implications for the planning of your advertising campaign. Whether the facts are supplied to you by the production staff or, as is more likely, you try the product for yourself, you must obtain all this vital information. Furthermore, you must ensure that you are notified, well in advance, of any possible changes. Having thoroughly studied the merchandise, you can now proceed to study the potential purchasers of your goods, known in advertising terminology as the 'market'.

YOUR MARKET

You must have a clear picture of the customers likely to be interested in your goods. Are they men or women? Married or single? What ages are they? What is their income? Of what 'class' are your customers – the man-in-the-street and his wife, or the 'professionals'? Who makes the actual purchase, and who influences the buying decision? The housewife may buy, but act in accordance with the wishes of her husband or children. Perhaps your potential customers are distinguished by a particular special interest, whether of race or creed, hobby or occupation. Sometimes the buyers may be other organisations rather than individuals, but it is equally important in such cases to know who makes the purchase and who influences it and the buying process.

Where are your customers located – are they local, in another part of the country, or spread throughout the world? Clearly this affects where you place your advertising. When do your customers buy, and how often? This information influences the timing of your campaign, and the frequency of the advertisements. Is your product bought on impulse, or only after careful consideration? How long is this consideration period?

This, too, clearly affects timing, and the type of campaign to be mounted.

What use do your customers make of your product, why do they buy it and why do they select one brand in preference to others? How strong is their brand loyalty? Are some people more likely than others to adopt your new products? How many potential buyers are there? Do some buyers use the product more heavily than others? An effective approach is to segment your market into Users and Non-users, and then further segment the former group into Light, Medium and Heavy users. And are their numbers increasing or decreasing, and if so at what rate?

Part 1 outlined the socio-economic categories into which much current research groups people, and those concerned with advertising planning have long been used to looking at demographic differences (measures such as age, income and social grade) between buyers and non-buyers. Sometimes, however, demographic measures alone fail to show real differences and, furthermore, many attitudes and interests which you might expect to relate to social grade are not, in fact, associated with grade.

Lifestyle classifications

Because of these weaknesses in the customary classifications, other techniques have been developed which try to distinguish buyers from non-buyers of a product by classification of personality type rather than conventional demographics. Lifestyle or psychographic analysis is an alternative approach to understanding your consumers. By gathering comprehensive information about people's attitudes, interests and activities, it produces generalised consumer profiles which are claimed to delineate 'real live people' in a superior way to the more traditional methods of classification. Protagonists assert that it demonstrates considerable potential in identifying new market segments and opportunities (as well as providing an extra creative input for advertising).

Anyone who has read the James Bond novels will recall how Ian Fleming's description of 007's clothes, cars and drinking habits give a far more realistic impression of his lifestyle than simply describing him as an A-grade consumer. (Bond enthusiasts who quibble that he is only intermediate rather than senior managerial, administrative or professional will not argue over his distinctive life-style!) This is an extreme example, but a more down-to-earth and practical approach has been developed which classifies people according to brief 'pen-portraits' which describe their background, attitudes and habits – rather than grouping them in social grades according to the chief income earner's occupation.

One approach is that of lifestyle profiling undertaken, among others, by NDL International (NDL). The basis of NDL's approach is the consumer link programme by which questionnaires are distributed in products and with services. 16,000 questionnaires are collected each day, eliciting lifestyle profiles on around 100 brands. Over time this has built into a database of more than 16 million individuals. Among the options provided by NDL is the *Lifestyle Selector* providing over 140 demographic and lifestyle characteristics options.

Another provider of consumer profiling data is Computerised Marketing Technologies Ltd, who issue the National Shoppers Survey compiled with the sponsored input of clients wishing to identify changing market trends and buying patterns. It has over 8 million records on five million homes.

This data is used to create the *Behaviour Bank*, a lifestyle database providing such information as

- hobbies
- sports and activities
- cultural pursuits
- betting and games
- hours of watching TV
- fashion, clothing and beauty
- appliance product ownership
- mail order buying
- business details
- pet ownership
- holiday and travel
- media consumption

Another approach to considering your market is in terms of *Sagacity Groups*, a lifestyle classification developed by Research Services Ltd. This alternative way of classifying consumers takes into account the individual's lifestyle, income and expenditure, and breaks the population down into groups according to whether they are 'blue or white collar', in the dependent, pre-family, family or late stage of life; in the last two stages respondents are also classified as better-off or worse-off, thus making 12 groups in all. Each group is designed to be as homogenous as possible, and contain respondents at a similar stage of their life cycle, with similar disposable income and cultural characteristics. These Sagacity groups are found to exhibit different behaviour patterns over a wide range of markets, in terms of media behaviour and product usage. The classifications are based on National Readership Survey data and give an interesting addition to the standard demographic classifications.

Geodemographic classification

Another way of considering your market is in Geodemographic terms, that is by obtaining information on individuals and the areas in which they live. The basic philosophy of geodemographic systems is that 'birds of a feather flock together': that by identifying existing customers who live in areas with similar characteristics, an advertiser can identify potential customers living in the same areas.

There are a number of providers of geodemographic systems who base their data on postcodes which are classified using various sources including census, electoral roll, demographic, financial, housing, retail trading and TGI data.

CACI's **ACORN** (A Classification of Residential Neighbourhoods) classifies the population of Great Britain into 54 Types which identify variations in lifestyle, purchasing and expenditure patterns and exposure to different advertising media.

The 54 neighbourhood Types (described in Chapter 7) are grouped into 17 groups (eg: group 1 is wealthy achievers in suburban areas) which in turn are described in 6 categories (eg: thriving, expanding, rising, settling, aspiring and striving).

There are various other ways of classifying your market geodemographically, including:

MOSAIC, developed by CCN Marketing is based on postcodes which are classified into 12 groups and 52 types. Examples of MOSAIC types include Clever Capitalists, Chattering Classes, High Spending Greys, Pre-Nuptual Owners. Other classification systems marketed by CCN include:

- **Psyche** a segmentation system based upon people's values and attitudes; it combines the 'why' people buy with the 'where' you can find them.
- **Financial MOSAIC** uses direct measures of financial activity to identify 10 groups and 36 types such as Captains of Industry, Over-Committed Owners and Welfare Dependency.
- **Regional Systems MOSAIC** provides segmentation systems for various regional needs such as Scottish MOSAIC and Northern Ireland MOSAIC, which reflect the differences in housing types. Another regional system is London Tribes classifying 300,000 London postcodes into 11 tribes and 40 sub tribes such as Affluent Opinion Formers, Ethnic Pride, Time-Saving Commuters and So-So Semis.
- **International MOSAIC** classifies over 700m consumers in 14 countries: Australia, Belgium, Germany, Ireland, Italy, Japan,

Netherlands, New Zealand, Norway, South Africa, Spain, Sweden, UK and USA. EuroMOSAIC classifies 310m European consumers into one of 10 EuroMOSAIC types such as Elite Suburbs, Luxury Flats, Rural/Agricultural.

Super Profiles is marketed by CDMS, part of the Littlewoods organisation. Two hundred and forty different variables are used to build Super Profiles, the core being the 1991 census enhanced with electoral roll data, credit information from Littlewoods mail order and finally, TGI.

There are 160 cluster groupings in Super Profiles, each one encompassed within a particular lifestyle (eg: Affluent Achievers). Within each lifestyle there are a range of target markets (for instance, Affluent Achievers encompasses three targets: very high income professionals in exclusive areas, mature families in stockbroker belts, and mature families in select suburban properties).

Special Workplace Statistics, another variation on the 'Where' question has turned attention to where people work, by means of a classification system developed by CACI. This operates in the same way as ACORN, in that it can function as a management/media information tool, for market identification and business location, and as an aid to market segmentation.

Comparing Geodemographic and Lifestyle Systems

Many advertisers utilise both lifestyle and geodemographic systems to analyse existing and potential customers. This dual approach is made easier by systems such as PORTRAIT, marketed by Equifax Decision Solutions, which fuses lifestyle and geodemographic data. It is a multi layered segmentation system allowing targeting at full postcode level by income, age and lifestyle. In addition to the typical constituent elements of geodemographic systems, PORTRAIT combines the NDL database, described above.

Media Usage

Another approach to classifying your buyers and potential buyers is to think of their *media* habits and attitudes. It is always salutary to remember that the easiest way to define a fashion-conscious woman is to point her out as 'one who reads fashion magazines'. Many firms already categorise their markets in terms of heavy, medium, light and non-users, and the same thinking can be applied to their 'use' of media

– are they heavy, medium, light or non-users of television, radio, newspapers, magazines or other media? Some advertisers now link their target markets with media audiences by relating them to the so-called Media Imperative groupings, which break the population down into four quartiles according to their media preference. Some women, for example, watch a great deal of television and are also heavy readers of women's magazines, others are more exposed to one of these two media than the other, while some women are difficult to reach through either medium. In this way, the population can be divided into four Media Preference Groups: Dual High (heavy exposure to both media), TV Preference (more exposure to TV than to print), Magazine Preference (those who read more than they view) and Dual Low (those with low exposure to both media). These preference groups, when related to heavy, medium, light or non-usage of your product, can be a most useful aid to media selection and planning. The classifications are based on Target Group Index data, and can provide a further interesting addition to the ways in which you can relate markets and media. Later, when selecting media to reach your chosen market, you should always bear in mind that advertising communication is a two-way process – how do your consumers use the media you are using to reach them?

In practice, you may well find that you have more than one homogenous target group, so it would be more accurate to refer to *market segments* than to *market*. For effective media planning, each segment must be clearly defined and sizes, trends and priorities established – without this knowledge, how can you start constructing a media schedule which delivers your advertising message to your selected target groups?

Knowledge of all these market factors is vital if your advertising campaign is to be effective. Considerable time and money can usefully be spent on research before planning begins, for unless you know your potential market segments you cannot select media to reach these people, nor create advertisements that will appeal to them. In addition you must bear in mind that your market is not static, but constantly changing as old customers leave and new ones come along. The replacement customers may perhaps be different and motivated by other desires, so that mere repetition of previously successful advertising may not show the same results. Market knowledge must be kept up-to-date, and your advertising policy adjusted accordingly. Study of market trends is, in fact, a never-ending task.

With knowledge of your firm and its products and market, you must now make a study – of how your company plans to sell these products to that market: in short, its marketing policy.

YOUR MARKETING POLICY

Advertising policy is affected by, and should reflect your company's marketing policy. The concept of marketing was outlined earlier, and your advertising campaign should bear direct relation to a number of marketing factors. Is the purpose of your advertising to launch a new product, a reminder campaign for an existing one, or an attempt to halt a decline in the market? If, on the other hand, your marketing decision is to increase sales, how is this to be achieved? Is the drive to be in a particular area? Is distribution of your product completely even across the entire country or is it regionally biased, or perhaps even limited to certain areas? Many companies divide their selling territory into areas, and the total marketing operation thus comprises a number of individual sales drives. A phased or 'rolling' product launch may be spread over a given time period, successively covering one area after another until national (or sometimes international) distribution is achieved. This will clearly affect media planning, since it calls for heavy initial advertising in appropriate areas during the launch periods, followed by a reminder campaign during the months that follow. Even where distribution is nationwide, your marketing decision may be to increase sales by pin-pointing a particular segment of the market (as distinct from a geographical area) for special attention, rather than attack on all fronts. Clearly, such marketing decisions directly affect media selection, and for effective use of advertising media you must appreciate the policy behind the choice made.

What is the structure of your sales force? How many sales staff does your company employ and how long does it take them to complete their round of calls? Do they call on all retailers, or rely on wholesalers to reach the smaller outlets? How dominant a role do the multiple shops and chains play? Or do you rely on direct mail or telemarketing to maintain contact with those intermediaries whom the sales force cannot visit frequently. Is your product extensively available or only in selected outlets? The need to feature names and addresses of local agents may have a marked influence on media selection. Are trade discounts competitive, or has your firm an advantage or disadvantage over rival producers? Promotional policies differ and manufacturers may adopt either a 'push' or a 'pull' approach – with the latter you give minimal discounts and use massive public advertising and sales promotion to pull your merchandise through the retail outlets. The retailer gets only a small amount per unit, but prospects of large sales stimulated by public advertising make him realise it will be to his advantage to stock your merchandise, so that he is ready to meet the public demand stimulated by your advertising. With a 'push' campaign, on the other hand, little is spent on public advertising, but heavy merchandising and attractive trade discounts are used to persuade the retailer to promote your goods, in view of the large sum he gets for every unit sold. In practice, naturally, it is rarely a question of operating at either extreme end of this push-pull scale but at some intermediate point, but clearly such factors determine whether or not to use the trade press and the timing of the support campaign.

With a thorough knowledge of firm and products, market and marketing policy, you must next study previous advertising.

PREVIOUS ADVERTISING

You must check carefully what advertising has appeared in the past and with what results, and see what lessons can be learned to increase the effectiveness of future campaigns. All too often money is wasted through failure to keep adequate records. Careful checking of results can lead to increased efficiency, bringing better results for the same expenditure, or achieving the same results for less outlay. Either way, the benefit to your company is obvious and previous advertising must, therefore, never be overlooked. Which advertising media proved effective in the past? What creative approaches appealed to prospective customers? What did these call for in terms of advertisement size, position, use of colour, and timing and duration of the campaign? Before planning future advertising you should check what you can learn from the past and, as has already been made clear, evaluation of the results of this year's campaign should provide the basis of next year's planning. This preliminary stage of situation analysis is thus directly linked with the final planning stage of evaluation of results, to which a later chapter is devoted.

CONSTRAINTS

In considering your future advertising plans, you may be faced with two different types of constraint – internal and external. Both should directly influence your advertising planning.

Internal The points considered here should have first arisen when reviewing your company and its activities under earlier headings. Is there a limit to the number of products your company can produce? There is no point in stimulating demand you cannot satisfy. Will financial constraints restrict your advertising budget? Is your distribution restricted to certain areas? This will influence your media selection. Do you have a list of dealers whose names and addresses must be featured in your advertising? This will affect choice of media, size of space booked and your creative content.

External Advertising practice is not a free-for-all with no holds barred. There are a number of legal constraints and voluntary codes that limit your actions. In some cases the constraint is fundamental and dictates media policy, eg you cannot advertise cigarettes on television or radio and they are severely restricted in youth magazines as well as poster sites in proximity to schools. Clearly your researches must make you fully aware of what you are (and are not) allowed to do and say – how else can you prepare an advertising campaign that satisfies these requirements? What constraints does the Data Protection Act impose on your direct mail database? What, if any, are the implications of the Financial Services Act? How will your advertisements be affected by the Advertising Standards Authority's British Codes of Advertising and Sales Promotion, the ITC's television code, or the Radio Authority's rulings? Detailed discussion of these legal and voluntary controls is beyond the scope of this book and, for the most part, they have creative rather than media implications.

COMPETITION

In investigating competition, you make not one study but at least six, since you must consider the competition faced from each of your rivals under the same six headings – firm, products, market, marketing policy, previous advertising and constraints.

What are the strengths and organisational weaknesses of rival companies? What products do your competitors make and how do they compare with your own? What are the strong and weak points of each? Who are your competitors' customers and how do they differ from those of your own company? And, most important, why do they purchase rival brands in preference to your own? Are your sales ahead or behind those of your competitors in the 'brand-share' table? Are you, or is one of your competitors, the brand leader and, if so, why? This may be due to differences in products or perhaps because of marketing policy, the next aspect of competitors' activity which you must study.

The marketing policy of competitive firms must be studied, item for item, against the points previously considered when investigating your own company's policy. Equal attention must be paid to the advertising campaigns of rival firms – which media do they use and what sizes and positions? How frequently do they advertise? What sales points are stressed in their advertisements and how are they illustrated? What are the constraints your competitors face? These may give you a competitive advantage you can feature in your advertising.

During World War II, Field Marshall Montgomery had a photograph of Field Marshall Rommel in his caravan HQ in the North African desert. He knew that only by getting inside the mind of his opponent could he expect to out-think and beat him. In planning your advertising, it is vital that you have a similarly thorough knowledge of the competition you face from others. A clear understanding of the indirect competition which your own and rival brands face from other product groups can be equally important.

MEDIA

As you would expect, your investigations should include gaining a first-rate knowledge of advertising media, the need for which was made clear in Part 1. This investigation is best approached from the concept of 'candidate' media, which should indicate those media that merit *in-depth* study. You may consider, for example, that to reach your AB target markets you should use 'quality national newspapers', but your plan must be far more detailed than that. To select between these newspapers, and to use them in such a way that they make the maximum contribution to achieving your campaign objective, you must first study them in detail.

This in-depth investigation should go far beyond simple statistics (such as costs, circulations, and comparison of costs-per-thousand) because Average Issue Readership (AIR) is only an estimate of the number of people who have read or looked at a copy of the publication for at least two minutes during its issue period. While this information is important, you should ask if there really is such a thing as an 'average' issue? As different readers look at some pages more than others, this calls for in-depth analysis of both editorial content and advertising format. What features does each publication carry on a regular basis, on which days of the week, and is adjacent advertising possible? The same advertisement could be made more effective, for example, by booking particular positions on specified feature pages which appear on certain days of the week in any given publication. Such positioning not only pin-points those readers with interests relevant to your product, but also ensures that your advertisement reaches them when they are in a receptive frame of mind.

Gaining such in-depth knowledge of media is no small task: it calls for daily study of every copy of each relevant medium – and its competitors – over numerous issues. Hence the importance of the candidate media concept, and having neither too long nor too short a list before beginning your detailed planning. Too long a list, and you will never complete your task. Too short a list, and you could perhaps overlook a medium which, through *effective* use, could make a positive contribution.

BACKGROUND

When undertaking your research and investigations it is important to recognise that you – and your competitors – do not operate in isolation, but against the background of a national economy increasingly influenced by international factors. To assist you in reviewing this background and placing your organisation in it, there are two useful acronyms: P-E-S-T and S-W-O-T.

P-E-S-T

These initial letters represent four background areas with direct implications for the success (or failure) of your organisation: *P*olitical, *E*conomic, *S*ociological and *T*echnological.

Political This analysis is not a question of whether you vote Conservative, Labour or Liberal Democrat, but simply recognising that political decisions in Westminster or Europe directly affect the day-to-day running of your business. Changes in tax structure, in capital allowances, or in development grants all illustrate how political decisions have immediate business implications. Changes in the law can be equally important.

Economic This area of course overlaps with the first, since different political parties have different policies for dealing with economic ills such as inflation, recession or unemployment. We must recognise, however, that our own economy is influenced by others – action on oil prices, changes in exchange rates, or other governments' decisions about interest rates all have far-reaching effects on the British standard of living.

Sociological Under this heading, you have only to consider the changing role of women and young people in our economy, the increasing number of single parents, general concern about health and environmental 'green' issues, changes to Sunday leisure/shopping habits, or the development of Britain's multi-racial society, to realise their direct implications on any advertising or marketing campaign. In some cases, of course, sociological and political changes interact, for example, lowering the voting age from 21 to 18, or legislation regarding racial, religious or sexual discrimination.

Technological We live in an increasingly technological society – think of the constant flow of new and technologically improved products. Even if your own product is not undergoing a technological revolution, your organisation is certainly affected by technological changes, particularly as these affect advertising media. Printing quality has improved for most press media, colour is increasingly available and copy dates are shortening. Television has been revolutionised by satellite and cable. Shortly, television and radio will both be revolutionised by Digital Broadcasting. As Internet technology speeds up, for instance to show video, advertising will be affected. Direct mail has also undergone a technological revolution. To varying degrees, all advertising media have been affected.

S-W-O-T

These initial letters come from a well-known marketing analysis which has equal application to deciding advertising policy. Bearing in mind the many factors just reviewed and likely future trends, what are your Strengths and Weaknesses, and what are the Opportunities and Threats facing your organisation?

THE IMPORTANCE OF RESEARCH

Without research into all eight points discussed above, it is impossible for you to plan effectively. Before thinking about future advertising, therefore, your first task is to make a full analysis of all these matters. Then, and only then, can you give thought to planning future advertising.

Research is vital for accurate media selection. Media planning can be likened to aiming a gun: you cannot hit a target unless you know what and where the target is, and it is research that frequently provides this information. Research also helps in timing your campaign, by indicating when your product is purchased and how frequently, and whether it is an impulse purchase or one that needs serious reflection, the latter calling for your advertising message to be delivered well in advance with subsequent reminders.

Research can equally be helpful to creative staff. Your product may have dozens of sales points, any one of which could be featured in your advertising, and it is of major importance to select the particular benefit that will attract attention and lead readers to study your advertisement more closely. Featuring the correct sales point attracts attention and, equally, featuring the wrong 'copy platform' loses attention – and sales. Should the creative work be based on something of lesser importance, the potential customers may not bother to read the advertisement and will thus miss the sales point which *is* of major interest – and would have clinched the sale had they known of it.

Research can thus make a significant contribution to media planning and creative work by ensuring that it is soundly based. Its purpose, however, is only to set the framework for media and creative work: it will not prepare a media schedule nor the creative content of your advertisements. Research does not dispense with the need for good media planners or creative staff, but does provide an efficient tool to make their work more effective.

Market research has been defined as 'the systematic study of products (and services) – existing or potential – in relation to their markets'. You could obtain information by going out to interview potential customers personally, but field research is both costly and time-consuming, and the necessary information may already have been collected by some other organisation. Research does not necessarily imply spending large sums of money calling in a professional market research company to undertake scientifically planned investigations – although naturally the information that results from such action can be invaluable. Research also includes your own reading, and the number of information sources you can consult is extremely large: there are numerous government surveys and reports, the many data sources detailed in the chapters on media research and on specialist sources, and there are the innumerable research documents published by media-owners, advertisers and agencies. If to this list is added information available from analysis of your own internal records, the research undertaken by trade, professional and technical associations and institutions, and the reports and publications available from other sources, then the wealth of information that is available, provided you know where to look, will be apparent – as will the invaluable contribution of desk research. Good desk research could make field research unnecessary by locating the information required, perhaps a bit here and a bit there, in the many different published sources, and so not only save the expenditure of several thousand pounds on a field survey, but save vital time as well. Any book on media must necessarily cover desk research and – as when field research was discussed in an earlier chapter – there is thus an in-built tendency for it to become a book on research as such. But a line must be drawn somewhere and so, having drawn attention to its role in providing information on which to base your planning, discussion of desk research will end here, other than mentioning that a good librarian could provide you with invaluable help in locating relevant information sources, either direct or through various directories in which such sources are listed.

PLANNING YOUR PROGRAMME

It is important to recognise that, although listed as the Advertising Manager's first task, these initial investigations must be approached as an on-going programme. Situation analysis is in fact a never-ending exercise – today's newspapers may contain news that directly affects both you and your target groups, and markets must be monitored throughout the campaign.

Pareto Analysis

Many newly-appointed executives recognise that research never ends; their problem is 'where to begin?' For example, how should you set about situation analysis on joining a company with an extensive range of products, selling to numerous types of purchaser, spread across a large number of different markets? One solution is so-called 'Pareto analysis', applying the 80/20 rule based on previous profits.

Such analysis frequently shows some products, purchasers or markets to be more profitable than others, usually in an 80/20 ratio. If 80 per cent of your profits come from only 20 per cent of your product range, it is logical to concentrate initially on finding out all you can about those particular products. For those selected products, the same analysis can reveal which target groups are the most profitable, and within which particular markets. In this way, you identify the relatively small number of big buyers who merit most attention.

The converse is that 80 per cent of your products, purchasers and markets account for only 20 per cent of profits, and Pareto analysis can identify the many small buyers making only a limited contribution to profits, who merit less attention.

As we shall see later when discussing media planning, advertising expenditure can then be allocated between the more and less profitable target groups in the same proportions, according to their 'market weights' or values.

Always remember, however, that all market situations are necessarily in a constant state of flux. While the 80/20 rule is a sound starting point, do not overlook that its very opposite – 20/80 analysis – can often make an equally positive contribution. Hence the importance of a never-ending study of trends, to identify those products, purchasers or minority markets which, although making only a small profit contribution at present, are the 'big earners' of the future. Fighting competitors for today's markets should not prevent you from cultivating tomorrow's profitable target groups, which your rivals may not yet have identified.

The alternative approach

Pareto analysis, which implies that past profit figures are available for analysis, may be inapplicable for entirely new products. How could you set about planning to launch – with no previous data – a revolutionary new service, highly relevant to a wide range of possible purchasers within a large number of different market segments? Conventional research is both costly and time-consuming and, in any case, in which of these many markets should you begin your investigations? An alternative approach is to formally recognise this absence of data, spend your money on advertising rather than conventional research, use advertising as a research tool, and plan your campaign on the 'shotgun' principle. If both purchasers and markets are unknown quantities, it is clearly impossible to mount a focused campaign, and your objective must therefore be to get possible prospects to identify themselves. Accordingly, your campaign can then feature a large number of small direct-response advertisements spread over a wide range of candidate media. Your initial advertising serves a research function: those market segments requesting further information clearly merit attention, and future campaigns can be focused accordingly.

THE NEXT STEP

With your initial investigations complete, you now have a firm base on which to undertake your next task. This is determining your advertising strategy, described in the next chapter.

Chapter 14

Determining Your Advertising Strategy

With a thorough knowledge of your firm and its products, its market and marketing policy, your previous advertising, the various constraints imposed, the competition you face, candidate media, and business background, you can now commence more positive action – problem analysis and determination of your specific advertising objective.

Advertising is a means of achieving an objective. Your firm may have more than one reason for advertising, and thus need to run two or more concurrent advertising campaigns. The underlying purpose of these campaigns may also change from time to time, with circumstances.

There is a remarkably wide range of reasons for advertising – one well-known analysis* contains a checklist of 52 advertising tasks! Even the more fundamental reasons are, surprisingly enough, a blind spot to many advertising people, who are so engrossed in the detail of their work that they overlook the need to define clearly the basic purpose of their advertising. Many times, when you enquire about the objective of a proposed advertising campaign, you receive a surprised look and the answer 'Why, it's to increase sales, of course' – as though you had asked a foolish question. But how are these increased sales to be achieved? 'Increased sales' is not a business objective but only an optimistic hope for the future. If these increased sales are, in fact, to be realised, then there must be a definite objective for, as you will see later, this will affect the type of advertising campaign, the media used and its creative content.

A useful exercise is to take a random selection of advertisements and try to 'read back' from the creative content just what was the *specific* objective. Very few participants in this exercise will achieve a 100 per cent strike rate, which surely proves two points:

* *Defining Advertising Goals for Measured Advertising Results* by R. Colley (see Chapter 20).

227

1 Many advertising people have a blind spot when it comes to analysing advertising effectiveness.
2 Many advertisements are not effective, simply because those responsible for the campaign failed to establish a clear objective.

This may be a 'Heads I win, tails you lose' argument, but why else should we not be able to achieve a 100 per cent success rate in analysis?

In no way should you underestimate the importance of creativity in advertising, but creativity is functional only when it contributes to achieving your campaign objective. Specification of a clear objective assists creative people by setting the parameters within which they should work: it gives a strong indication of the creative approach necessary, quite apart from being essential for good media planning. This book concentrates on direct media aspects, but these cannot be treated separately from creative considerations.

ANALYSIS OF SPECIFIC OBJECTIVES

Analysis of advertising campaigns in a wide range of media revealed a large number of different specific objectives: these are discussed below, but not necessarily in any order of importance. The list is not exclusive, nor should the objectives be considered as separate 'water-tight' compartments. You may wish to achieve two or more purposes simultaneously – or perhaps your company has an objective not included in the list (I readily admit my own blind spot). The main point is the essential need to set out clearly, before starting to plan your campaign, *precisely* what you hope to achieve. Planning and creativity will then follow that much more easily. This implies that, in order to be accountable, objectives should be SMART. This acronym stands for:

Specific
Measurable
Achievable
Realistic
Timed

Some critics have argued that any systematic analysis must restrict the creative process. On the contrary, it should liberate creative staff, by ensuring that their efforts are concentrated on providing the ideal creative solution to the *real* problem facing the advertiser. Possible campaign objectives might include the following.

Reminding existing users

You must constantly remind users of your wares. Why 'must'? Well, human memory is short, and frequent reminders are necessary. Moreover, there are innumerable distracting factors which soon make memory fade. In some cases, it may be the advertising of rival firms. There is also the competition for attention faced from makers of totally different products: television sets face indirect competition from washing machines, holidays abroad, or new furniture. Taking a still wider view of the many factors competing for public attention, there are thousands of non-selling influences at work to make people forget your products – the latest news at home and abroad, the activities of family and friends, new events at work and the latest films and television programmes. The manufacturer who expects to be permanently remembered amid this host of competing calls on public attention is more than optimistic. An apocryphal story tells how Wrigley, the chewing gum magnate, was once asked during a train journey why he spent so much money on advertising. Surely, his questioner asked, everybody knew Wrigley's chewing gum and everybody chewed Wrigley's chewing gum? Why the need for such heavy advertising? Wrigley supposedly replied that he would answer if the questioner told him how fast the train was going – and promptly denied he was changing the subject. When told that the train's speed was about 70 miles an hour, Wrigley immediately asked 'Why keep the engine on the front?' Reminder advertising maintains momentum in the same way and, if this is your objective, there are clear implications as to choice of media and creative content. Furthermore, constant reminders through advertising can enhance your firm's reputation and standing, and play their part in cementing customer loyalty. Reminder advertising is, however, quite distinct from the need to reassure previous purchasers – another specific purpose discussed below.

Reassuring previous purchasers

The need to reassure previous purchasers is a task quite different from that of simply reminding existing users. For many products, particularly where major expenditure is involved, current owners are key figures in the decision process of potential purchasers. If you reflect on any major purchase you have made, you will realise that in almost every case you sought the advice of somebody who had already bought the product. *Their* view was far more influential than any salesman, and much current advertising therefore takes account of the theory of 'cognitive dissonance'. This theory is based on the idea that if a person knows various things that are not psychologically consistent with each other he will, in a variety of ways, try to make them more consistent in order to reduce this dissonance. To illustrate how advertising planning should allow for this, take the case of someone who so dislikes waking up in ice-cold rooms that he installs central heating. After some months, the unpleasantness of cold mornings will fade from his memory, and all he remembers is the previously non-existent heating bills. Ask such a person for his views on central heating and you will hear how expensive it is to run and not a word about the benefits. As such negative reactions would put off prospective purchasers, much advertising recognises this and aims at reassuring previous purchasers just as much as attracting new ones. If your product comes into this category, the need to 'keep customers sold' has clear implications for both media choice and creative content.

Countering the natural decline in the market

Reminder advertising can be most effective in maintaining sales, but you must face up to the fact that your existing customers, through no fault of yours, are steadily decreasing in number. The manufacturer who claims there is no need to advertise because he has all the business he needs ignores the fact that people leave the area or the country, change their circumstances or just stop using his product. The quality of your product may remain as high as ever, but sales will steadily decline through the natural diminution of the existing market. As Lord Keynes once pointed out, in the long term we're all dead! New customers must be attracted to counter this decline, and advertising is one of the means available to achieve this end.

Informing the constant flow of potential customers

The population is ceaselessly changing, not only in size but also in composition. As they grow older, people change from schoolchild to teenager, to young married to parent, and perhaps to grandparent. As they move from one consumer group to another, so their needs change; they become potential customers for goods which previously were of no interest to them. Similarly, in the technical field, firms change in size and in the scope of their operations, and need to purchase new plant, equipment or facilities. They become new prospects, and advertising can convert them into customers. Many firms mistakenly assume that, just because they have been advertising for years, people must know about the merchandise they have to offer. This ignores the fact that many prospective customers entered the market for the first time *today*, and earlier advertising therefore had only a limited effect. Research has proved that people look at advertisements for products which interest them, and ignore others. Yesterday these potential purchasers were not in the market, so were unlikely to respond to advertisements for the merchandise in question.

The constantly changing market

The fact that the market is ceaselessly changing is a blind spot for many advertisers. Markets steadily decline through natural causes, there are always potential new customers in need of information and, in the meantime, you need to remind and perhaps reassure existing customers. If you consider your own journey through life, the practical implications of this obvious statement become apparent. In your infancy you were, through your parents, in the market for nappies and talcum powder. As you left this market, the manufacturers of these products needed new customers to replace the sales lost when you no longer needed their merchandise. Your life can, in fact, be described in terms of products which you use for the first time, others about which you need reminding, and those which you eventually no longer need. Such a list would include school clothing, bicycles, razor blades and cosmetics, engagement and wedding rings, homes and furniture, baby clothes and push chairs, and so on through to false teeth and hair pieces. Such analysis has been extended to describe markets in terms of the dependent, singles, mating, breeding, full nest and empty nest stages. Population trends are important here, in recognising the increasing numbers of 'golden wrinklies', for example. We all finish up in what has been given the macabre title of the coffin and cremation market! At every stage of our lives we represent, simultaneously, lost customers for one producer and prospective buyers for another. Advertising planning, if it is to be effective, must take account of these never-ending changes in the market.

Information about new developments

Present customers may know of your goods, but do they know of any improvements made, or of new lines added to your range? Firms devote a great deal of time, money and effort to improving their products, but this is of little purpose if customers are left in the dark about them. They must be informed about new or improved products, new packs, or the delivery of eagerly awaited goods. Prices and products are constantly changing, and it is a great mistake for any manufacturer to believe that, just because *he* knows about these things, his customers are equally well-informed. Potential customers will not become purchasers unless they know of the new developments, and advertising helps to keep them informed. Furthermore, changes in your product line may open up new market segments, for whom your earlier products were not of interest. Again, there are clear media and creative implications.

Stabilised production

For a number of advertisers, their objective is not to increase sales but to stabilise demand. If demand for your product is unsteady, your factory has to work at full capacity – perhaps even overtime – while sales are high, but when demand falls off machinery lies idle. A sales graph with great peaks and troughs makes for uneconomic production. Advertising can help to even out the graph in two different ways.

One solution to problems arising from uneven production is to plan your advertising to fill the troughs. There is a net increase in sales but you stimulate the market only at specified times of the year. The other way of levelling out your sales graph is by shifting sales from peaks to troughs: in this latter case there is no increase in sales but, by using advertising to persuade consumers to make their purchases in slack rather than peak periods, expenses are reduced with an obvious increase in profit. Stabilised production as an advertising objective can be applied not only seasonally but also between days of the week or even hours of the day.

Advertising can facilitate making the most efficient use of your resources and such considerations directly affect the timing of your campaign and its creative content.

Fighting declining sales

The purpose of your campaign may be not to increase or stabilise sales, but to hold off a decline. This overall category, in fact, masks various types of decline, for which different advertising approaches are necessary. One advertising campaign may have as its purpose countering the natural decline in the market, mentioned above. Another purpose might be to sustain an existing brand against competition. Other purposes might be to slow down a permanent trend, or to reverse a temporary decline.

Where the market for your product is steadily diminishing, it is unwise to expect advertising to work miracles and reverse the permanent trend: it may, however, be able to make some contribution by slowing the rate of decline, thus giving you time to seek new opportunities in other directions. Where advertising can make a far more positive contribution is in countering temporary falls in sales. The

Chancellor's budget, for example, may introduce tax changes in relation to specific groups of products, or impose credit restrictions which inhibit sales. Positive advertising, emphasising value for money, can help people adjust more swiftly to the new conditions.

Increased advertising is one method you can adopt to avert a slump, but the underlying causes call for different types of advertising campaign.

Overcoming resistance

Many companies seem to assume that the public is merely waiting for a suitable advertising message to stimulate them into buying the product. But people are wary of buying unfamiliar products, and retailers equally shy of stocking lines unknown to their customers. More than this, people may even be hostile: consider, for example, the reluctance of many drivers to change their drinking habits, and how successive 'don't drink and drive' campaigns have contributed to reducing road accidents. If your product encounters such resistance, advertising can do much to overcome this sales barrier by building up a favourable image in the public mind.

'Prestige' advertising

The popular 'title' for this type of advertising covers allied uses – you will come across references to mood-selling, image-building, corporate or institutional advertising. Certainly some organisations may need to concentrate on their image rather than their products but, alas, in many cases this approach is misused, or even taken as an easy way out! Many cynical creative directors have remarked that, when all else fails, you can always rely on the old stand-by of an aerial view of the factory and a picture of the Chairman to keep everybody happy! But for this type of advertising to be effective, you must ask very fundamental questions. Whose opinion are we concerned about? What opinion do these people hold now? If your image is bad, is this, in fact, well deserved? If it *is*, then no amount of so-called prestige advertising can rectify matters: the true solution is to put things right and only then set about advertising. For this type of advertising to be effective, you must know who constitutes your market, what these people think now, and precisely what you want them to think in the future. Unless you have the answers to these questions you can neither choose media nor decide upon creative content.

Whilst in the general area of consumer opinions, you should also consider those cases where manufacturers attempt – perhaps at the same time as achieving the main aim of 'selling' their products – to change consumer attitudes. In such circumstances, it is vital to distinguish between basic beliefs and short-term behaviour. Many consumers have deeply entrenched views based on their total experience of a product – or product group – perhaps going back to their childhood days. As you would expect, it is no easy task for advertising to shift such views, which may be paralleled by market trends. Whilst advertising can be very effective in influencing short-term buying behaviour, changing long-term beliefs or market trends is a very different matter. Advertising can rarely reverse a negative trend (see 'fighting declining sales' above) but it can help encourage a positive one.

'Umbrella' campaigns

The underlying purpose of many corporate campaigns is not prestige as such, but to link various separate activities. Examples are often found where organisations are active in various fields, with separate divisions marketing separate products to separate markets via separate advertising and selling campaigns. Many such organisations realise that linking their self-contained business operations would benefit all the component companies. To illustrate how this applies in practice, divisions A, B, C and D might each have sales campaigns for their separate industrial markets, with appropriate advertising in the relevant professional or technical press. National press would normally be ruled out as too few readers come within the specified categories of buyer. But as many industrial purchasers buy not only product A but also perhaps B, C and D as well, the separate advertising campaigns in specialised press can be made more effective by an 'umbrella' campaign in more general media, on the creative theme of 'If you need advice on A, B, C or D, we are the experts'. Sales representatives from the individual companies then cross-refer enquiries, as necessary. Such an advertising objective clearly has a much more functional aim than a so-called 'prestige' campaign, and there are clear implications for both media choice and advertisement content. The same effect can apply, however, even within a single company, as is explained in the following section.

Benefit to other lines

A similar effect to an umbrella campaign may apply within a single organisation. One obvious effect of advertising is to increase sales of the item featured, but a secondary result may be increased sales of *other* lines. A retailer, for example, is likely to find that people make more than one purchase when they call at his shop to buy an advertised product. Multi-product manufacturers also benefit correspondingly when the publicity afforded their brand name by advertising one item helps other lines in their range: hence the importance of establishing, at the earlier investigation stage, whether there is any family branding or corporate communication theme which links the autonomous profit centres which produce your various products.

If advertising is likely to have a beneficial 'spin-off' for your other products, this added advantage must be borne in mind when planning your campaign. The chapter on the advertiser mentioned the existence of 'brand managers' and the question then arises of whether a company with this marketing structure is likely to adopt such a co-ordinated approach.

Launch a new product or service

For new products or services, reminder advertising is clearly inapplicable: here the task is one of basic education – informing potential customers of the benefits they will reap by purchasing your new product. A side effect of this may well be, in due course, a counter campaign to fight declining sales by the manufacturer whose product is no longer in favour.

Market Research

The previous chapter pointed out that, on occasion, the Advertising Manager must accept that the information necessary for an effective product launch is not available. In such circumstances, two possibilities present themselves. One is to commission the necessary market research. The alternative is to proceed despite this lack of data, spend money on advertising rather than field surveys, use advertising as a research tool, and prepare a campaign (often on a 'shotgun' basis) to make prospective purchasers identify themselves. Consumer response is then carefully evaluated, to identify target groups ripe for subsequent development through focused campaigns in targeted media. As the database marketing section pointed out, this alternative approach – planning campaigns in such a way as to obtain all necessary information – could replace conventional market research in some product areas.

Even for those firms not able to develop their database so directly, this advertising objective clearly links with the later planning stage of *Evaluation of Results*. As Chapter 20 makes clear, evaluation is a vital stage, whatever your campaign objective.

Extending distribution

In some cases, your advertising may be aimed not at the public but at stockists. A manufacturer who finds his product in insufficient outlets will seek to widen his distribution and would use advertising as a tool for this purpose. Trade press advertising is obvious in this respect but consumer advertising is equally effective, when sales representatives take round specimen advertisements which they employ as a most persuasive argument in getting retailers to stock and display your merchandise. If extended distribution is the purpose of your campaign, it is often to your advantage to book advertisements of a larger size than is strictly necessary to convey the creative message, simply because of the impact this larger size has on retailers in getting them to anticipate a heavy demand.

Stimulate existing distribution

As with the previous case, advertising is used for its effect on retailers rather than the general public. The difference is that your product is widely distributed but you consider the stockists insufficiently active in promoting sales. To rectify this, you can use heavy local advertising to persuade hitherto passive retailers to give your products more window and in-store display. As before, larger sizes than are strictly necessary can be most helpful when using advertising in this way as a sales tool for representatives. In both this and the previous case you may find it advantageous to feature the names and addresses of stockists, perhaps on a co-operative basis. Such considerations clearly influence the choice of media, and the way in which you use it.

An extreme example which shows clearly how the need to influence distributors can affect media planning concerns a less than active builders' merchant. Booking poster sites immediately facing and adjacent to his shop contributed markedly to overcoming his former apathy!

Back-up for sales representatives

As in the previous two cases, the underlying target for your advertising is not the general public – here, its aim is to stimulate your representatives. Salesmen, in the field all day and thus out of contact with your sales office, soon feel cut off and may become dispirited. One important activity here is to keep the sales force informed with copies of media schedules and advertisements. It is very discouraging for the sales force when the first they hear of an advertising campaign is from a customer! Advertising can give your sales representatives a much needed psychological boost. Where representatives sell to industrial buyers rather than to retailers who then sell to the public, this back-up role can be vital. Advertising aimed at extending or stimulating distribution can also be considered under this heading, for its indirect effect in boosting your salesmen's confidence and thus encouraging them in their efforts. A classic McGraw-Hill advertisement, designed to promote advertising in its specialist publications, showed a steely-eyed industrial buyer looking at the reader and saying:

'I don't know who you are.

I don't know your company.

I don't know your company's product.

I don't know what your company stands for.

I don't know your company's customers.

I don't know your company's record.

I don't know your company's reputation.

Now – what was it you wanted to sell me?'

MORAL: Sales start before your salesman calls – with business publication advertising.

McGRAW-HILL MAGAZINES
BUSINESS •PROFESSIONAL •TECHNICAL

Leads for sales representatives

This use of advertising differs from the previous instances in that it is aimed at the consumer, but the salesman is still a key figure because the purpose of the campaign is to provide him with sales leads on which to call. Salesmen's time is valuable and at a premium, and following up contacts who have indicated positive interest by, for example, returning a coupon is far more productive than cold canvassing. This was the main advertising function for one client whose account I handled: the aim was a steady stream of leads to keep sales staff busy. Although planned on a long-term basis, scheduling was extremely flexible with advertising activity being stepped up when necessary or cut back when the representatives had more business than they could handle. For this client, effective advertising clearly demanded flexible media planning.

Direct selling and mail order

Much the same type of strategic planning may be necessary for those who sell direct to the consumer, using advertising to spread information about their products and to solicit orders. As was the case when keeping representatives supplied with sales leads, a flexible media plan is necessary to keep demand and supply in balance. This objective links clearly with the concept of database marketing discussed earlier – as does the next objective.

Building up a mailing list

Some advertisers have found it profitable to vary this pattern when selling direct. The initial mailing list is built up by public advertising and direct mail then used to obtain orders from those who have expressed interest. Direct marketing is the primary aim of the campaign, and general advertising is used to 'top up' the mailing list from time to time since this must necessarily suffer the natural decline inherent in every market.

Clearance of surplus supplies

Advertising is often used on an occasional rather than regular basis, and the 'sales' which feature so prominently on the retail scene reflect this. Sales advertising often serves two quite distinct purposes – one is to boost sales at an otherwise slack period (as described above) while the other purpose is to clear shelves of last year's stock to make way for new merchandise. The retailer makes the old stock more attractive by cutting prices, and makes this reduction known through his Sale advertising. Additional benefits come from the fact that valuable storage space is cleared to make way for new merchandise, and cash provided to pay for it.

Dispose of by-products

In other cases, the purpose may be to market by-products rather than to clear dead stocks. In manufacturing its main product, your company may produce a by-product which it wishes to sell at a profit.

This exercise differs from the main selling operation in that sales volume is dictated by the main product, demand for which determines production levels, which in turn control the amount of by-product produced. The aim of the by-product advertising campaign is thus to sell just so much and no more, since there is little purpose in stimulating a massive demand for this secondary product when supplies could not be increased without creating an unsaleable surplus of the main product. Any promotional plan thus has a 'cut-off' point dictated by the main sales programme, which your media scheduling must clearly take into account.

Utilising other marketing strengths

There are other circumstances in which advertising planning is determined by your company's overall marketing programme, rather than by demand for the single product for which you are preparing a campaign. This can occur when manufacturers review their product range and make a work study of sales force effectiveness. A producer may find, for example, that his representatives are not working to full capacity: this is no reflection on his sales staff and their efforts, but simply recognises that the present product range does not keep them fully occupied. There is thus spare sales force capacity, and the question then is: 'What additional product, which would be of interest to current buyers, could your salesforce carry and sell effectively?' If a further item is added to round out your company's product line, this is another case where promotional planning will be determined by factors outside the usual considerations, depending on the main marketing programme.

Advertising as an aid to buying

Advertising has been defined as 'making known in order to sell' but on many occasions your aim may be the very opposite – not to sell, but to buy. Many business needs are put out to tender, the contract being advertised and the order going to the firm submitting the best bid. Similarly, 'Situations Vacant' advertisements are the recognised way of locating suitable applicants to fill staff vacancies. At the start of this chapter mention was made that the various reasons for advertising should not be considered as water-tight compartments, and that two or more purposes may be applicable at any one time: 'Situations Vacant' is an example of where this applies. Many firms realise that, whilst a small classified advertisement might be sufficient to convey the bare facts of a post, they face competition for the best applicants who are more likely to respond to a prestige advertisement which conveys that they would be working for the leading company in the field. Employers realise also that not only potential applicants see these advertisements but also many others, including the public at large, suppliers, shareholders and customers. Such positive recruitment advertisements can also help weaken competitors' morale!

Arbitrary reasons for advertising

This section should not be here but, alas, it would be unrealistic not to recognise the sad fact that, whilst there are many sound reasons why advertising can be the most effective way of helping you achieve your purpose, there are also a number of other 'reasons' for advertising which are less rational. To give one example, it is not unknown for a producer to advertise out of personal pride: it gives him satisfaction to see his name (together with his picture and an aerial view of his factory!) in print or some other advertising medium, and to feel that his friends and acquaintances think of him as an important man.

Media selection can also be influenced by arbitrary factors – the advertiser's motivating force may perhaps be tradition: his firm has always used the medium in question. Alternatively, he may feel 'forced in' because he does not wish to be the odd man out. Or again, he may feel he has a 'duty' to support the relevant trade magazine or exhibition. Sometimes this latter aim is not as irrational as it appears: some firms realise they *need* the publication or exhibition, and equally appreciate that the media-owner's sales revenue from copies or admissions is insufficient to make the venture commercially viable. Since the manufacturers have a clear need for this particular means of communication they support it, and advertising thus has in it an element of subsidy. In other cases, by booking space in special programmes, firms use advertising as an indirect means of making donations to charity.

Increased sales

This reason for advertising has deliberately been left until last: not because it is unimportant – far from it – but because it demands greater attention and more detailed analysis than the other reasons so far discussed.

The so-called aim of 'increased sales' is perhaps the most frequent blind spot in the whole advertising and marketing process. It is a great weakness that many firms, both large and small, regard 'increased sales' as a sufficiently clear objective on which to base an advertising campaign. But 'increased sales' is *not* a specific objective – it is only a wish for the future. What percentage increase are you aiming for? By which date? Where are these increased sales to come from? How are they to be achieved? The lucidity of the answers to these questions will influence the effectiveness of your advertising campaign, and directly affect not only media choice but also the way in which the selected media are used in terms of size, position and frequency. Equally fundamental is the influence of these answers on the advertising content, in terms of creative approach.

Too many people overlook the fundamental fact that different routes to increased sales call for different types of advertising campaign, in terms of both creative content and media strategy. One well-known marketing matrix suggests four basic ways of increasing sales:

- existing products to existing markets
- existing products to new markets
- new products to existing markets
- new products to new markets

These possibilities can be evaluated against a 'risk' scale, with the fourth clearly being the most risky.

While this matrix can assist marketing planning, it is unsatisfactory for advertising purposes since it fails to take account of competition, nor does it consider campaigns which persuade customers to switch brands. An alternative approach is therefore necessary, and the matrix below facilitates both media and creative planning.

A first essential is to stop thinking in terms of increased sales, and to think instead of increased *purchases* – or, more specifically, possible purchasers and their buying patterns. Viewed in purchasing terms, there are three ways in which you can increase sales of existing products.

1 Increased purchases by existing users Such a campaign will convert light into medium users or medium into heavy, and your aim is to extend the range of uses they make of your product, or increase their frequency of use. This will increase the value of the market, but not its size in terms of people.

2 Purchases by new users With such a campaign, your aim is to educate non-users (who have not used your own product nor that of any rivals) about the benefits of your product, thus converting them to its use. Advertising of this type will increase the size of the market in terms of people, as well as its value. But see the warning note below.

3 Purchase by competitors' customers Your campaign aim here is to persuade buyers (existing or potential) of rival products to switch brands. This will not increase the 'size of the cake' – only the way it is divided.

These three routes to increased sales of existing products facilitate advertising planning more effectively than the earlier matrix which suggested only two markets – existing and new – and ignored opportunities for brand-switch sales.

The new matrix does not yet allow for *new* products. This term could encompass replacements for existing products, or extensions to an existing range, as well as entirely new product lines, so clearly advertising analysis must now extend beyond the three possibilities so far considered. A full planning matrix should also allow for:

4 Purchases of new products by existing customers There are many advantages when planning such a campaign – you know who your present customers are and can perhaps reach them through, for example, direct mail. Furthermore, your advertising messages can build on existing knowledge: there is (hopefully) a wealth of goodwill to assist in launching your new product.

5 Purchases of new products by new users This is similar to the second possibility (purchases of existing products by new users) in that the target group has not used the new product and needs educating about its benefits. One significant difference is that as the product is *new*, there is no track record on which to build: the testimonial approach of 'thousands of satisfied users' is not applicable. Secondly, there is no goodwill from which to benefit. And there is, again, a warning note, discussed below.

6 Purchases of new products by competitors' customers Although similar to route No 3 (purchases of existing products by competitors' customers) the differences are again significant – there is again no track record on which to build, and furthermore you must fight established goodwill to rival companies.

If the new product is a multi-use one, this six-route matrix can be extended by subsequent campaigns which suggest new product uses (or, for a single-use product, reasons for more frequent use). This completes the circle by returning to the first route to increased sales – existing users to use more.

A warning note

In considering sales to 'new users' – and indeed *all* purchasers – you must be careful to distinguish between long-term basic beliefs and short-term current needs. Advertising can be most effective in influencing short-term buying behaviour but, as earlier paragraphs made clear, changing beliefs is a very different matter. A simple example is wedding dresses, which at first sight would appear to be 'purchases by new users'. In the strict sense this is of course true, but you would be very unwise to plan your advertising appeal on this basis – there is no need to 'educate non-users about the benefits of your product, thus converting them to its use': women *know* the use of a wedding dress! Equally, no woman is going to rush out and buy one because of new styles, low prices or easy credit terms: the purchase of a wedding dress depends directly on her long-term views on marriage, on accepting a proposal, and on her deeply entrenched views about white weddings. In this sense, the sale of a wedding dress is a brand-switch operation: the woman's decision is made, and your objective is to persuade her to buy a wedding dress from your company. The same reasoning applies to another example, this time for the (mostly) male market – a new exhaust system for your car. This time there are few (if any) 'basic beliefs' but in no way will you spend money on a new one until it is essential to do so: the decision to replace your exhaust system is made for you by circumstances, and your task – aided by suitable advertisements – is to decide where to go to get it. In this case you will actually seek out information, so this is another example of how people *use* advertisements that are being used to reach them. Both examples illustrate the need to consider the long-term and short-term effects of your advertising, as well as consumers' entrenched beliefs and short-term needs – your immediate campaign aim might be to attract possible customers who are in the market for a product *now* but, at the same time, your advertising will also be seen by others who – although they have no need of your product at present – may want it in future and, when the time comes, may recall your company name in this respect.

Wedding dresses and exhaust systems are extreme examples and, in most cases, 'sales to new users' means just what it says, and your task is to explain to non-users the benefits they will get from your product. If your analysis is correct, they should be grateful for the information and buy the product, to your mutual benefit.

If the increased sales/increased purchases analysis is reduced to the most fundamental level, it will be apparent that media policy and basic creative content can then be entered on a chart as shown overleaf.

A campaign designed to meet one of these objectives is unlikely to be as successful in achieving the other five since they call for different advertising in terms of both media and creative content.

Type of sales increase	Media policy	Creative content
EXISTING PRODUCTS		
1 Existing product to existing users	Maintain insertions in current media	Suggest new uses for your product, or reasons for more frequent use, building on existing contacts and goodwill
2 Existing product to new users	Consider new media	Explain the basic benefits of your product, and your company record, to people unaware of them
3 Existing product to users of rival products – brand-switching	Consider competitors' media patterns	Comparison campaigns pointing out the advantages of your product over rival brands, and of changing established buying habits
NEW PRODUCTS		
4 New products to existing customers	Maintain insertions in current media	Explain basic benefits, building on existing contacts and goodwill
5 New products to new users	Consider new media	Explain basic benefits, and company record in other fields
6 New products to competitors' customers	Consider competitors' media patterns	Explain basic benefits, and overcome established goodwill

From the creative standpoint, a campaign aimed at existing users, suggesting further uses for your product, may not be understood by new users who are unaware of your product's basic function, let alone additional uses. A campaign designed to explain your product's basic benefits to potential purchasers may bore existing users, who are already well aware of its function. Neither will it be effective in influencing the brand loyalty of buyers of rival products. Equally, a campaign prepared to persuade buyers of rival products to switch brands, by stressing the advantages of your product over others, is likely to be less successful in educating new users to the product group's basic benefits. Campaigns for new products call for similar basic differences in creative content.

Much the same can be said of media policy: to increase sales to your existing customers you would clearly wish to continue (but strive to improve) your present media pattern, whilst to reach new prospective buyers you may have to use new media. Playing 'follow my leader' rarely results in effective advertising but, if you seek brand-switch sales, clearly you will wish to influence your competitors' customers and would *deliberately* aim at the same market – and are thus likely to use the same media. This is a very different matter to blindly following your rival's lead, for lack of anything better to do.

Advertising should thus be seen in context as part of your total marketing operation. It is not a separate activity but must be based directly on marketing objectives, which should be clear and detailed. Sales force activity must equally be aimed at achieving the identical marketing objective: advertising and selling should be complementary.

Thus different types of sales increase call for different types of media schedule as well as different creative content. Like most fundamental truths this is all very obvious – once it has been pointed out. But for too many organisations it appears to be a blind spot. Of course, the matrix over-simplifies for ease of analysis, and the six types of increase are not self-exclusive. Furthermore, there certainly *are* advertisements which achieve sales in two or more of the possible ways simultaneously. Much successful advertising recognises the distinct ways of increasing sales and accordingly the campaign is not a single entity but comprises several interrelated components, each aimed at one distinct target group. These components are not only successful in their own right but, because they are clearly linked, each component reinforces the effectiveness of the others. Synergistic advertising such as this can be achieved only by design, never by accident.

Summary

The essential message of this chapter is the need to define clearly, before starting to plan your advertising, precisely what the underlying objective of the campaign is to be. It is more than obvious to state that you cannot hit a target unless you know what that target is – why should it be less obvious that it is impossible to prepare advertising proposals to achieve an objective unless you know precisely what this objective is? A great deal of current advertising is, alas, ineffective simply because this fundamental truth has been ignored. Analyse your marketing objectives properly and your advertising effectiveness must increase.

A later step will be to convert these advertising objectives into communication objectives – what information must you convey and what should be you say, to achieve your desired campaign objectives?

THE NEXT STEP

Having decided what you hope to achieve, you can now proceed to the next step – deciding how much you should spend on achieving this objective.

Chapter 15

Budgeting

The first essential for effective use of advertising media was gathering information on which to base your planning. Next came problem analysis and determining your specific advertising strategy. With these two tasks completed, you can now tackle your third problem – deciding how much to spend on achieving your chosen objective. It is appreciated that not all readers will be directly involved – some may be on the receiving end, and have to work to a budget set by someone else. Nevertheless, it is helpful for them to appreciate the ways by which the advertising appropriation can be decided. Furthermore, if their advice is sought on whether a proposed sum is suitable, or if any agency or media-owner hopes to persuade an advertiser to spend more, then this knowledge is even more important.

ADVERTISING AS AN INVESTMENT

Advertising is a cost, but it is usually incurred in increasing sales, from which come profits. If sales are increased by the advertising campaign, then profits are increased, and the extra profits can more than pay for the advertising. Increased sales can also lower costs, and thus enhance the margin of profit. Production in large quantities spreads overhead costs over more units of output and brings other economies of scale (such as better terms for purchasing raw materials in bulk) which lower the cost per unit produced, and thus make possible lower prices.

Increased sales, as we have seen, is by no means the only possible reason for advertising – stabilised sales make for more economic production and thus lower costs, higher profits and/or lower prices. Advertising can make a positive contribution to profitability in many

247

ways, depending on your particular business objectives. The number of firms which imagine that advertising adds to the cost of goods, and that therefore they risk being undersold by competitors who do not advertise, are few: most firms realise that advertising is a cost, but a cost which brings savings in its wake. The problem lies not in deciding whether or not to spend money on advertising, but in deciding *how much* to spend. This, strangely enough, is another blind spot for too many organisations.

It is important to consider the advertising budget in context, as part of your total complex business operation. There are in fact several stages to the financial planning involved. Businesses need a business plan, and within that a marketing plan that integrates the product you manufacture (or service you provide) with your pricing, distribution, selling and advertising policies, all geared to achieving sales in a chosen market.

An overall allocation of funds is then made: so much for plant and equipment; so much for raw materials and labour; so much for selling effort; so much for advertising support, and so on. In this way a total budget is drawn up, showing the various financial commitments involved. It soon becomes apparent that fixing the advertising budget is a *management* decision, and part of a process of balancing expenditures when different activities compete for funds.

It is, therefore, desirable to approach this exercise from the viewpoint of ROI (Return On Investment) or ROC (Return On Capital) rather than spending money. For management to approve an advertising budget, you will need to convince your directors that advertising, rather than any other use of funds, will be the most productive form of expenditure, and make a positive contribution to profitability. Should your Board view advertising as spending without results, you are unlikely to have any budget approved.

Some companies regrettably see advertising budgets as a sub-set of profit in that they mistakenly reduce the budget when they need to show an increased short-term profit. This thinking is fundamentally flawed, as inappropriate reductions in advertising budgets can lead to reductions in market share, and thus to reduced profit in future years.

BUDGET DEFINITION

The amount to be spent on advertising is known as the 'appropriation' and appropriation policy is usually initiated by the advertising manager and then confirmed by the Board, some three months or so before the start of the marketing year.

The term appropriation can be defined as 'the total amount to be spent on advertising during a given period'. Like all definitions it sounds simple, but two points merit special comment – for very practical reasons.

One point relates to 'a given period'. If you have an advertising budget of £X,000, you can have no idea whether this is a sufficient sum, or too much or too little money, unless you know the period of time for which this amount must provide advertising support. Most appropriations are for twelve-month periods, either the calendar year starting on 1 January or the financial year commencing on 5 April. Some appropriations are longer term whilst others are for shorter periods, say three months, with four appropriations per year, but the annual appropriation is more usual. Often, accounting practice makes this inflexible, so that towards the end of the period you are not permitted to 'borrow' from your next year's budget: equally, accounting practice forbids your carrying over any unspent funds. You must, therefore, be clear as to the time period to be covered by the money available, otherwise you cannot budget to cover it effectively. This, surprisingly enough, is less of a problem than the second point regarding the definition, namely the meaning of the word 'advertising'.

In its broadest sense, advertising could be taken to include anything featuring your company name or symbol, but more usually it is restricted to the conventional forms of advertising: press, posters, cinema and television and radio commercials and so on. Firms take differing views of what they include under the heading of advertising and may depart from the ASA's definition of 'paid-for media space or time'. Some exclude production costs for leaflets, exhibitions or display material, the money for these coming out of a separate budget. Others include them, together with such items as postage on direct mail, all of which come out of the advertising appropriation. In some firms the salaries of advertising personnel are set against the advertising appropriation, whilst in others they are considered as general staff costs. Public relations activity may have a separate budget or come out of an overall promotion budget, and the same applies to merchandising and sales promotion. In short, there is no hard and fast rule as to what comes out of the budget and what does not, and practice varies from firm to firm. However, the point is a basic one – if you are responsible for the appropriation you must have a clear idea of what it does and does not cover. It would not do for you to plan carefully how to spend your appropriation and then, towards the end of the period, get an unexpected invoice for something you did not consider as advertising, but which the accountants do.

There are many sad stories to illustrate the practical need for this clear understanding. A newly appointed advertising manager was told, three-quarters of the way through the year, that he had overspent by several thousand pounds. Even after repeated checks he still considered himself well within budget, and the difference of opinion arose because he considered sales literature as coming under the sales manager's budget, whereas the accounting staff considered it an advertising charge. As a result, the advertising manager was obliged to cancel some insertions, in order to make up the amount of money in dispute, so upsetting his carefully planned schedule. This deprived his company of valuable advertising support at a time when it was greatly needed, which resulted in lost sales which, in turn, meant loss of profits. A clear understanding of what his appropriation covered would have prevented this.

This is an extreme case, but even minor items can pose a major problem since many activities do not fit neatly into one category or another and soon add up to a considerable total expense. Is the new shop front or the new sign outside your factory an advertising expense, or should it come out of general building costs? What about the charges involved in special painting of delivery vans? Is the cost of 'Situations Vacant' advertisements to be charged against your advertising budget? There is a tendency for other departments to pass unwanted invoices (and who wants invoices anyway?) to the advertising manager, and if these are paid for out of the so-called advertising appropriation there is less money available for genuine media expenditure. The possibility of invoices being 'passed sideways' is, of course, increased by the fact that different departmental heads compete for funds. It is therefore directly in your own interest that you are absolutely clear about what your budget does and does not cover.

THE NEED FOR A PROPER BUDGET

With the period of the appropriation and what it is to cover clearly defined, you can then make plans, and so fixing the budget is clearly a vital step. On what basis can you avoid spending too much or too little on advertising? Before reviewing the various methods, consider three alternatives.

1 No budget It is vital that your advertising is carefully planned. Sometimes you may encounter a manufacturer who suddenly feels 'It's time we had an advertisement' or, occasionally, you may come up against one who advertised simply because a media representative asked for an order! Such an off-hand attitude is unlikely to bring results. If the manufacturer does not plan his advertising, the chances are that a bit of money will be spent in one medium and a bit more in another, some this month and some the next. Before long, someone will get round to adding up how much has been spent on advertising: he will usually be horrified at how expenditure has mounted up, and decide that advertising is a waste of money. And, face facts, advertising in this way *is* a waste of money. To be effective, your advertising must be planned, and planned well in advance. Your plan should be flexible rather than rigid to allow for the opportunities – and setbacks – of business, but a plan there must be. Advertising is not a separate activity unconnected with your company's other activities: advertising, sales and display effort must all be co-ordinated. When this is the case, retailers' windows, in-store displays and shelves feature the merchandise you are advertising, and selling activity ties in with your advertising and display effort. With effective planning, sales staff have advance information about the merchandise advertised, and have been coached to draw attention to these goods. In this way your prospective customer's interest is awakened by advertisements, displays give effective reminders, and the sale is completed by counter staff. When sales staff are ignorant of the advertising, sales are lost and bad impressions created. Think of the occasions on which you asked a shop for an item currently advertised, only to find that sales staff knew nothing about it: your impression – correctly – is that the shop is slack and inefficient which, of course, it is. This is more than likely the result of unplanned and uncontrolled advertising expenditure.

2 The arbitrary 'guesstimate' Picking a figure out of the air, by hunch or whim, rarely leads to successful advertising. This method is adopted by fewer and fewer advertisers, and most give careful thought to the amount they spend. But beware of those who disguise this approach to budgeting by claiming that 'My twenty years' experience tells me that we should spend £X,000'. Has this individual really had twenty years' experience – or only one year's experience twenty times? Certainly, as will be seen later, true experience can make a most valuable contribution, but all too often the term is used to defend what is, in truth, only a guess. The 'method' still exists, however, and so it must be mentioned – if only to point out that it has little in its favour.

3 'Chairman's Rules' This 'method' is encountered in companies where the advertising manager has no say in deciding the appropriation, but a figure is dictated to him by his Board. A sub-set of this so-called method is the 'Finance Director's rules': when the basis of the board decision is a negative one of cutting the advertising budget to achieve some financial goal. This method sometimes occurs in paternalistic or product-oriented organisations where advertising is seen not as an investment but as a cost which can be cut to provide funds for other purposes such as the purchase of new plant or maintaining profitability. In many cases, the company *does* know what it is doing, but in some instances there is no real basis for the Board decision. A figure is decided, but those concerned have little idea of whether they are budgeting too much or too little. The 'method' nevertheless exists and so must be mentioned if only to stress that – like the 'arbitrary guesstimate' – it has no sound basis.

Methods 2 and 3 above, however, are not entirely without merit. They set a sum for advertising, and this in itself means that someone is *forced* to undertake at least basic planning. Somebody will have to ask fundamental questions such as 'There are twelve months of trading, so how shall I spread my spending over the year?' and 'There are *x* products needing advertising support: how much shall I allocate to each?' From the planning point of view, he will be forced to apportion his money between media, and decide which to use and so, in that these two methods are likely to result in some fundamental planning, they are not without merit – but, either could result in too much or too little being spent on advertising.

Most readers will know the saying attributed to Lord Leverhume – 'Half the money I spend on advertising is wasted – the trouble is, I don't know which half'. Whenever I hear this story, I always recall my visit to the merchandising vice-president of a gigantic one-stop shopping centre in Midwest America. In reply to my question as to how many people worked in the centre, his laconic reply was 'About half of them'.

Your aim must be to ensure that *all* your advertising money is working for you and, if the 'no budget/arbitrary guesstimate/chairman's rules' methods have so little in their favour, what alternatives are open to you?

There is no single best way to decide on how much to spend. A great deal depends on circumstances: for established products, fixing the appropriation may be an annual ritual, while with the launch of a new product it may be regarded as a capital investment. Many methods are in use, each with its advantages and drawbacks, and all are used with varying degrees of success according to the circumstances in which the company operates.

BUDGETING METHODS

Though there are many different methods, they can be considered under seven main groupings. Each of these categories has numerous variations – in some cases the necessary arithmetic can be done on the back of an envelope whereas in other instances the same method is applied in a more complex manner using a computer to undertake intricate mathematical calculations: it is, nevertheless, the same basic method. The fundamental choices open to you are outlined below, together with their advantages and drawbacks.

1 Percentage of last year's sales

Many advertisers take a set percentage – say half per cent or five per cent – of the previous year's turnover as the basis for their appropriation. If you use this method it has the advantage of safety, as you are spending money in accordance with established sales. There are, however, two drawbacks to this method. First, there is the problem of deciding what percentage it should be – half, one, two or five or more per cent? When you consider that some industrial advertisers spend less than a quarter of one per cent of sales on advertising, while consumer product advertising could account for up to a quarter of the selling price, this gives you a more than wide range from which to choose! Some categories of firm have an advantage in that trade statistics are published showing the average for their particular industry. But this advantage is not as helpful as it seems, since an average is only an *average*. Remember that half the people in the UK are below average height (the other half are above average height: that's why there is an average!). If there is an average percentage, that is because many firms are, quite rightly, spending more than the average and others, equally correctly, are spending less than average. The first drawback to this method is determining what percentage *you* should spend.

The second basic weakness of the method is that it looks to the past rather than the future. A bad year means lower turnover and so even less on advertising – in a never-ending downward spiral. The answer to lower turnover might be for you to spend *more* on advertising rather than less, to counteract the decline, in the belief that advertising causes sales. Even if sales do not drop the method still has weaknesses: if your market is, in fact, growing by 25 per cent a year, then a sales increase of only 5 per cent means that you are losing out by some 20 per cent each year. Furthermore, it is a chicken and egg situation – did sales rise because you spent more on advertising, or did you spend more on advertising because sales had risen? In spite of its weaknesses, this method is, nevertheless, used by a large number of organisations. Others prefer to look to the future and use expected sales as their criterion.

2 Percentage of anticipated sales

This method can lead to a realistic appropriation if, for example, your aim is for a marked increase in sales. It suffers, however, from one of the same drawbacks as the previous method, that of deciding just what the percentage should be. A second drawback is that future sales cannot be precisely estimated: the sales have yet to be made and over-estimation could lead to over-spending on advertising. Examination of the 'expected sales' decision-process will reveal three broad categories:

(a) Solo decisions In many small firms all management decisions are taken by a single individual. Since he is responsible for all aspects of his firm's activities, he usually has his finger on the pulse of the market, and takes a realistic approach.

(b) The sales versus advertising split With some larger firms, responsibility for the two functions is divided, the sales manager being responsible for the buying/selling operation, and the advertising manager for the advertising: this can lead to considerable problems in practice. Most sales managers have a strong optimistic streak – the nature of their job calls for it! Consequently, they frequently over-estimate unintentionally. Problems begin when expected sales are not achieved, since the advertising manager will blame the sales manager and *vice versa*. The advertising manager will point out that the advertising cannot work miracles, and he is not to blame if the sales manager chose poor merchandise. The sales manager, in his turn, will ask how on earth can he be expected to sell merchandise with such pitiful advertising support? When the unsold stocks come to management attention the old game of 'pass the buck' commences and, in 'pecking order', sales usually ranks above advertising. The managing director will reprimand the sales manager, who vents his wrath on the advertising manager, who promptly takes it out on the agency, the account executive finds fault with the media department, and blame eventually passes to the media representative, whose medium has 'proved' itself ineffective! This is a game in which nobody wins but unfortunately is played all too often, as most media representatives will confirm.

(c) The marketing approach Here the decision is again taken by a single individual, but this is a very different matter to the one-person approach described above, since the marketing director has reporting to him executives responsible for sales, for advertising, and for market research. The sales *versus* advertising problem just described has led manufacturers to devote considerable time and effort to sales forecasting, in order to better decide the appropriation, as well as the more obvious benefit of fixing production levels with greater accuracy.

3 The unit percentage method

This approach uses detailed cost analysis as the basis for deciding the amount to spend, thus overcoming the problem common to the last two methods, of arriving at a suitable percentage figure. A costing study is made of the product: so much for raw materials, so much for direct production costs, so much for overheads, so much for packaging and so on. These figures may total, say, 35p, and if you wish to sell to the retailer for 40p this leaves a 5p margin. Of this, you can decide to keep 4p as profit and spend 1p per unit on advertising, keep 3p and spend 2p, keep 2p profit and spend 3p per unit and so on. This costing exercise can be extended to include distribution charges through to your final selling price to the public rather than stop at the factory gate but, in essence, the advertising appropriation is fixed as a residuum with profit: the difference between the selling price and all charges is a fixed amount which you spend on advertising or retain as profit. If you use this method, you are unlikely to overspend, since with a 5p margin you would never dream of spending 6p per unit on advertising. By the two previous methods, however, you could unintentionally overspend, as we have seen.

Even this method, scientific as it may appear, is not without its drawbacks. It is strictly inward-looking, since it is based on the factory floor and takes little account of the outside market. Even within the factory there is the danger that the amount per unit may not be revised as conditions alter, raw materials change in price or wage rates increase. Furthermore, overheads vary with output: the more units there are produced, the more widely costs are spread and the smaller the charges that must be borne by each unit.

Finally there is the fundamental point that all these figures are costed with a certain level of sales in mind, whereas it is possible that you may not achieve these sales. However, providing you estimate sales accurately and revise costings whenever necessary (so that the unit percentage is not passed down over the years without alteration) this method can provide a useful guide to what you can afford.

The three methods so far discussed are alternative answers to the question 'How much shall we spend?' The next method asks a very different question: 'How much are *they* spending?'

4 Competitive parity

Another way to fix your appropriation is to look at what competitors are spending and to decide your own expenditure accordingly. This method can be useful when entering a new market, for in such circumstances competitors' spending provides a useful indication of the amount of money you need to inform the market.

The weakness of the method is that although your competitors are similar they are not *identical* but vary in product, market and marketing policy and their problems are therefore different. Moreover, there is the difficulty of finding out just what competitors *are* spending. Press advertising expenditure can be calculated to a reasonable degree of accuracy and without too much trouble, simply by checking competitors' advertisements against publishers' rate cards. For the more important advertisers the task is even simpler in that you can quantify their expenditure by consulting Nielsen Register-MEAL or MMS, both described in Chapter 5. These figures are however often at rate card cost or use an estimation of the discount obtained, whereas an effective media buyer may well have achieved considerably better discounts. For other media, such as direct mail or display material, it is even more difficult to estimate the scale of competitors' financial expenditure. And, even if this information is available, who is to say that the rival companies were correct in the first place? One advertising manager remarked, with some justification, that basing expenditure on your competitors is like cheating in an examination by copying the candidates next to you – you can't see all that clearly, and you don't know that they're right anyway! A further drawback to this method is that a new entrant to the market must have some effect on competitors' sales, with the result that they may spend more on advertising, so forcing the newcomer to increase his appropriation. This method, then, gives a useful opening indication, but should not be allowed to lead to an advertising 'war' wasteful to all parties.

5 Advertising share

A variation which overlaps several methods already discussed is the 'Share of Voice' approach which looks not only at your advertising expenditure in relation to your competitors, but also at your relative sales. Earlier chapters indicated sources you can consult for this information, and in both cases the figures are examined in terms of 'share'. The question then is 'Are the sales for your product the same share of the market as your advertising share?'

Analysis of this kind may result in interesting information such as an average advertising-sales ratio for the product group and whether you are 'working harder' (in terms of advertising expenditure) than your competitors and – much more important – what result is this having on sales? Observation of what happens in the market place may reveal, for example, that firms which increase their share of advertising also increase their share of the market. (Or, of course, *vice versa.*)

This study of advertising and market share may be extended over time by what has been called the 'dynamic difference' approach which looks at

Sales share in one year less sales share in the previous year

as against

Advertising share in one year less advertising share in the previous year

The overall weaknesses of this method are those already outlined under the 'competitive parity' method and, furthermore, it does not *prove* that increased expenditure results in increased sales. Even if a sales rise is associated with increased advertising, the question then arises of *how big an increase*? One firm, for example, might increase its share of advertising, but at a *lower rate* than its main competitor who might have stepped up his advertising expenditure for some very good marketing reason which has no immediate connection with advertising.

6 The marginal method

The methods so far discussed all have one thing in common: they ask the same question, namely 'How much shall we (or do they) spend?' The marginal (sometimes called *zero-based*) method poses a very different question, and asks 'How much *extra* shall we spend?' Attention is shifted from deciding a total amount to deciding 'layer by layer', and each additional expenditure must justify itself. The claim that 'Advertising will increase sales' is frequently made: the manufacturer using the marginal method asks *how much* will it increase sales? The method is an extension of the unit percentage method, and is based on a careful assessment of the results of each *additional* amount spent on advertising. If, for example, a manufacturer makes a profit of £10 per unit sold, then an advertisement costing £1,000 must sell at least 100 additional units if it is to pay for itself. 'Increased sales' of only 50 units would be of little appeal to this advertiser, since this would involve a *loss* of £500. If you can relate sales to advertising in this way, the marginal method can prove extremely helpful. But do bear in mind just *what* you are evaluating, since the advertisement's content clearly influences its effectiveness. Your money has, in fact, bought you the most useless thing in the world – a blank space! There is no point in blaming a medium for proving ineffective in bringing increased sales, when the fault lies really in the use you have made of the space purchased. Some advertisers, in the fortunate position of having a direct response they can measure, extend the marginal method to measure creative aspects as well as media, checking creative idea A against creative idea B, headline C against headline D, illustration E *versus* illustration F and so on. Returning to the media aspects, however, the marginal method can be applied more specifically. Colour costs more than black and white and special positions are more expensive than run of paper insertions – are they worth it in terms of increased returns? Economists talk about the 'Law of Diminishing Returns' and supporters of the marginal method check this out in practice – large advertisements cost more than small ones and weekly insertions are some four times as expensive as a monthly appearance, so is it worth it? The fundamental question asked by those applying this method – who are in the fortunate position of being able to evaluate the answer – is 'If it costs x per cent extra, do returns increase by more than x per cent?' A later chapter covers evaluation of results in more detail but it should already be apparent that this method is ideal for those who can make their advertising 'sit up and beg' when it comes to measuring response. Many advertisers, however, are unable to establish so direct a connection and must therefore look to other methods of fixing their appropriation.

7 The target sum method

This means of determining your appropriation is on an entirely different basis from all the methods so far considered. Instead of asking 'How much (or how much extra) shall we spend?' the target sum (often called *Objective and Task*) method asks 'What will it cost?'.

In short, the method jumps ahead to the next planning stage – Preparation of Proposals – and then works back from media-owners' rate cards. If you decide that to achieve a given level of sales you need, say, half-pages every week in a selected list of publications, your appropriation can thus be calculated by multiplying the cost of these advertisements by the number of insertions. Thus a schedule of weekly advertisements costing in total £10,000 for each appearance in a selected list of publications gives you an appropriation of 52 × £10,000 or £520,000 plus production costs. In practice, of course, the schedule would be more complex and the arithmetic more involved.

The method is realistic in taking into account the cost of advertising – ignored by all the previous methods. A weakness common to the other methods so far considered is that if media rates increase by, say 10 per cent, the outcome is that you are forced to book 10 per cent less space or time, since no allowance is made for actual media costs.

The problem with the target sum method lies in deciding the variables – who is to say that half-pages are the correct size, that weekly appearances are necessary and which media should be included? The danger obviously lies in being greedy: what most advertisers would really like is saturation campaigns comprising full colour pages every day in every publication, posters on every hoarding, heavy television and radio campaigns, leaflets distributed door to door, and so on! In such circumstances, *all* your company's money would go on advertising. However, if you take a realistic view of what weight of advertising is really needed to inform your potential customers, this is a sound method of fixing your appropriation.

8 The composite method

This chapter began by stating that there were seven main groups of methods for fixing your advertising budget, so you may well be surprised at arriving at number eight! The eighth 'method' is, however, simply to use two or more of the previous methods together and strike a figure somewhere between those produced by the several calculations – which in any event are unlikely to be vastly different. When reviewing the various methods of fixing the budget against your own particular situation, some will immediately appear more relevant, and others less practical. By making the necessary calculations for the selected methods, you arrive at a range of figures giving your minimum and maximum expenditure levels. To 'pick a figure' somewhere in this range may sound haphazard, but consider what you have in fact achieved. Rather than any arbitrary guesstimate you have determined that, under no circumstances, should you spend less than a certain sum. Equally, you have scientifically and logically calculated a maximum figure. Your range of uncertainty has thus been narrowed down in a most practical manner, and it is at this point that experience becomes truly valuable.

This chapter warned earlier against those who made claims that 'My experience tells me we should spend £X,000' but there is a vast difference between vague guesses and the practical application of true experience. And it is experience in assessing the overall marketing situation which will tell you where, within the prescribed range, you should fix your own particular appropriation. For example, an advertising manager might consider that, with a depressed economy and consumers having little disposable cash, the signs indicate that a high budget is necessary. On the other hand might be the facts that his company's merchandise has a distinct product and price advantage, and that his main competitor's sales force and distribution are currently weak. Taking into account the strengths and weaknesses of the situation, he might decide to fix his appropriation at the lower end of the scale rather than the higher level which at first appeared necessary. Your own experience can be invaluable in reaching a decision relevant to your own particular situation, and certainly the results of your previous year's advertising should be considered also. Advertising policy thus becomes a 'circular' procedure, the results of one year's appropriation serving as a basis for establishing the subsequent year's expenditure which, in its turn, will also have to be revised to meet the needs of the following year.

In search of the perfect method

Any reader mistakenly seeking the impossible – a single universally applicable method of fixing the advertising budget – will be disappointed. I often recall, however, a colleague taking issue with my earlier writings on this subject – why was I so general, when his brand-leader organisation calculated its budget precisely? When I enquired how, he proudly presented a mathematical model calling for estimates of some dozen variables, and he used a computer to resolve them into a recommended budget figure. When I pointed out that most advertisers did not have estimates of so many variables, nor a formula to inter-relate them even if such data was available, and that the research budget to acquire this information (let alone the cost of devising the mathematical model and then processing the data) far exceeded most companies' total advertising expenditure, he did admit that his 'perfect' method was specific to his firm, and that having a brand-leader's budget did make quite a difference!

Completing the loop

Even if there were a single perfect method, there is considerable difference between fixing a budget and then a) using it and b) spending it. The circular procedure of last year's results helping determine this year's expenditure should also be influenced by two later stages in the planning process: preparing and executing your advertising proposals.

When using your advertising budget, how strong will your creative proposals be? A powerful selling proposition, made to 'come alive' in a compelling way, will produce results with less expenditure than a weak creative campaign.

Equally important is the efficiency with which you buy your advertising. A good media buyer, by hard bargaining, will get you more for your money or, putting the same thing another way, will buy you the same amount of advertising for a smaller budget.

Various budgetary methods, all with many variations, are thus currently in use, each with its advantages and drawbacks. The outlines given perhaps over-simplify some variations, which are based on econometric approaches and complex mathematical models. In the absence of a single perfect mathematical model, however, these are the main methods from which you can choose. Indeed, any method is preferable to the 'bit-here-and-a-bit-there' approach, in that it must lead to planning and thus to more effective advertising.

Budget divisions

Before leaving the matter of your appropriation, various additional points must be made. One is that your company, rather than have a single figure, may require several appropriations, one for each of its products or divisions. It may even need an additional appropriation to promote an 'umbrella' campaign for the group as a whole, rather than for any individual line.

Furthermore, the appropriation may be divided into two – for 'above the line' expenditure by the agency and a 'below the line' budget retained by the advertiser. Also, part of the budget – described as a 'Contingency Reserve' – may be set aside to cater for unexpected opportunities or setbacks. These sub-divisions within the overall appropriation are discussed elsewhere.

You may also encounter division of the budget for yet another reason: to set aside funds for manufacturer/stockist co-operative advertising. Many firms find it productive to share with retailers the cost of advertisements in local media, announcing that they stock the merchandise featured in the campaign. When retailers consider their advertising budgets, they should clearly take into account this possible source of additional funds. Some advertisers also set aside funds as a contribution to a co-operative advertising campaign mounted on an industry-wide basis, to increase demand for their product group as a whole.

The question 'Who pays for a pan-European advertising campaign?' often proves a vexed one. Similar questions are also asked about funding corporate or umbrella campaigns within a single country. Many multi-national companies have for years adopted a philosophy of decentralisation, with individual operating companies generating their own advertising budgets. In many cases, a central advertising budget did not exist. The availability of satellite-delivered Pan-European television has lead many multi-national companies to institute new procedures for funding advertising campaigns which appear simultaneously in different countries. There are two alternatives: 'top down' funding (a central advertising budget above and beyond those of the operating companies) or 'bottom up' (whereby the operating companies contribute to the central fund). Similar 'top down' or 'bottom up' considerations apply to the funding of corporate or 'umbrella' advertising campaigns.

Long-term planning

Finally, mention must be made of long-term budgeting. The various methods described all imply an *annual* appropriation, but the custom of yearly decisions is largely an artificial one arising from accounting practice, and many companies now take a longer-term view. When launching a new product, they accept that it will be impossible to realise a profit within a calendar year. It is unrealistic to expect a new venture to show a profit situation within a day, a week or a month – why should you expect to move into a profit situation within a year? It is long-term prospects which are important, since your company plans to be in business long term. Indeed, one difference between UK and Japanese companies is that some UK companies work on a financial year, whereas many Japanese companies work on a five year plan, particularly when launching into new markets. Their plans cover the time needed to capture that market. The first year of operation may involve a considerable loss, in the second year the company breaks even, the third year shows a sufficient profit to offset the first year's loss and a true profit is not made until the fourth year. The first-year loss is a calculated situation, and that year's appropriation is regarded as an investment to be recouped by subsequent sales. Some conventional accountants resist the concept of advertising as investment, since they see no tangible assets they could sell off in the same way that they can dispose of production plant. But since machinery is purchased not to sell but to produce, surely advertising should be treated in the same way? Accountants are more than accustomed to the concept of 'depreciation', spreading capital expenditure over a number of years, so it is surprising that many find it difficult to adopt this approach with advertising.

Long-term budgeting calls for a 'pay-out' schedule. In simplest possible terms, the company calculates two cash flows – the rate at which money is being spent, and the rate at which it is coming in. As we all know from personal experience, we soon run into difficulties if cash goes out faster than it comes in, and the same applies to companies. They must therefore work out how much capital is needed to keep things going until a profit situation is reached: it would be more than unfortunate to run out of capital on the very eve of showing the first true profit. So this is where the accountants should come into their own – a marketing-orientated accountant can make a most valuable contribution.

Equally, any advertising and marketing executive will find a knowledge of financial skills and terminology a most useful asset – even if only in arguments with the more conventional accountants whose instinctive reaction in times of recession is to cut the advertising budget. Most advertising and marketing people have this argument more than once during their careers!

At the start of the chapter, mention was made that fixing the appropriation is a management decision, and it is to this point we must return before concluding. The appropriation is decided at director level, and advertising and marketing staff must learn to live with this figure. There is always a temptation to ask for more money to take advantage of some special offer. This temptation should be avoided, for the appropriation was decided after very careful thought. Even if you do decide to ask for more money, there may be no Board meeting for some weeks and, in any event, is the Board likely to view this special offer – a very minor event in the total company operation – with the same enthusiasm as you do? Covering such events is the function of the contingency reserve described later: this is a very different matter from a *major* overall review of company policy. Should the economic situation, for example, change to such an extent that your company's marketing plans are no longer valid, the Board would swiftly meet to deal with the new situation as a matter of urgency, and would review all aspects of business activity – production levels, prices and, of course, advertising. Such a major review is a very different matter from coping with the temporary and minor setbacks which are an unfortunate but unavoidable feature of business life.

The Next Step

Now that your budget is known, your next task is preparation of campaign proposals to achieve your advertising objective.

Chapter 16

Preparation of Advertising Proposals

Advertising planning is only part of overall marketing, and for effective use of media you must think in terms of your marketing objective – that you manufacture a product (or provide a service), with product, pricing, distribution and advertising policies and selling effort all geared to achieving sales in a chosen segment of the market. To talk of campaign planning is misleading, however, since this implies a *single* campaign, whereas effective planning is more complex. Quite apart from the need to 'aim' your product correctly, including its branding and packaging, your promotional activities must also seek to achieve the same marketing objective and here it is usually more correct to talk of *campaigns* in the plural.

Before the purchaser can buy your product it must be available; before your product can be in the shops your sales staff must put it there; and before they can do so they must be fully briefed. Any successful campaign, therefore, has at least three components – a campaign to potential purchasers, a second to distributors, and a third aimed at your own sales force. Each of these groups could be the target of several types of promotional activity: advertising, created media, merchandising and sales promotion, and public relations. This book is concerned with the advertising aspect alone, but you must consider this in context, if you are to plan effectively. Media planning, although vital, is only one part of your overall promotional campaign, and must interlock with the others.

THE MEDIA BRIEF

If you ask any media planner to tell you, in confidence, what causes the most problems, the majority will say it is a request for media proposals unaccompanied by adequate information. Many will complain of clients – or even agency executives – who rush in to demand 'a £750,000 schedule for new product X'. Such individuals fail to appreciate that a full briefing is essential for the effective use of advertising media. The adequacy of this briefing directly affects the effectiveness of the media planning. If an inadequate briefing is given, there is no firm basis on which to evaluate the advantages of the different media, or on which to construct an effective schedule. For this reason, it can be vital for the media executive to contribute to the formulation of the media brief, rather than play a passive role 'on the receiving end'.

The earlier chapters on situation analysis and advertising strategy detailed much of the information you need if you are to prepare the most effective media plan. Part of your media brief has yet to come, however – the creative aspects.

CREATIVE/MEDIA INTERACTION

The two aspects of preparation of proposals – choosing the media and creating the advertisements – are complementary activities and, whilst this book is concerned primarily with media, you are directly affected by creative considerations. If your schedule provides for half-page advertisements in certain publications, this implies a creative decision that the insertions are to be of half-page size in press media and, at the same time, it is equally a media decision – to book half-page advertisements in selected publications on certain dates at a cost of £X. Creative and media decisions are therefore usually taken simultaneously, but the dominant aspect may be either media or creative. For example, media selection may be determined by the creative need to show your product in colour or to employ a medium which demonstrates its use. Alternatively, creative needs may take second place to the market requirement of informing a clearly defined target group, which one medium covers more effectively than others.

The attention factor

Media decisions overlap with creative considerations in another way, when attracting potential purchasers' attention to your advertising message. It is insufficient simply to place it before them by choosing a suitable advertising medium: you must also decide how to attract their attention. The first essential for effective advertising is attention, for without this your advertisement cannot communicate. There are various devices for attracting attention: some of them concern creative work alone, but others have media implications.

All these devices have one thing in common, however: their full utilisation implies a media knowledge which goes far beyond circulation or readership statistics alone. Hence the importance of the concept of 'candidate media' discussed earlier, and the need to study each of those in depth. What is the format of the medium, and what regular (or occasional) features does it have? What advertisement positions are available, and on which pages? These factors in fact suggest an alternative title for this book: The *Creative* Use of Advertising Media. Creativity and media planning/buying should be considered as interactive, rather than treated as separate activities.

Size

A large advertisement in itself attracts attention (and is more impressive to those who see it, as well as giving greater scope for creativity and the inclusion of more information). The creative/media decision to use advertisement size as the attention device has clear scheduling implications. You should always bear in mind, however, that sheer size is no substitute for creativity and may be extremely wasteful – full pages in broadsheet newspapers may be *too* big to be read comfortably, except at arm's length. For this reason, many media-planners prefer to book 'page killer' sizes: solus position large enough to dominate the page.

Position

A press advertisement on the front page, or facing or next to editorial matter, or in a solus position without competition from other advertisers, is likely to be seen by more people than one appearing alongside others within the body of the publication. Positioning on particular pages also serves as an attention filter, by placing your advertisement before those readers who, by the very act of reading the selected editorial, indicate that they are likely to have an interest in your product. Additionally, such positioning is more likely to attract attention, simply because these self-selecting readers are in a receptive state of mind. Again, the decision to use position as an attention device directly affects your media plan.

Colour

Colour is often used as an attraction device. Printing in a second colour can attract (and highlight parts of the advertisement) while full-colour advertisements also permit you to show your product in its natural colours which, with some merchandise, is a vital factor in influencing consumers' buying decisions. The creative need for colour to attract attention clearly influences media planning, particularly if creative staff stress high quality colour reproduction.

Illustration

A product well-illustrated is often more than half sold, and advertisements featuring illustrations usually have greater impact than those without. 'Action' pictures, showing your product in use with people enjoying its benefits, have strong attention value. Whilst these are mainly creative considerations, it is obvious that the quality of reproduction required directly affects media selection.

Movement

Movement, as in an 'Ultravision' poster panel that rotates, a moving display at an exhibition or a retail outlet attracts attention through contrast with the static background.

Demonstrating your product in use can also attract attention through movement, and not all media permit this. Once again, creative requirements have strong media implications.

Sound

The human voice can quickly attract attention and also convey a message. Music and other sound effects can similarly attract attention as well as influence the mood of the listeners, who become more receptive to your advertising message. The need for sound to fulfil these functions again influences media selection.

Headlines (and body copy)

Writing headlines which serve as an attention device is the copywriter's speciality, as is producing interesting and compelling text for the body of the advertisement. There is a simple formula which provides a helpful checklist in preparing (and evaluating) advertisements. It is expressed mainly in terms of press advertising, but the points made apply to most advertisements, subject only to adaptation for the medium in question. There is an easy way of remembering the formula – the initial letters of the four checkpoints form the title of an opera: AIDA. These creative checkpoints – all of which have media implications – are:

Attention
Interest
Desire
Action

AIDA is not the only model of how advertising works – another suggests an Awareness/Comprehension/Conviction/Action process, while the ATR model is an analysis based on Awareness, Trial and Reinforcement. Detailed examination of these models is outside the immediate scope of this book, but the purpose of mentioning them is to point out their relevance to media planning. Taking the AIDA model as an example, the first and last checkpoints have immediate media implications. The use of media planning (rather than creative devices) to attract attention has clear scheduling implications, and the same is true of many 'Action devices'. If your advertising objective is consumer *action* (rather than, for example, reminder advertising or image-building) this has direct media implications, since this may demand selection of a medium which facilitates action by your potential consumers. Examples such as coupons in press advertisements, reply cards in magazines or direct mail shots, or reply services on television and radio, all clearly illustrate how the final action checkpoint has media implications which are just as direct as the opening attention factor. Even the other two checkpoints – interest and desire – cannot be considered as having creative implications only, and thus not influencing media selection: never forget that the mood of your potential purchasers, when your advertising message is received, is an important criterion for media comparison.

Advertising strategy determined your campaign objective. This must now be translated to communication objectives: what must you say to whom, and how, for your advertising to be successful? Effective media planning and creation of persuasive and attention-getting advertisements are thus complementary activities and both are essential for effective advertising. Clearly there is little point in placing your advertising message before those who are not potential buyers, nor in buying media if your advertisements fail to capture attention or feature the wrong sale propositions or are not sufficiently persuasive. It is, therefore, vital that both media and creative staff agree that the market could best be reached by advertisements of a certain size, in an agreed broad group of media. The media staff must feel that this broad plan gives them sufficient scope for effective scheduling, and the creative staff must similarly consider that the plan permits them to express the selling message persuasively. Creative and media departments then work independently, the creative staff preparing their copy and design proposals, and the media planners calculating the scheduling possibilities within the broad media groups agreed. The next step for the media staff is to plan in detail how to spend the appropriation so as to get maximum effect for every penny spent.

MARKET WEIGHTING

Your media problem is not simply to decide whether or not Medium A is to appear on your schedule. The problem underlying all media planning is how your appropriation should be allocated over time, how it should be divided between the different sales areas and what weight of advertising should be directed to different segments of the market. This is sometimes decided on what is described as the 'case rate' method, by which expenditure is in direct proportion to sales. Thus, if Sales Area A accounts for 30 per cent of total purchases, it would seem logical to devote 30 per cent of your budget to media that will stimulate that area. The spread of expenditure across the year may be decided in the same way, according to each month's sales figures: months when the market is ripe in terms of actual purchases will thus receive heavier advertising than the months in which sales figures indicate that the market is not in a buying mood. Case-rate spending thus provides a sound basis for media scheduling: as we shall see later, however, there are often good reasons for departing from this planning base.

MEDIA ALLOCATIONS

A first step in constructing the schedule most suitable for achieving your marketing objective is often to divide the overall appropriation into separate allocations for each of the different media groups on which your campaign is to be based. Amounts are allocated to individual media groups – so much for television, so much for national and local press, so much for posters, and so on. This is sometimes called the 'Media Split' stage, or the 'inter-media' decision.

Newcomers to advertising are often surprised that media planning is both precise and empirical, and that the perfect media schedule is rarely produced at the first attempt. There is in fact no one right answer, and so media planners consider innumerable ways of spending the appropriation, assessing one schedule against others, before making final recommendations. The schedule that is finally booked may well be the end result of first calculating and then contrasting perhaps dozens of possible alternatives.

The same practice applies when allocating between different media. Should the appropriation be divided, for example, between press and television, then possible schedules will be constructed for these two media groups and the overall costings compared: if good press coverage can be achieved without spending the provisional allocation in full but additional money is needed to obtain an adequate television schedule (or *vice versa*) then the media split will be changed and the inter-media allocations adjusted accordingly.

DETAILED PLANNING

Within any group of media, the same constructing of different schedules, and consequent adjustment, is also the rule. Taking into account the target market and advertising strategy, in terms of the duration of your campaign, the advertisement size selected, the required frequency of appearance, and the list of candidate media that initially appear most suitable (probably on a cost ranking basis, as described below), the first step is to cost a preliminary schedule. The chance of this basic arithmetic resulting in a sum that exactly balances the allocation is small, so several possible schedules are costed out. Should the preliminary costing exceed the allocation, then expenditure must be cut back and you must evaluate the best way to do this. In the simplest possible terms, there are just four ways in which your preliminary schedule can be adjusted. These are:

1 Advertisement unit One solution might be to reduce the size of your advertisement, or to abandon the use of colour, of special positions or of peak time. If essential creative or other considerations make this impossible, then you must consider other alternatives.

2 Frequency Another approach would be to reduce frequency and have, for example, alternate week instead of weekly insertions. Marketing requirements, however, may make this solution unacceptable and you must, therefore, consider other possibilities.

3 Duration Another alternative would be to curtail your campaign and maintain it for only (for example) 11 months instead of a full year, omitting periods when the market is dead. There is, however, a fourth possibility you must consider.

4 Media list Another solution is to reduce the number of candidate media included in your schedule, in order to maintain the weight of advertising in those retained.

The variables you can use for media planning permutations are thus basically four: dominance (in terms of size, position or colour), frequency of appearance, duration/continuity of campaign, and the media list. In every case, except the last, you must take into account *non-media* considerations, since the advertisement unit can be changed only after consultation with creative staff, and the frequency of appearance and length of campaign are determined by marketing factors such as how often your buyers must be reminded, and the duration of your selling campaign. These problems are magnified by the fact that rate cards tend to be only indicative of cost, and are really often only a starting point for negotiations at the later buying stage.

Often, these considerations lead inevitably to a reconsideration of the case-rate spending method. Case-rate spending, with expenditure proportionate to sales, can be likened to a chicken and egg situation. Should you spend 30 per cent of budget to maintain the 30 per cent of sales – or have you achieved 30 per cent of sales in that month or this area simply because you have always devoted to it 30 per cent of your advertising expenditure? This leads to a marketing-cum-media re-examination of the cause-and-effect of the case-rate situation: from this re-examination two other strategies may arise. The two alternatives – increased or decreased expenditure – are both based on consideration of *potential* as distinct from actual sales.

1 Increase You may decide to boost a particular month or area by devoting *more* than the case-rate amount on the assumption that, although according to past sales figures it merits only, for example, 10 per cent of expenditure, there is in fact a far greater potential which would respond to added stimulation. Hence the media/marketing decision to step up the advertising in the selected area, market segment or time of year. But with limited funds, where is the additional expenditure to come from, if not from the standard four variables already mentioned? The other alternative to case-rate spending, in fact, releases funds rather than calling for additional expenditure.

2 Decrease Here, your assumption is that demand is relatively stable: in economic terms, it is 'inelastic'. People have perhaps got to buy a certain minimum amount of your product. After heavy Christmas spending, for example, many people have no funds to spare and keep their spending to a minimum. No amount of heavy advertising can persuade them to buy more, since they just do not have the cash to do so. Conversely, however, there is a minimum amount they must buy – and would do so even without any advertising stimulus. Alternatively, on a more positive note, you may consider that one particularly brand-loyal market segment would maintain its level of purchases, despite a reduction in advertising frequency. Hence you may take the media/marketing decision to reducing advertising activity in a particular month or market in the belief that demand is inelastic and sales will remain at that level even when advertising is cut.

OTHER VARIABLES

The balancing of advertisement unit, frequency, duration and media list, and re-examination of these four variables against the case-rate method, by no means exhausts the media scheduling possibilities open to you. Other variations should also be considered.

Multiple-size campaigns Many campaigns call for more than one size of advertisement so that, rather than use one uniform size throughout, you plan your media schedule using two or more sizes – and a new possibility in the media 'balancing act' is thus open to you. For example, you may open your campaign with a half-page advertisement, followed by quarter-page advertisements in each of the following three weeks, reverting to a half-page advertisement and more quarter-pages in a repeating pattern. Use of two sizes enables you to get the best of the two worlds of impact and repetition, and many campaigns are based on this principle. Sometimes a third and very dominant size, perhaps a full-page advertisement, may be used to launch your campaign, simply to impress retailers and assist your salesmen in persuading them to both stock and display your merchandise.

Multiple sizes can also be used with other media such as television, where you will often see a combination of longer commercials and shorter 'edited' versions. This is yet another example of where media and creative staff must work together. Research has proved that such creative/media co-operation can be most effective. When shown a shortened version, many of those interviewed often respond with total recall of the full commercial screened earlier!

Drip versus burst A variation on the increase versus decrease and multiple-size approaches is to base your planning on a 'Burst' rather than 'Drip' advertising. A campaign based on the drip approach calls for steady advertising over a period, on the premise that 'constant dripping wears away a stone'. The burst approach on the other hand concentrates resources into a limited number of weeks to achieve greater impact (larger sizes, greater frequency or more extensive media list) within the period. A typical burst campaign might consist of four weeks on/twelve weeks off/four weeks on, in a repeating pattern. This variation of the multiple-size campaign incorporates the increase versus decrease approach to planning, the difference being that one of the multiple 'sizes' is zero, ie advertising is abandoned in certain weeks in order to boost the others. Although the burst approach offers advertising advantages by concentrating campaign impact, it can present marketing problems by complicating the retail stock control of advertised products. There is also the problem of 'decay' – will your market forget you in the intervals between bursts?

Media in combination Few campaigns are based on a single advertising vehicle but rely on various media used at the same time. Economists refer to the 'Law of Diminishing Returns' and this applies just as much to media planning as to other types of expenditure. You may feel that one medium has received a sufficient weight of advertising, and that it would not be worthwhile spending any more money in it. You therefore consider other media for this reason, and also because it permits you to reach the same market but by other means, for fresh impact. The chapter on budgeting outlined the marginal method of deciding your appropriation, and this approach can be applied to the use of media in combination – will the last £X,000 spent on your first medium bring as good a result as the same £X,000 spent on the alternatives?

The term 'media in combination' masks two separate considerations: *inter*-media and *intra*-media comparison. The former concerns the 'media split' stage, and thus refers to multi-media campaigns which cover, for example, newspapers *and* television *and* magazines. The intra-media consideration concerns media *within* a group, eg within press using publications A *and* B (*or* C?). With both aspects of the term, you encounter the problem of distinguishing between 'duplication' and 'net extra coverage'.

Duplication Duplication means reaching the same market by different media. To some extent all media duplicate since people read newspapers and magazines, watch television and see posters, and advertisers contact them through all these media. Duplication, viewed from another standpoint, represents an increase in one of the four basic variables: frequency. If monthly contact with prospective buyers is your aim, monthly insertions in two media whose coverage overlaps means that those who see both media see two advertisements each month instead of one, and therefore receive double the frequency you think necessary. Two alternatives are open to you: to maintain monthly insertions in one publication and delete the other from your schedule, or to use the two publications in alternate months, thus maintaining regularity but giving this part of your market a monthly stimulus through alternative means, for variety of impact.

Net extra coverage If duplication and thus unwanted repetition is to be avoided, you will seek media giving you the greatest net extra coverage. Two additional candidate publications may be under consideration, one of which has a much larger readership than the other and therefore, on the surface, seems a better proposition. However, if most of this larger readership is already covered by media already on your schedule, this means you would contact these people with higher frequency than is necessary. If, on the other hand, the publication with the smaller readership gives little duplication, then by using this medium you will reach entirely new prospects to whom no advertising message has yet been delivered. By seeking net extra coverage, you thus increase the overall *penetration* of your campaign.

The two factors of duplication and net extra coverage reflect contrasting marketing objectives. If your marketing aim is to reach as many prospective buyers as possible (even if with only a single advertising message) then you should aim for net extra coverage and thus maximum penetration. If, however, your marketing objective is to achieve maximum repetition, duplication of coverage is preferable. In practice, however, you are unlikely to want to operate at either *extreme* end of this scale.

Cumulative coverage (or reach) Coverage is the proportion of the target group who have at least one opportunity of seeing your advertisement. Although the number of people reading the average issue of a publication remain constant, the same people do not always read every issue. Thus additional advertisements in a series can add new readers, thereby increasing your cumulative audience (as well as giving those already covered an additional opportunity to see your advertisement). Cumulative cover in this sense reflects the penetration of your campaign.

Opportunities-to-see How many advertisements will your target groups see? The average frequency is often called the average 'OTS' or opportunities-to-see (or hear), and is defined as the number of potential exposures received by the average reader/viewer/listener. Any average OTS or OTH figure must be treated with care when considering a possible schedule, for it can mask wide variations in the number of opportunities received by different members of your target group.

Frequency distribution This will give you a more detailed breakdown of opportunities-to-see across your target groups in terms of coverage. Coverage is very often linked with the levels of opportunities-to-see, *viz* 2+, 3+, 4+ and so on, showing the number (or percentage) of the audience likely to have that stated number of opportunities to see your campaign. Frequency distribution should reflect the marketing priorities of your market segments, and the market weighting discussed earlier. The vital need for a full media briefing is again apparent.

SOME UNCHARTED TERRITORIES

The fact that you can pump statistics about net extra coverage *versus* duplication through a computer to see the effect of adding publication A rather than publication B to your schedule has led many people to think the 'science' of advertising is at a very advanced state. And, taking data-processing aids into account and setting aside any research weaknesses (what *is* a reader/viewer/listener?) then our industry has made enormous strides in recent years – and is light years ahead of those countries which do not have authentic circulation figures, let alone reliable viewing, reading or listening figures.

It would be a false kindness, however, to omit mention of any weaknesses. When it comes to the basic matter of how advertising *works* and how the whole marketing communications/purchasing-decision process operates, it must be bluntly stated that there is a great deal more to know before we can claim complete mastery of advertising as a business tool. It would need another book to discuss these uncharted areas in full, so they can be touched on only briefly here. The fields in which we need more knowledge include the following:

Campaign period

This is not a matter of whether your campaign runs for 6, 8 or 12 months, but of the campaign's effects on consumers. What is the 'life' of an advertisement or of a campaign, and what would happen if you stopped advertising? Chapter 14 described the natural decline built in to any market and the need to remind those remaining but, should you stop advertising, how fast would its effects 'decay' and how swiftly would your sales start to fall? How strong is brand loyalty to your products, and what part does advertising play in maintaining this loyalty? As campaign duration is a basic variable in your media-balancing act, more information is needed. Under this heading – but beyond the scope of this book – you should also consider the creative use made of the space booked. How quickly will your current campaign 'wear out', and how swiftly should you replace it with a new one? This may in turn be affected by the next factor – the frequency with which people see your advertisements.

Frequency

This is another basic variable, but little is known *in detail* about its effects. It is all very well to have rules-of-thumb about weekly reminders for weekly products and so on, and these do perhaps give a guide to the minimum frequency required. But what about *maximum* frequency? Is increased frequency necessarily beneficial? Can you always equate heavy usage of your product with heavy exposure to your advertising? And can you, in fact, dissociate this from your campaign's *creative content*? Will over-exposure perhaps be counter-productive? People have argued, for example, that some heavily repeated television commercials have an irritation factor which harms rather than helps sales. All of us have seen humorous commercials which were extremely amusing at first viewing but for which we dreaded subsequent screenings and, with some people, hard-sell commercials have the same effect. Cultural differences may be important, since different things irritate (or motivate) different groups. There is very little published data on this area.

Multi-media campaigns

You can compare with relative accuracy the results – in numerical terms – of adding Newspaper A rather than B to your schedule, or Magazine C instead of D. When it comes to comparing different media groups – comparing *Newspaper* A or B with *Magazine* C or D – you are on less certain ground. And when it comes to assessing these in comparison with a totally different medium – whether this be television, cinema, radio, outdoor or any other media – you are in largely uncharted territory. While *intra*-media research (comparing publication A with B) is relatively advanced, *inter*-media research is still at the experimental stage. When looked at in terms of the way advertising works and the purchasing-decision process, there is certainly no 'map' to help you find your way. There are, however, a few 'pointers'. If, as the Law of Diminishing Returns suggests, you should use more than one medium or one media group, it is best to examine the possible ways which you could use them, and then evaluate these alternatives against your advertising objective. In making such an assessment there are marketing and creative as well as media considerations. Multi-media schedules can achieve various objectives.

1 Additional coverage By adding new media you can increase your cumulative cover and thus the total penetration of your campaign. A variation on the same theme is to rectify any weaknesses in the coverage of those media already on your schedule. Clearly this is a matter of marketing/media rather than creative considerations.

2 Added frequency Through a multi-media campaign, your target market may have more opportunities to see your advertisements. This again has mainly marketing/media considerations, but you should consider how your customers will react to this increased frequency.

3 Different media The aim here is the very opposite of (1): rather than increase penetration, you wish to reach the same people. It overlaps with (2) but, even though you may deliver the same message more often, your target audience receives it through a *new* medium, often with a different environment (at home or work or while travelling) for fresh impact. This is not a simple matter of added frequency and there are important creative considerations, as some media groups are more complementary than others when used in combination. The term 'synergism' (or visual transfer) is used to describe, for example, the degree to which people exposed to a given TV campaign can re-create the visual component with only the TV soundtrack to trigger their memories. TV *plus* radio is the obvious example, but the same principle of beneficial 'transfer', with one medium reinforcing the other, applies to other combinations. Some combinations, eg TV and Radio, have considerable 'built-in' synergism, while others have it to a lesser degree. Where there is minimal media synergism, this should be achieved by creative means.

4 Strategy variations All three variations so far described assume your advertisements have the same creative content: the variables are *who* you reach, *how* you reach them and *how often* – not *what you say*.

Should this be so, or should you consider variations in creative strategy? The concept of 'mood' is nothing new in media evaluation, and the same is true of creating advertisements to suit the media that are to carry them. Even if reaching the same people in demographic terms, many advertising practitioners put these two concepts into practice, and develop different creative approaches to suit the different media. Others ask if you will, in fact, reach the same *kind* of people, even if the standard demographic characteristics are similar? Are the people you reach through one medium more (or less) likely to buy – or try – your product than the people you reach through alternative media? The Media Preference Groups analysis described earlier has shown marked differences in the purchasing patterns of people reached by different media, even though the demographic descriptions are the same. Should your media selection and creative content change accordingly?

Added cost

In addition to considering these possible ways of mounting a multi-media campaign, you must also bear in mind you have changed yet another variable: cost. Quite apart from the fundamental cost of buying an additional medium there is the added expense – in terms of time and effort as well as money – of preparing advertisements for the new medium.

Multi-media campaigns thus have implications far beyond media choice alone, and these fundamental questions give a new importance to problem analysis and the vital need to establish a *true* campaign objective. Before leaving these relatively uncharted areas, you should bear in mind that a great deal of exploratory work is being done – with some very interesting results, so you should keep up-to-date with new developments. However, much of this pioneer work is undertaken to gain a competitive advantage and, understandably, the results are not always published. But Part 1 listed sources of media news, and you should therefore consult these regularly to keep up-to-date with new developments.

RESPONSE FUNCTIONS

Balancing cover against repetition has always been a difficult planning problem, and most decisions have been taken after analysing schedules rather than applying a 'Response Factor' in advance when preparing the media proposals. Given a fixed budget, the variable of cover as against repetition is the amount of advertising each individual receives and, when a mathematical response model is used, you must state the objectives of your campaign in numerical terms. These numbers describe the response you expect from the individuals exposed to your advertising.

A response function is a weighting system for overall schedule construction, based on your subjective judgment of how your advertising works and specifically how many exposures are necessary for your advertising to be effective. A *cumulative* response function is a set of numbers defining the relative value to the advertiser of an individual in his target group receiving one, two or more advertising impressions, and must be distinguished from the corresponding *additional* response function – the added value given by each separate additional exposure.

Response functions are often employed when using a computer optimisation program (see below) to construct a schedule. Although expressed numerically to give the computer a weighting factor for each successive advertising exposure received by the individual, graphs are often used in formulating response functions and as a basis for discussing the type of advertising campaign best suited to achieve your chosen objective. Such discussion must necessarily be general, involving creative and marketing considerations as well as media. In that these graphs reflect the 'shape' of your campaign, five possible response functions are illustrated here, rather than in the later discussion on computers.

RESPONSE FUNCTIONS

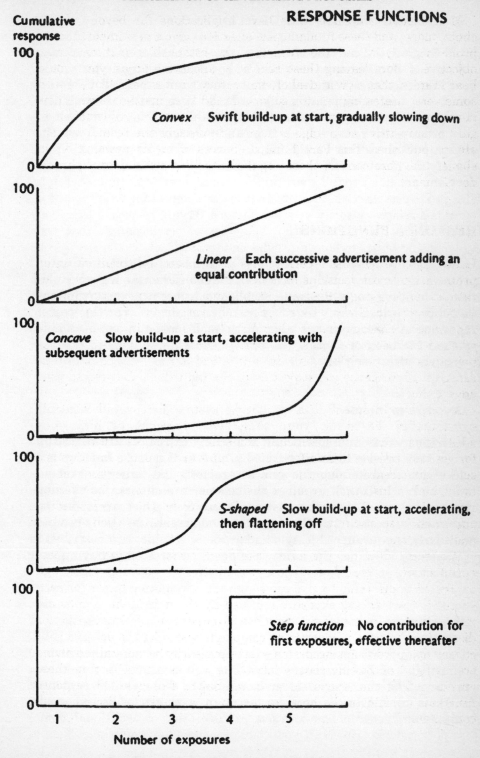

Cumulative response

100

Convex   Swift build-up at start, gradually slowing down

0

100

Linear   Each successive advertisement adding an equal contribution

0

100

Concave   Slow build-up at start, accelerating with subsequent advertisements

0

100

S-shaped   Slow build-up at start, accelerating, then flattening off

0

100

Step function   No contribution for first exposures, effective thereafter

0

1   2   3   4   5

Number of exposures

RESOLVING THE INEVITABLE CONFLICT

In balancing all these variable factors, there is necessarily some element of conflict, and you must be aware of the danger of trying to meet *all* requirements, since it is unlikely that you can meet them all. Somebody once said that a camel looks like a horse designed by a committee. Similarly, if you try to balance the variables by merely reaching a compromise, the result is likely to be an ineffective schedule. In another sense, however, all media planning is necessarily a compromise – if you satisfy the requirement for one of the variables in the media balancing act, you are likely to fall short on the others. It is important, therefore, for you to establish whether coverage is more important than repetition, and the relative priority of other factors. Trying to please everybody may lead to the appropriation being so widely dispersed that your advertising ceases to have any solid impact.

A generally accepted rule is to give each medium a sufficient weight of advertising before adding others to the schedule. One way to avoid a weak compromise is the well-established 'concentration-domination-repetition' principle advocated by many practitioners. For this reason, the suggestion that you cut back 'just one' insertion in one medium to permit inclusion of another in your schedule, is unlikely to result in effective advertising.

The rifle principle

With the increased sophistication of media research, it is often possible to be very precise in selecting media, just as if using a high velocity rifle with accurate sights to aim at precisely the target market you wish to reach. BARB describes the television audience, for example, but fusion of BARB data with a consumer panel identifies the programmes watched by those people who actually buy your product. Similarly, the fusion of lifestyle and geodemographic data described in Chapter 13 identifies the location of people interested in buying your product.

The shotgun principle

The very opposite approach to media planning is the 'shotgun' principle often followed by advertisers launching new products into unknown markets. The same approach can be applied by those whose fragmented markets cannot be defined in terms of age, gender, social grade, occupation, geographical location or any other conventional demographic criteria. How can you communicate advertising messages to clear but widely diffused markets (such as people who need glasses, have bad breath or back trouble, or suffer from haemorrhoids) when there may be no medium, or group of media, which gives particular coverage of these target groups? If it is impossible to achieve concentration, domination and repetition, one alternative is to pepper the market on the shotgun principle, often with a wide spread of small advertisements which, through their headlines, select potential purchasers from the total audience reached by the media in which they appear.

As we have seen, 'shotgun' schedules can also be used as a market research tool. In such cases, the actual campaign would be executed on a flexible basis, according to results. Three 'separate' planning stages – preparation of proposals, execution, and evaluation – are thus all directly inter-related.

Scheduling stages

There are thus two distinct stages in scheduling. First, there is the arithmetical work of costing and balancing alternative schedules taking into account cost ranking and other variables discussed below. Second, and more important, is the work of evaluating these schedules to select the best. The second task involves just as much arithmetic as the first, in assessing facts about coverage and cost per thousand, quite apart from value judgments about qualitative factors such as the means of transmitting your message, and the mood of prospective purchasers when they receive it. The process of schedule construction, calculating possible alternatives and contrasting each to see which gives the best results, means a tremendous amount of work in evaluating media research data and in sheer arithmetical calculations. Most major advertisers, agencies and media-owners therefore now use computers to make these calculations.

THE COMPUTER IN MEDIA-SCHEDULING

Most data processing experts stress that a computer is nothing more than an incredibly fast and accurate idiot, which does exactly what you tell it and nothing more. The way in which a computer is instructed is known as a 'program': note that this is spelt differently from the conventional theatre 'programme'. The names of these programs are often acronyms based on initials: thus AASAM stands for Area Allocation System for Advertising Money, SORBA stands for Systems for Optimising Regional Budget Allocations, BAR stands for Budget Allocation by Region and BAT for Budget Allocation over Time – all four programs are variations on the case-rate spending method, which take into account a wide range of different variables. One leading agency even developed ABACUS (Advertising Budget Allocation and Co-ordination Utility Systems), ARENA (Agency Rating Expenditure Network Analyser), PREFACE (Predictive Formula for Audience Coverage Estimation) and SESAME (System for Evaluating, Setting and Allocating Media Expenditure). The computer experts even have a name for the program which reveals the computer's idiocy – GIGO, standing for 'Garbage In, Garbage Out' or, in more British terms – 'Ask a silly question and you get a silly answer'.

The term computer is a catch-all expression and covers huge mainframes down to the hand-held palm top. It also includes the use of external bureaux, of internal networks, or of stand-alone PCs and Apple Macs.

Computers have influenced the effective use of advertising in various ways, and earlier chapters have already briefly reviewed the spectrum of their use from housekeeping to media planning.

The introduction of computers has led to far greater efficiency in office routines, with faster, more up-to-date and accurate housekeeping as well as greater flexibility in media planning.

Speeded-up paperwork can lead to invoices being paid more promptly. The computer cannot extract money, but it can 'invite' people to pay earlier, simply by sending out invoices more quickly. Similarly, payments can be made by the computer which can also write out cheques.

The availability of low cost computing means that media planners now have on their desks the ability to undertake calculations quickly, simply and accurately. Most agencies use external computer bureaux to support their individual requirements, usually in an on-line mode so that reports are received virtually instantaneously.

Computers can make a positive contribution to the effective use of media, but it is important to bear in mind that the underlying principles of media planning remain the same whether or not a computer is used: data processing merely helps you to work more efficiently. The contribution the computer can make to media planning depends on the information it is given and the calculations it is asked to make.

Input

The information supplied to a computer, as the basis for its calculations, falls into two broad categories.

1 Factual data Research statistics, such as the size and composition of the media audience and the wealth of data described in Part 1, can easily be put into the computer's memory, as can information about costs.

2 Quantified value judgments This involves you in assigning 'weights' to various qualitative factors, such as whether you think mood and the time spent reading a publication make magazine readers more 'valuable' than newspaper readers. Similarly, you might wish to assign relative media values to high quality reproduction, or to colour as against black and white, or to availability of sound and movement and so on.

If you value a magazine reader as 1½ units and a newspaper reader as only 1, because you believe that magazines are better able to communicate your advertising message, this will clearly bias the results in favour of magazines. Value judgements are not infallible simply because they are processed by a computer. Effective use of media is still based on media research data backed up by media judgement, a situation no different from that encountered in the past. The task is basically unchanged whether an external bureau, internal network or stand alone PC is used.

Calculations

Software can be obtained to undertake various types of operation:

1 Cross tabulation This is an analysis examining one set of variables against another, and is frequently used to provide additional analyses not included in the standard tables. A cross tabulation could, for instance, identify the target market for a campaign by analysing age within specific classes.

2 Cost ranking Candidate media can be ranked in cost-efficiency terms against your target market, taking the price to be paid for the space available and relating this to the readership. In this way the computer establishes an order of priority for candidate media to appear on your schedule, expressed in terms of cost efficiency. If desired, you can include your own weights for the demographic constituents of the market and for the media themselves.

3 Schedule optimisation Because of the speed of operation, it is possible for the computer to contrast literally thousands of possible schedules within a very brief space of time, and select the best according to specified criteria. If maximum coverage of a selected market group at the most economic cost is your aim, you can instruct the computer to calculate the combination of media which, for a given expenditure, produces the highest total coverage at the lowest cost per thousand. Value judgements, as well as research data and costs, can also be taken into account if required.

4 Schedule evaluation The purpose of this approach is not to say whether a schedule is the best possible, but to estimate what a schedule will achieve. You can use it, for example, to estimate what total coverage would be achieved for each market group for each month of your schedule. An evaluation program can compute the coverage, the gross opportunities-to-see, the average frequency, the schedule cost, the cost per thousand opportunities-to-see and the frequency distribution of these opportunities. Evaluation techniques tell you what you get for your money, leaving you to make your own decision.

5 Performance evaluation The computer can be instructed to evaluate schedule performance over time (comparing the results of one advertising period with another) to improve advertising scheduling to suit marketing objectives.

Whichever task the computer performs, you are free from the chore of innumerable mathematical calculations, and can concentrate on your main task of planning. Consideration of alternative schedules need no longer be limited by the work involved in producing them.

An indirect advantage of using a computer is that media are no longer vaguely assessed. To use the computer, you must draw up precise criteria by which to judge media, and you no longer evaluate them by loose 'experience and judgement'. Media planning moves from vague personal preferences into the area of facts, clearly stated value judgments and specific performance criteria.

Most major agencies and media independents make extensive use of the DDS (described in Chapter 11) database which contains complete records of TV transmissions over the last five years: every spot on every station with ratings for over 200 audiences. Analysis can be undertaken on-line and competitive expenditure costed.

Another facility worth describing is that of Telmar Communications Ltd. Many of their systems are designed for the interrogation of standard media research databases such as TGI, NRS, RAJAR, CAVIAR and JICREG as well as a selection of specialist studies including:

National Medical Readership Survey
Businessmen's Readership Survey
European Businessman's Readership Survey
Pan-European Survey
Hospital Media Study
International Air Travel Survey
Computer Readership Survey
Youth and Premier TGI

Additionally Telmar can load a client's own research data to provide analysis to suit individual needs. Typical services available from Telmar include

Press Planning programs which:

- rank by cost, cover, or audience composition
- evaluate schedules with reach and frequency calculated instantaneously
- schedule frequency distribution with the facility to evaluate effective response
- cumulative coverage to measure the additional coverage built with increasing insertion levels
- schedule optimisation to budget or coverage goals.

Timeplan evaluates cumulative readership over time using research into reading patterns for weekly and monthly magazines.

Correspondence Analysis to help understand different brands by analysing lifestyle statements. The computer illustrates the differences graphically.

THE NEXT STEP

With your campaign proposals prepared, your next step is to evaluate them as carefully as possible, to ensure to the best of your ability that they will achieve your chosen objective.

Chapter 17

Approval of Advertising Proposals

Approval of proposals is far more complex a matter than it appears, and you will need time to review the proposals overall, to check the reasoning behind the media schedule, to study the creative proposals, and to ensure that all the component parts of the plan interlock. When your campaign is a large and complex one, this task may take some weeks. Sometimes, campaign approval is an on-going procedure rather than a single task but, even with relatively simple proposals, it is rarely possible to give an instant OK, since approval has repercussions far beyond advertising alone.

Before you can approve campaign proposals, you must check them from several different standpoints. The approval process has both interesting and routine aspects: where many executives slip up is that in their eagerness to consider the more glamorous creative aspects they sometimes overlook checking the duller internal and external background on which their campaign is based. In consequence, basic errors often pass unnoticed.

While it is important to scrutinise proposals meticulously before giving your approval, it is equally important to do so as swiftly as possible. Early approval gives more time for execution, thus preventing the mistakes which so often occur with rush jobs. Delay in approving proposals, quite apart from increasing the likelihood of expensive errors, can result in missed deadlines. What a waste of money if you have no advertisement to appear in the spaces for which you are legally liable to pay! Swift approval can also lead to cost savings: undue delay could result in your finding all the best positions already booked by competitors, and having to bid at high rates for the few remaining spaces!

INTERNAL ASPECTS

Before planning any advertising proposals, your first step was investigations into firm and product, market and marketing policy, previous advertising and competition. You must bear in mind that preparation of proposals took time and that things may have changed since the investigations, on which your proposals were based, took place. For example, the original plan might have been to market your product in a choice of colours, but subsequent production problems necessitate a reduction in the range. Clearly your creative proposals must be amended, for there is no point in stimulating prospective customers into demanding a colour which will not be available. Such action is likely to result in disappointed buyers and perhaps an increase in sales of competitors' products. This is only one example of changes that may have occurred since your original investigations.

In addition to checking your proposals from the product/creative changes standpoint, you must also ensure that the media aspects still dovetail in with your company's marketing activities. If your advertisements are to list branch addresses and phone numbers, has the list changed since the initial briefing? Many an advertising executive has been castigated for giving out-of-date details, for lack of attention to this very point! Campaign timing is vital, for consumer advertising must not appear before your goods are in the shops, ready for people to buy. Your campaign plan must therefore allow for the delivery time needed to get goods to the shops once the order has been received, and further allowance must be made for the time needed by salesmen to get orders. To assist salesmen in their work, your consumer campaign may be supported by trade advertisements, and further help provided by heralding your salesman's call with a letter. The timing of each campaign stage must match the other marketing and promotional activities.

The timing of these many aspects of your overall marketing campaign does not depend on the advertising manager alone and, accordingly, you must check to ensure that your proposals interlock with salesforce movements and with other parts of the overall plan. Delivery dates might have changed since your first investigations – will the product in fact be in stock and on display when your advertising breaks, or has there been some unexpected hold-up? If for some good reason or other things are not proceeding according to the original plan, then clearly you must take action to remedy the breakdown in the plan or alternatively amend your proposals to take account of the changes.

Advertising proposals are designed to solve a particular problem, and the facts of this problem may have changed: you must therefore check these marketing aspects before executing your campaign proposals. Clearly, approval cannot be given overnight, for you may need to consult the sales manager, production manager, transport manager, and many others.

EXTERNAL ASPECTS

Before considering your campaign's more creative and media aspects, it is necessary to check proposals from another less interesting but nevertheless crucial aspect: that of background constraints.

This is a creative/marketing matter for the most part, but it is nevertheless necessary to discuss it in some detail, and for you to remember the numerous legal and voluntary controls which affect advertising, and thus your own campaign proposals.

You should certainly obtain a copy of the *British Codes of Advertising and Sales Promotion*, which is under the general supervision of the Advertising Standards Authority and has the support of the major organisations representing advertisers, agencies and media-owners, whose representatives constitute the Committee of Advertising Practice (CAP). The Code is published by CAP, whose address is Torrington Place, London WC1E 7HW. CAP is responsible for advising the industry, and you can get free and confidential advice from the CAP Secretariat.

The general principle is that all advertisements should be legal, decent, honest and truthful and as the Code points out, its rules are not the only ones to affect advertising. There are many provisions, both in the common law and in statutes, which can determine the form or the content of your advertisements. The Code is not in competition with the law: its rules, and the machinery through which they are enforced, are designed to complement the legal controls.

TV commercials

The *British Codes of Advertising and Sales Promotion* do not apply to broadcast commercials. Television advertisements are subject to a separate closely related code administered by the Independent Television Commission (ITC) at 33 Foley Street, London W1P 7LB.

The ITC *Code of Advertising Standards and Practice* is a comprehensive document of general rules, and five main appendices deal in more detail with advertising in relation to children, finance, medicines and treatments, charities and religion.

It is a condition of the licenses granted by the Independent Television Commission (ITC) and the Radio Authority (RA) that broadcasters ensure that all the advertisements they transmit comply with the ITC or RA Codes and that they have in place the checking procedures to enable them to do so.

To fulfil their licence conditions, as well as to provide a service to advertisers and advertising agencies, broadcasters have set up the Broadcast Advertising Clearance Centre (BACC) located at 200 Grays Inn Road, London WC1X 8HF. Previously known as the ITVA Copy Clearance Department, the BACC is responsible for pre-transmission examination and clearance of television commercials. BACC's services are free of charge to the advertiser or agency.

With the exception of a minority of local commercials which may be cleared by the broadcaster concerned, a finished commercial must be viewed and given BACC clearance prior to transmission. Although the submission of pre-production scripts is not compulsory, the great majority of advertisers and agencies avail themselves of this service. Consequently it is unusual for a finished commercial to be rejected by BACC and only a small proportion require some amendment before being cleared for transmission.

An 'Appeal Court' function is provided which comprises senior executives from broadcasting companies.

Radio Commercials

Control of radio advertisements is equally thorough. Special arrangements for copy clearance are necessary in view of the differences between the two media. Some 90 per cent of television advertising is for nationally-marketed products, and most is planned many weeks prior to transmission dates. This enables the central copy-clearing machinery to ensure that all TV commercials comply with the ITC code.

Much radio advertising, however, is local – in some cases the proportion is higher than 70 per cent, and even national advertisers on local commercial radio often give a 'local' flavour to their commercials. Equally, much radio advertising is mounted at short notice, taking advantage of the medium's operational flexibility. Because of this, there is a different control procedure.

Copy clearance is a voluntary system operated by the radio companies and designed to protect both advertisers and radio stations, just as much as listeners, as no fewer than 58 Acts of Parliament (together with detailed regulations made under them) affect radio advertising! Commercial radio therefore operates the Radio Advertising Clearance Centre which provides a clearance service responsive to the special characteristics of commercial radio.

Central clearance Clearance of radio scripts by the Centre is required for all 'national' advertisements, that is all commercials intended to be run in more than one region. Clearance is also required for all commercials in the following special categories: medical products, contraceptives, feminine hygiene, financial, consumer credit, alcoholic drinks, environmental claims, cigars and pipe tobacco, food and nutrition claims, 18 certificate films and videos, betting and gaming, commercials claiming environmental benefits, charities and religion as well as being recommended for pilot or test campaigns.

Regional clearance A commercial to be broadcast in one region of the UK can be cleared by the Regional Copy Clearance executives for that region.

Local clearance Commercials to be run on only one station, and not falling within the special categories listed above, can be cleared by that station.

These procedures help ensure that scripts are swiftly processed and commercials transmitted with minimum delay, allowing advertisers to take full advantage of the radio medium's speed and flexibility.

Other media

Cinema commercials are checked by the Cinema Advertising Association which is the trade association of cinema advertising contractors in the UK. Its role is partly one of a watchdog, acting to ensure that professional standards are met and maintained by the cinema advertising industry. As a member of ASA, it is responsible for vetting all commercials prior to screening in cinemas, in order to ensure that they conform to the British Codes of Advertising and Sales Promotion. Commercials of 30 seconds or longer must also be submitted to the British Board of Film Classification for certification. Direct Mail is monitored by the ASA and other media have their own special standards. The *British Codes of Advertising and Sales Promotion* also enable the ASA to investigate complaints about new media such as CD Roms, video games and the Internet.

The need for careful pre-clearance

Pre-clearance of advertisements for media implies a thorough knowledge of the Codes *prior to preparing your proposals*, quite apart from the need to check your proposals against them afterwards. The earlier chapter on situation analysis stressed, under 'Constraints', the need for you to be aware of the legal and voluntary controls which affect advertising, but these controls are not static: like your product or the marketing situation they too may have changed since your first investigations, so rechecking, under the general heading of approval of proposals, is a necessary safety measure. Quite apart from being desirable in its own right, such double-checking can avoid the unfortunate consequences of failure to comply – two to three per cent of finished television commercials being unacceptable may seem a small proportion, but consider the position of those advertisers who find themselves deprived of advertising support through lack of any commercials to screen, quite apart from the considerable funds wasted in producing a useless commercial. Careful attention to this matter will ensure that you are not numbered among this unfortunate few.

ADVERTISING ASPECTS

Checking campaign proposals is something that *everybody* thinks they can do – show an advertisement to a layman and he can always suggest improvements! Too many people look only at the pieces of paper in front of them and fail to 'think back' to see how these integrate with the marketing objective which underlies the whole campaign. Before approving any media schedule or creative proposals, you should ask four fundamental questions:

1 What is your specific advertising strategy? As was made clear earlier, it is no use hoping that an advertisement will 'increase sales'. Where are these increased sales to come from – increased purchases by existing users, conversion of new users, or brand-switch by the buyers of rival products? These and many other possible objectives were discussed in Chapter 14: your specific campaign objective affects media selection as well as creative content. A good advertisement clearly indicates the advertiser's marketing policy and whether increased sales are to be achieved by a brand-switch from competition, by bringing new users into the market for the first time, or by persuading existing purchasers to use more of the product.

2 What fundamental proposition has been selected to appeal to your target group? Of the many appeals you could make to potential buyers, which is the correct copy platform, key attribute or unique selling proposition that will trigger them into action? Cheapness? Effectiveness? Value for money? Better performance? If you select the wrong proposition, you will fail to achieve your objective. This question is a creative one and thus outside the scope of this book, but the answer has media implications: there is little point in constructing an effective media schedule, only to have it deliver the wrong message to your potential purchasers.

Good creative work is vital for effective advertising, but you must avoid the mistake of seeking creativity for its own sake. Your campaign must relate to your specific strategy and, when approving any proposals, you should beware of advertisements which sell creative gimmicks rather than your products.

A good advertisement gives a clear portrait of the target purchasers and their motivation in buying the product.

3 How effectively will this proposition be conveyed to the selected target groups? This in turn breaks down into two separate checking operations – creative and media. Could the creative proposals be improved – does the illustration convey the selected appeal effectively, and is this backed up by equally persuasive copy? Has the single-minded selling proposition been made to 'come alive' in a compelling and memorable way? Will the advertisement convey your message to maximum advantage as regards printing or transmission?

Equally important, and more the subject of this book, is checking your advertising proposals from the media standpoint – is the schedule as effective as possible in media selection and in the way the selected media are used – sizes, positions, frequency and dates, and duration of campaign? The chapter on preparation of proposals outlined the two-stage process – construction of various possible schedules, followed by evaluation to select the best, so there is no need to describe this process again. What *is* necessary is to set this checking operation in the context of the two preliminary questions – what is your specific objective, and what appeal did you select for your target group? Only after the answers to these two questions are clearly established is it worth checking the efficiency of the media schedule – a missile aimed with great accuracy at the wrong target does not win any battles, except by accident!

4 Are your proposals comprehensive and cohesive?

Comprehensive This book concentrates on the effective use of *advertising* but, if your campaign is to make its maximum contribution, it should be supplemented by optimum use of all forms of marketing communications. Chapter 4 stressed the importance of the editorial route, of possibly creating other media, and of considering the full range of your target market's message sources.

Cohesive Approval must also ensure that the various components of your campaign all fully interlock. This may mean checking each campaign component separately, but an overview is essential. Your marketing communications efforts will be wasted if the advertising campaign delivers one promotional message while public relations adopts a different theme, and merchandising and sales promotion follow separate paths. Under such circumstances, your target market would be very confused.

Rather than such fragmented efforts, you should strive for a synergistic approach whereby the separate campaign components reinforce each other, thereby multiplying the media effect.

Similarly, your proposals should be cohesive over time, so that all new marketing communications build on and benefit from earlier campaigns.

THE NEXT STEP

Once you have approved your campaign proposals from these three standpoints – internal, external, and advertising aspects – and are sure that your advertising proposals in their final form will make the maximum contribution to achieving your campaign objective, the next step is to put them into effect.

Chapter 18

Execution of Advertising Proposals

Once you have approved your campaign proposals, the next step is to put them into effect: this is a more difficult task than it would appear at first sight. Some campaigns may include hundreds or even thousands of individual advertisements in a whole range of media, and the execution of such a plan calls for meticulous attention to detail.

The task of converting a media schedule – which is nothing more than a plan on paper – into formal orders placed with media-owners is discussed below, but mention must also be made of the creative side, which also calls for considerable detailed work – commissioning artwork and marking-up the copywriter's words for typesetting. Appropriate material must be sent to the selected publishers, and advertisement proofs checked. Other media call for similar creative and production work.

Accuracy is vital in its own right, but the need for accuracy is emphasised by the time limits imposed by the media-owners' 'copy dates' which allow little or no opportunity to correct errors. If a media-owner's copy date is 1 September, this means that material for the advertisement is needed by that date if it is to appear on time. Media-owners' copy dates are difficult if not impossible to postpone.

The task of executing creative proposals may, like the work of preparing them, be undertaken in a variety of ways. The advertising department may do the work itself, it may be handled by an agency, or it may be divided between the two. Some smaller advertisers may rely on the media-owner's service facilities for help in implementing the proposals as well as advice on preparing them.

IMPLEMENTING YOUR MEDIA SCHEDULE: PLANNING VERSUS BUYING

The task of converting your media plan into firm orders placed with media-owners is more than simply an administrative task, and here the difference between media planning and media buying becomes all important. For example, your approved media schedule might show a series of television commercials to be transmitted in various time segments on certain dates. When the plan was drawn up, however, it was impossible to know the programmes that would be transmitted or the viewing figures that would be achieved many months ahead. So a great deal of skill is called for in negotiating the best possible spots at times when your commercials will be seen by the largest number of people in your target market group. Similar detailed negotiations will be necessary with the owners of other media.

The up-to-the-minute buying function contrasts sharply with the earlier planning stage, which produced only an outline plan to be implemented in the light of subsequent information. Media buying calls for a highly competitive cut and thrust approach which many find more exciting than the abstract planning stage which, in contrast, seems a rather boring arithmetical exercise. The buying role is complex and skilled: it involves diplomacy and negotiation skills, and a detailed knowledge of the market place. A good media buyer, with a good working relationship with media-owners, can save many tens of thousands of pounds, and perhaps get preferential treatment over competition. Some practitioners argue that the personal qualities called for in planners and buyers are so very different that few individuals can do both jobs properly.

The vital importance of the buying side is illustrated by the growth of the media independents, by the separation within many agency media departments of the planning and buying functions, and by the fact that advertisers have been known to move their accounts from one agency to another simply because of its better buying performance. In such cases, media considerations clearly have just as high a priority as the creative side of advertising.

SCHEDULE IMPROVEMENT

Few advertising campaigns ever appear exactly as originally planned, and you should keep your schedule under constant scrutiny and make whatever improvements are possible. A marginal improvement of, say, ten per cent in coverage is equivalent to a 10 per cent increase in your appropriation, so you should keep your schedule under review and adjust it in the light of subsequent information.

Systems such as DDS, described earlier, provide a dynamic buying facility which allows an agency or media independent to book TV spots on-screen in the context of a schedule, and see instantly the effect on costs and ratings. Amendments can be undertaken by the system, and the file updated instantly.

The next chapter deals with evaluation of results as such, but it would be very wrong to consider this an exercise to be undertaken only *after* your campaign: you should monitor performance throughout and, with television advertising, schedule improvement is just as important as the original plan. Changes are less frequent with press or other media but the case for schedule improvement is just as valid. The publication of new circulation or readership data, the issue of a new rate card or the launch of a new publication, for example, should lead you to re-examine your current media plans. The media world is a fast-changing one with new information becoming available almost day by day. Under these circumstances, it would be true to say that anyone who executes a media plan exactly as written, without effecting any changes or improvements, must be asleep on the job!

OTHER CHANGES

In addition to the normal on-going work of schedule improvement, it may be necessary for you to make other changes, to cater for the inevitable set-backs – and unexpected opportunities – which occur from time to time in normal business practice. These can be considered under three main headings – minor, on-going and major changes.

Minor changes Although media planners always complain that the appropriation is never sufficient, you will find they rarely budget to spend *all* the money at their disposal. In preparing your own advertising campaign, you would be well advised to keep back part of your appropriation, in recognition of the fact that no amount of forward planning can predict every possible future event, and that some unforeseen eventuality is bound to occur. Rates may increase or attractive offers be made by media-owners, and a 'Contingency Reserve' allows for such events, and also for unexpected set-backs.

In a highly volatile market, it may be desirable to keep back a considerable contingency reserve, while in a stable marketing situation a nominal reserve may be quite sufficient. In fixing your contingency reserve, you are in fact attempting to predict the unpredictable: this is a most difficult decision, for if contingencies are under-estimated and call for more than the amount set aside then you must cancel some advertising to provide the necessary money, and your carefully planned schedule will be ruined. If on the other hand you over-estimate the amount, there is a temptation to fritter away this too large reserve at the end of the year, rather than leave it unspent and face criticism from your firm's financial staff when seeking budget increases in the future. There is also the danger of this contingency fund being seen as surplus to requirements, and 'taken back' when things get tight, thereby removing your ability to make tactical moves. The correct amount can perhaps be determined only through trial and error over the years.

Other advertisers take a different approach and, rather than establish a contingency reserve in advance, build one up over the campaign period. Aggressive media buying, while executing the media plan, provides another way of coping with the unexpected, the money saved being used to fund a contingency reserve. In some cases, however, the unexpected may occur on such a scale that no contingency reserve, however large, can possibly cope. Such an eventuality is discussed below, under the heading of 'major changes'.

On-going changes When launching new products or services into diverse and unknown markets, with no previous data on which to build, and when the research to provide market information would be unduly expensive, some campaign plans are often deliberately left open-ended. Rather than book a series of 12 advertisements (which would secure a series discount, but commit expenditure to media or market segments of yet unknown value) the initial space order is for only a few insertions in candidate media, with the bulk of expenditure deliberately held in reserve.

Response to these advertisements is then evaluated: those media giving value for money remain on the schedule, while those with poor response are removed. The 'Shotgun' approach, referred to earlier, involves peppering the market and then targeting specific campaigns at those market groups which, through their response, revealed themselves as likely purchasers. In such circumstances the four stages of investigation, planning, execution and evaluation are inseparably linked, with advertising serving a market-research function.

Major changes You may bestow great care, time and effort on preparing your advertising campaign only to have your work wasted, through no fault of your own. One advertiser's national campaign was at proof stage when a new competitor unexpectedly changed the marketing situation to such an extent that the whole advertising campaign had to be scrapped. The thinking behind the proposals had been correct at the time they were put forward, but the unexpected changes meant that the campaign no longer applied to the new marketing problem. Similar situations have arisen following major economic changes or governmental action such as alterations to tax structure or credit restrictions. The task then is to produce another campaign to deal effectively with the new situation, in the shortest possible time. In such circumstances, resilience and the ability to 'bounce back' when all your work is scrapped are just as important as being able to handle the new situation with a clear head and without getting flustered. Hopefully, however, there will be no major upheavals and contingency reserves will enable you to cope with such unexpected changes as do occur.

In other circumstances, however, major changes may take place that make no call on contingency reserves: to the contrary, you are forced to cut back your advertising. The outbreak of fire or an explosion or strike which stops your production line all illustrate this point, for in such unfortunate circumstances you might well call a halt to advertising aimed at stimulating a demand your company is incapable of satisfying. After an initial advertisement announcing the cause of the delay, you might cancel all advertising other than interim reminder advertisements, until your production line is rolling again.

If all goes well, however, such problems will not arise and your task in implementing your media plan will then be as described earlier – part administrative and part buying/schedule improvement.

MEDIA ADMINISTRATION

The agreed schedule shows an overall picture of your proposed campaign: for press media it will include name of publication, size of advertisement, whether this is run-of-paper or a special position, black and white or colour, together with the cost per advertisement, number of insertions, total cost and dates of appearance. For other media, similar details are given. A television or radio schedule, for example, shows region and contractor, length of commercial, the time segments in which the commercials are to be screened, cost per transmission, total cost and transmission dates. For other media, this information pattern is adapted to show the relevant details. The schedule, however, is nothing more than a plan on paper and must now be converted into firm bookings.

In preparing media proposals you frequently make advance contact with media-owners to check if certain sizes or positions will be available on certain dates, for it is a waste of time to prepare suggestions if these are not realisable. The agency which obtained its client's consent to book a certain schedule, for example, only to report later that few of the spaces suggested were in fact available would look more than foolish in the client's eyes. The same would be true of an advertising manager who obtained Board approval only to report later that the plan could not be put into practice. Accordingly, you may have sought the media-owner's co-operation by asking that certain spaces be reserved for a given length of time pending formal approval. In any event, no firm bookings have yet been made and you now have the considerable task of sending out confirming orders to all media included in the schedule.

You should not under-rate this routine task of converting a single document into a number of individual orders, for accuracy is vital. A media schedule may include insertions in a large number of individual media: on more complex schedules there may be dozens of different publications – national and local newspapers, consumer and business magazines – as well as transmissions on television and radio, and bookings for cinema, posters, exhibitions or other media. Some media groups may offer some form of central-booking or single-order service, but in most cases your media plan must now be translated into individual orders for each of the media-owners concerned, who may possibly total a hundred or more. Each individual order will contain numerous items of information, and must be accurate as to name of medium, sizes and positions and dates of advertisements, as well as costs and discounts.

A simply typing mistake can cause a great deal of trouble or even jeopardise an entire campaign. If your media schedule features an advertisement to appear on, say, the 9th of the month and the order to the media-owner is incorrectly marked for the 19th, your company would rightly be more than annoyed at lack of advertising support when expected, at what would most certainly be a vital time. This simple typing error could endanger the success of the complete campaign. If the fault lay with the agency, it would find itself in an exceptionally difficult position. In such circumstances the agency might, for example, be too late to cancel the booking for the 19th but would be legally liable to pay the media-owner for it, whereas the client need not pay the agency since he had not authorised it.

Similarly, carelessness in checking could bring trouble of a different kind. If, for example, the true cost of £950 for an advertisement is, by mistake, shown on the client's schedule as £590, then £590 is the amount the client has authorised the agency to spend on his behalf – or which the Board has given the advertising manager authority to spend. Or again, orders have sometimes been sent to the wrong media-owners and advertisements included in the wrong media: this is not as unlikely as it sounds, as many publications have similar names and can easily be confused. Needless to say, no client would be under any obligation to pay his agency for such unauthorised insertions. Accuracy in paperwork and meticulous checking for possible errors is therefore essential.

Even when the individual orders have been typed, checked and posted, however, your administrative work is not at an end. It is necessary to retain and file reference copies, and also to check carefully that every order is acknowledged by the media-owner to whom it was sent. Mere posting of an order does not ensure appearance of your advertising, for there is always the possibility that the order may go astray. Such a mishap rarely occurs but when it does the consequent absence of advertising support could have very damaging effects. To facilitate the order-checking procedure, many order forms have a tear-off acknowledgement slip for media-owners to complete and return. Some media-owners use these slips, while others prefer to use their own 'Acknowledgement of Order' forms: but either way the responsibility for checking that orders have been received and acknowledged still rests with the advertiser or his agency.

Even after a schedule has been planned, booked and acknowledged, changes may become necessary, for the reasons discussed above. For example, should demand so exceed supply that further advertising would be an embarrassment, it may be desirable for you to cancel some insertions. Alternatively, it may be necessary to transfer a booking from one date to another. Often there are special forms for these purposes and, when cancellations are called for, then special 'Stop Orders' – frequently printed in red for immediate attention – might be used. Similarly, there may be 'Amendment Orders' to affect changes within a series of insertions. As before, stop or amendment orders must be meticulously checked, and care taken to see that they are duly acknowledged.

Before leaving this administrative aspect of media, it should be pointed out that a great deal of the drudgery has been taken over by the new technologies. The chapter on specialist services drew attention to the computer services available to advertiser, agency and media-owner which, in addition to their positive contribution to media planning, can also do much of the 'housekeeping' work, thus freeing staff for more constructive activities. The chore of checking nevertheless remains – an incorrect order is still incorrect, even if it is processed by a computer!

THE LEGAL POSITION

Orders sent to confirm bookings and requests for cancellation both raise the legal aspects of contracts with media-owners. This is a complex matter which was admirably dealt with in Diana Woolley's *Advertising Law Handbook*, published by Business Books on behalf of the Institute of Practitioners in Advertising, by whose permission the following paragraph is quoted:

> .. *media-owners specify in rate cards the conditions on which they will sell space or time to agencies, and it is an advertising trade custom that such conditions will apply to all contracts for purchase of space or time, even if no reference is made to them in the media booking form, which may be an extremely simple document. So,*

when an agency books space or time, if it wishes to avoid any of the media-owner's conditions, it must expressly exclude them in its order and, unless its exclusion is accepted by the media-owners, the agency will be subject to all the conditions regardless.

Although the book is now out of print, this quotation is still the best summary of a very complex matter.

THE NEXT STEP

A final step before executing proposals is to double-check follow-through arrangements, as described in the next chapter: there is little point in stimulating the market, if your company does not respond to the demand generated.

Chapter 19

Follow Through

This chapter is brief – and ideally should not even be here! It is self-evident that, if any organisation invests considerable sums on advertising to stimulate the market, it should gear up to respond swiftly to the interest generated.

In practice, however, advertising is alas sometimes not integrated with other activities. Hence this warning: any executive responsible for advertising would be well advised to double-check follow-through arrangements, and to ensure that colleagues are ready to take whatever action is necessary, whether this be coping with telephone enquiries, posting out literature, or following up sales leads.

There are many cases where, alas, advertising staff have taken 'follow through' for granted, to their cost – unacceptable delays have occurred before action was taken and, in one extreme case, there were even complaints that an advertisement had caused so much work in answering enquiry letters!

While you are not *directly* involved with efficient follow-through, this does not relieve you of responsibility: internal marketing communications should ensure that your colleagues are fully briefed in advance, and ready to take whatever action is necessary (whether this be handling telephone enquiries, despatching literature, or following up sales leads) thus averting wasteful dissipation of effort. Incredible though it may seem, one recent survey (across a wide range of product and service areas) revealed that, on average, some 90 per cent of enquiries are never followed up!

Quite apart from being sound practice, tactful reminders are also a useful form of self-defence – if sales targets are not achieved, there is always a temptation for colleagues to blame poor advertising!

If necessary, extra work can be contracted out to other organisations to relieve you of administrative chores: Chapter 12 mentioned the wide range available. For example, some external services not only handle telephone enquiries but also store and despatch literature. Alternatively, if your advertisements feature the offer of an informative booklet, the Royal Mail's *Admail* service (described earlier) can be most helpful. Subject to agreement, this facility allows you to cite your Head Office or other prestigious address in your advertising, but have enquiries redirected to a different office, or perhaps to a 'fulfillment house' (which stocks all necessary material, and posts it on your behalf). This can encourage response and at the same time reduce administrative costs, by eliminating internal re-routing of customer enquiries. It also saves valuable time, thus reducing delays in responding to these requests. But beware – are such costs to be charged against your advertising budget?

THE NEXT STEP

With your campaign now running, your next task is to evaluate its results, to see what lessons can be learned for the future.

Chapter 20

Evaluation of Results

Skill in evaluating results is an important talent for you to develop if you are to use advertising media effectively. This task should be approached from three standpoints – checking backwards, allowing for other influences and looking forward.

CHECKING BACKWARDS

Evaluation of results involves, first, the relatively straightforward task of ensuring that you got value for money. For every insertion booked, you should carefully check the voucher copy sent by the publisher (or obtain a voucher if the media-owner has overlooked sending one). Has your advertisement appeared as booked: in the selected position on the appropriate page on the correct date? Where no special position was booked, did the media-owner place your advertisement wisely, or does its position compare unfavourably with those of competitors? What about adjacent editorial matter? An advertiser of tinned food would rightly be annoyed if his advertisement was foolishly placed on a page featuring an article on food poisoning. If your advertisement featured a coupon, does this back upon another advertiser's coupon on the reverse side of the page? Should this occur, neither advertiser can obtain maximum results. What is the standard of printing? Has the illustration been reproduced to maximum effect? With full-colour advertisements, is your product shown with true colour values? For food or cosmetics, even a slight variation in colour can detract considerably from your advertisement's effectiveness. Has the publisher, in fact, inserted the correct advertisement? It is not unknown for a media-owner to repeat a previous advertisement instead of replacing it with a new one as instructed. There may be few occasions in the year when you need to

304

take up any of these matters with media-owners but such mistakes do occur and you must, therefore, examine every voucher copy and carry out similar checks with other media.

ALLOWING FOR OTHER INFLUENCES

When keeping records, you should make a note of those events – other than advertising – which influence sales and, unless allowed for, would give you a mistaken idea of your campaign effectiveness. Such influences should be categorised under four inter-related headings – Favourable or Unfavourable, Once-off or Repeat.

A heatwave, for example, will push up sales of cold drinks and ice-cream and, whilst advertising can help channel demand towards your product, it would clearly be incorrect when evaluating results to conclude that advertising *caused* increased sales. By all means bask in reflected glory, but be sure to protect yourself against possible blame for decreased sales by noting those events which had an adverse effect. Both favourable and unfavourable influences may be regular or isolated incidents.

A whole host of events can affect your results, including special incentives to sales staff, entertainment and sporting events, strikes, bank holidays and so on. A record of such influences is vital in evaluating past performance and also provides a useful guide for future planning, indicating desirable or avoiding action you should take when preparing next year's campaign. Annual events such as the Cup Final will push up sales of some products at the same time as they depress others and, if your market is affected in this way, you should clearly make allowances in your media scheduling.

LOOKING FORWARD

Ensuring that you got value for money is important, but a far more significant aspect of evaluating results concerns checking effectiveness. Here your aim is different: your concern is not what happened in the past, but improvements for the future.

Did you achieve your objective? This question takes you straight back to the second basic requirement for effective use of advertising media. The first task was investigations, gathering information on which to base your advertising planning. The second task was deciding your specific strategy and the point was made that planning should be a 'closed loop' with evaluation of results of this year's campaign providing additional information on which to base next year's planning.

The direct link between the evaluation of results and the determination of specific objectives is best illustrated by reference to the DAGMAR concept. These initials stand for 'Defining Advertising Goals for Measured Advertising Results', an approach that was developed by R. Colley. To put this another way, unless you know where you are going, how can you know whether or not you have got there? At its most basic, the DAGMAR approach points out the vital need for a specific objective, and then asks if you achieved it. If not, why not? Failure to achieve your objective could arise from one of two reasons – either your objective was wrong (perhaps too ambitious) or alternatively your advertising campaign was at fault. This is an over-simplification, as there are other alternatives – circumstances may have changed during the year, or perhaps your method of measuring is not as accurate as it should be. But, whatever the reason – wrong objective, wrong campaign, wrong evaluation or change of circumstances – the DAGMAR approach leads to a re-examination of the advertising plan and its inter-relationship with your total marketing operation. If you did not achieve your objective, it is not necessarily the advertising that is to blame – perhaps the marketing was at fault. But even if your objective was achieved, this is no cause for complacency – could your advertising have done better? Hence the need to analyse advertising results meticulously. As a first step, you must establish whether you are considering direct response or alternatively evaluating results indirectly by some form of survey of retailers or consumers.

Direct response

The improvements you can achieve by evaluating results are best illustrated by the example of those fortunate enough to be able to relate advertising directly to its results. Such is the case with many retailers, organisations with showrooms, or advertisers selling direct or whose advertisements feature reader request coupons. Direct response can also arise through various reply service facilities provided by media-owners.

When you invite such a direct response, you can 'key' each advertisement so that respondents indicate in which publication and on what date they saw your advertisement. Inclusion of a 'key number' such as 'SE7' would indicate that the coupon came from an advertisement in the *Sunday Express* on the 7th. The principle of keying advertisements is simple, but you must take care that your system is foolproof. Does 'DM13' indicate *Daily Mirror* or *Daily Mail*, and does '13' imply the date of insertion or the thirteenth appearance in that publication? You must ensure that your system tells you, without fail, the source of every coupon. Even if your advertisement includes no coupon, it can still be keyed by asking readers to write to a certain department or to address their reply to a certain individual, to Desk Number X or Room Y.

Increasing postal costs have resulted in people thinking more carefully before writing for leaflets, so many firms now take advantage of the Royal Mail's Business Reply or Freepost services whereby they rather than prospective purchasers pay the postage. It also provides a further incentive in that some potential purchasers might be willing to pay postage but simply do not have a stamp handy: these response services can help overcome this inertia on the part of potential buyers. Increased postal costs have also resulted in an increase in showroom enquiries rather than coupon response, and many advertisers therefore take care to include these enquiries since evaluation of postal response alone clearly gives a very incomplete picture.

Parallel services are available for telephone response through Freefone 0800, lo-call 0345 or National call 0990. 0800 numbers are free to callers. With 0345 numbers, the caller pays only the local rate no matter where the call is made in the UK. 0990 numbers provide a single national number whether or not you have local branches, and the caller pays the national long distance charge.

Respondents to advertisements have two additional methods of responding to them: FAX and Internet.

Most businesses, and a growing number of individuals have fax machines and use them to send messages in preference to the post. Business advertisers increasingly feature FAX numbers in their advertisements to provide the opportunity for speeding-up consumer response.

Similarly with the Internet. The growing number of businesses and individuals with a modem can use the e-mail facility to send a message. Those of us with easy access to the internet find it a simple and easy method of sending and receiving messages.

A sensible advertiser provides the response opportunities expected by their targets. And provides the systems needed to ensure that response is quick and accurate. Anyone sending an e-mail message, for instance, would expect a same day response, personalised to their enquiry.

Finally, advertisers need to record response. The labour needed in checking keyed responses must not be underestimated, and you should ensure you have the necessary staff to undertake this vital chore. Much valuable information is thrown into the wastepaper basket for lack of staff to make the necessary evaluation – yet the improvement which could be achieved would more than pay for the labour costs involved, and even make a major contribution to profits! Should your advertising feature coupons regularly, there may be thousands or even millions to handle annually, and this necessitates establishing a carefully planned sorting and checking operation. Imagine yourself responsible for an advertising campaign which includes perhaps a hundred or more advertisements every month, all featuring coupons and appearing in numerous different publications – national and local newspapers, and magazines of various types. What could you learn from a careful study of coupon returns (or some other form of direct response) and what improvements could you recommend for the future?

Product offer Since all depends on the fundamental content of your advertisement, the product (or service) must appear at the head of the list. With direct response campaigns, the advertiser may vary the basic product offer featured and so judge the relative merits of different prices, packs, products, or product versions. Here, the old truth about making sure you get the offer right should be underlined in red. The head of a mail order company is quoted as saying:

> *'The product has to be central to your offer and, depending on how you present that offer in your advertising, you can expect a fluctuation in response of about 10 or 15 per cent. A good offer badly presented will still bring the response.'*

This quotation calls for comment. A fluctuation in response of 10 to 15 per cent, according to how you present your products, certainly puts advertising into perspective, but we must not overlook the vital importance of this difference in effectiveness. At worst, it can mean the difference between profit and loss and, at best, a significant contribution to profitability. Some of the advertising factors which can account for this fluctuation include the following:

The medium The number of coupons brought in by one medium can be compared with the response produced by others. If comparing press media, for example, publications can be listed in response order and publications with poor returns could then be eliminated from the schedule and the money spent to better advantage elsewhere. When listing media in order of productivity it is important to consider not only media but also production charges. The longer the media list, the higher the production charges; thus there may be a double saving when uneconomic media are deleted from the schedule.

Area of coverage Where do the coupons come from? One medium may bring a good response when measured in numbers of coupons, but many may perhaps come from outside your sales area. For a local advertiser, or one with a restricted sales or service area, this factor is of major importance. Area response can be very important even for an advertiser with national distribution, and if one region responded more than others, you might decide to follow up this local interest by booking additional insertions in local papers. Alternatively, returns might be extremely poor in one area and this would lead you to investigate the cause of the low response. You might then discover your company faced severe competition from a small local company and that the competitive strategy in the area needed reconsideration. Another reason for weak response in a particular area is the fact that even so-called 'national' media vary in their intensity of coverage in different parts of the country: should this be the case, low penetration in a particular area might call for reinforcement advertising support in local media.

Type of response Careful analysis of the type of person returning your coupons can also yield valuable information. Are the coupons mostly completed by men or by women? Where coupons appear in technical publications, one industry might show more interest than others when judged by coupon response and therefore be ripe for specific targeting by a special sales drive.

Cost per reply Numbers of coupons, completed by respondents of the right type and within your sales area, can be evaluated in terms of value for money, and cost per reply calculated. High numbers are insufficient in themselves: coupons must be returned by prospective customers and at an economic rate. Publications with uneconomic returns can then be eliminated. The chapter on budgeting mentioned the 'Marginal Method' of fixing the budget, which is based on such an immediate evaluation of results.

Conversions Where customer response provides leads for sales force activity, you can calculate the number of enquiries which result in actual sales. One medium might have a low response rate, but if every enquiry leads to a sale it will clearly merit retention on your schedule. Conversely, if the conversion rate of another is low, you would no doubt want to cancel further insertions.

The advertisement unit: size, position and colour Large advertisements cost more than small ones and special positions or colour also increase costs. Comparison of response rates can indicate whether the added expense was worthwhile.

Repeat Sales Source Organisations with databases which record repeat sales to individual customers can put a source marker against that customer's record. This makes it possible to record not only the media source of individual sales, but also identify those customers who provide the most profitable mix of repeat sales.

Frequency High frequency costs more than less regular appearances: evaluation of results can indicate if the additional cost was worthwhile.

Does the profile of heavy and light users of your product match in with heavy or light exposure to your advertising? If not, why not?

Timing Timing can be a matter of seasons, weeks, or days. By analysing response records you can discover the most suitable days of the week for your advertisements, or when the buying season starts.

Non-media aspects Some response measures mentioned above clearly have *marketing* as well as media implications: they may indicate a new potential market or likely sales area, or touch on other marketing activities. Other response aspects also have implications for marketing, or for creativity. These include:

Creative theme The chapter on approval of proposals asked 'What fundamental proposition has been selected, to appeal to your target group?' The results of two alternative creative themes can be contrasted and keying used to show which is the more effective.

Creative expression The approval of proposals chapter also asked 'How effectively will this appeal be conveyed to the selected target group?' A given creative theme can be expressed in a variety of ways whilst the fundamental appeal remains unchanged – the theme can be conveyed by different headlines, illustrations, copy and typefaces. Analysis of which version pulled best has clear implications for creative staff.

Creative life Whilst an advertisement might prove itself effective, it may not last indefinitely – evaluation of results might reveal that a given advertisement reached 'wear-out' and the time was therefore ripe to stimulate your market in a different way. This may be linked to the earlier matter of frequency, in that the more often people see your advertisement the quicker it may die. For this reason, some advertisers base their campaigns on a series of advertisements, which they feature on a rotating basis for change of impact. Other advertisers, particularly those who concentrate on the constant flow of new entrants to their markets, have found the same advertisement continues to pull year after year.

Sales promotions Some campaigns 'top up' their appeal for prospective customers to respond by offering an incentive, eg a free booklet or gift, or a product on bonus terms. Evaluation of results can indicate the effectiveness of various alternatives, but it is essential to refer back to 'conversions', and also to give a warning. It is easy to get a response in this way, but it may be response of the wrong kind – from those who want something free, rather than to make a purchase. Care should be taken, therefore, to select an incentive which, by its very nature, appeals mainly to your target group.

Reply devices The aim of a direct response campaign is consumer *action*, but you may experiment with various alternative types of response, some of which prove more productive than others. Examples of different ways in which you can invite customer response include

1 *Post this coupon* – with or without Freepost, and with one or more addresses. Variations are advertisements designed to serve as reply-paid folders, or inclusion of business-paid reply cards.
2 *Payment method* – where the direct response calls for payment of money, various alternatives are possible, eg: credit or debit card, cheque or postal order, either for the whole sum or a deposit.
3 *Call at showroom* – this overlaps with the first category in that respondents, rather than post a coupon, will call in. Other advertisements suggest such a call directly, without use of a coupon.
4 *Telephone this number* – this can be the advertiser's own number, Freefone or Lo-call services (described earlier), or a specialist answering service.
5 *Fax or e-mail* – are of growing importance in a business environment.

Needless to say, these types of response are not exclusive – some campaigns feature two or more. Under this heading, rather than under 'Creative Expression', it is relevant to mention action devices such as coupons featuring small scissors which serve as a visual trigger; corny perhaps, but they *can* work!

Cross comparisons The various comparisons listed above cannot be considered in isolation, as they frequently overlap. For example, people in a particular area may be attracted by one offer rather than another *and* respond more on a particular day of the week (perhaps affected by a major employer's pay-day). These regional and other differences will then be fed back, in a closed loop, into subsequent media and creative planning, and will lead to appropriately different advertising patterns.

Other types of response

The direct response achieved by coupon advertising is an extreme case, and if you have such a clear indicator to the success of your campaign you are indeed fortunate. Even where no such direct response exists, however, you must nevertheless attempt to evaluate results and to follow up leads which could improve your future advertising: this might be by sales audits or consumer surveys.

Sales and retail audits Many retail advertisers have direct results not in coupon form, but in sales. Manufacturers with showrooms take into account over-the-counter enquiries as well as coupon response when assessing overall results.

Other manufacturers without their own outlets attempt to evaluate results by analysing their salesmen's order books (another example of desk research) to check seasonal or geographical variations in relation to advertising effort. 'Sales in' to retailers are not always followed by 'sales out' however, so factory sales figures are an insufficient measure of success, since goods despatched from your factory might sit on retailers' shelves for months, with no sales resulting. Some companies therefore measure results by retail audits, subscribing to one of the research services which provide this data on a commercial basis. In essence, the idea is a simple one: if the stock held in a shop at the start of a month is known and deliveries made during the month are taken into account, the difference between this figure and the total remaining at the end of the month is an accurate indication of the quantity sold over the counter. If your advertising objective was to extend your present distribution or to stimulate your current outlets, a retail audit will give you the answer. A good retail audit will in fact give you a wealth of additional information – where are you placed in the shop and how many *facings* (numbers of your product actually on the shelves) has the retailer given you? Equally important, how are you faring in comparison with your competitors – who is winning the battle for maximum display at point of sale?

Consumer surveys Rather than evaluate results indirectly via retail audits, you may wish to measure customer action, researching purchases rather than sales. A retail audit may reveal an increase of say 20 per cent in comparison with the last period, but it does not tell you *how* this increase was achieved. If your sales increased, you need to know in which of three ways this came about – increased purchases by existing users, conversion of new users, or buyers of rival products switching brands. If the specific purpose of your advertising campaign was to persuade existing users to use more, consumer research can give you valuable information which no form of retail audit can ever reveal. Various research organisations maintain representative panels of consumers, which can make this information available to you.

In some cases, rather than measure actions such as sales or purchase, you may wish to measure changes in, for example, consumer recall of your advertisements, or in their awareness of your product in relation to its competitors. If your specific campaign purpose is to change consumers' attitudes, you may wish to commission research to ascertain their viewpoints before and after the campaign. Even here, however, a specific purpose is essential since 'attitude' is a very broad term. What precisely do you wish to change – your brand image, the degree to which people believe your product claims, their liking for your firm, or the likelihood of them buying your product?

Test marketing Evaluation of results may even extend to test campaigns. A national launch, however carefully planned, is an expensive and risky undertaking: marketing is increasingly competitive and great amounts of capital are involved. Many manufacturers therefore attempt to reproduce in advance, on a smaller scale, the conditions they will encounter on a national basis. By evaluating the results of the test campaign, the manufacturer can spot any weaknesses in his marketing plan, and adjust it prior to the national launch.

When planning a test campaign, your aim must be to reproduce the entire national campaign in miniature, in both selling and advertising. The advertising schedule must recreate in the local campaign the same proportionate weight of advertising to be mounted nationally. If, for example, the national TV campaign is to be launched with one 30-second peak time and two off-peak commercials each week, then this is the amount of advertising to be booked in the TV area selected for the test. Similarly, if half-page advertisements are to appear each week in the national press, then this weight of advertising must be booked in the local press. This general principle of using the equivalent weight of advertising applies to all media, for there is no point in forcing the campaign to be a success by mounting a level of advertising which your company cannot afford on a national basis.

In planning the schedule for your test campaign, account must be taken of the comparative coverage of the national media that would be used for the main campaign and of the local media to be used in the test campaign, and allowance made for any qualitative differences, eg class coverage, male/female bias, printing quality, editorial environment, etc, between them, before a realistic assessment of the 'real' national equivalent of a test campaign can be made.

One prime purpose of test marketing is to reveal any weaknesses, and to adjust your advertising plan accordingly. In other cases, two parallel test campaigns may be run, to evaluate the effect of different product formulae or prices, to select that most acceptable to the market. Different weights of advertising expenditure, different media schedules (or alternative creative themes) can be tested in the same way.

FUTURE ACTION

The purpose of evaluation is *action* and this can be of two different types.

1 Follow up leads Evaluation of results can lead to your taking action, eg addressing a target group not included in your original market definition but which, by its response, has proved its interest in your product. Evaluation of results thus leads to changes in marketing activity, rather than advertising alone. Alternatively, the target market may remain unchanged but, by evaluation of results, you improve the productivity of your advertising campaign by getting better results for the same money.

2 Elimination of weaknesses The reverse side of the 'better results for the same money' coin is 'same results for less money'. Elimination of weaknesses permits you to use the 'saved' money to buy what you could not afford before – and always remember that no budget is ever sufficient to do *everything* you wanted.

In defence of unproductive advertisements

An advertisement which does not bring results is not *always* a waste of money. Depending on your viewpoint, it can also be an investment. The 'investment' comes from the fact that you found out – the hard way – that it did not work, and this prevents further waste in future. Alas, a great deal of advertising money is wasted by those who make *no* attempt to evaluate results in the mistaken belief that it is impossible to do so. In such cases, their campaigns continue repeating unproductive advertisements year after year in unproductive media: this is a very different matter from investing money to prevent future waste.

Closing the loop

Schedule improvement is as important as the original plan, and monitoring performance during your campaign is equally as important as post-campaign assessment. Advertising planning must be a closed loop: this chapter completes the circle since what you learn from evaluation of results provides the basis for your future planning. Closing the loop also raises yet again the important matter of advertising briefing and client/agency relationships, as discussed earlier. Many agencies complain of minimal feedback from clients about the results of campaigns mounted on their behalf. Without such information, how can the agency be expected to improve future advertising effectiveness.

A salutary note on which to finish is that if you tell your agency that the brief is 'the same as last year' then you should either resign or fire the agency, since 'no change' means that all the time, effort and money spent on advertising over the past year has apparently had no effect whatsoever!

THE NEXT STEP

Return to Chapter 13 (or perhaps Chapter 18) – you now have new information on which to base your future use of advertising media.

Index